The Berlin Defence

A Novel

Andy Mack

The Berlin Defence: A Novel
Author: Andy Mack

Typesetting by Andrei Elkov (www.elkov.ru)
Cover page drawing by Anna Fokina Illustration Studio (www. fox-artwork.com)
© Andy Mack, LLC Elk and Ruby Publishing House, 2020
Follow us on Twitter: @ilan_ruby
www.elkandruby.com
ISBN 978-5-6041770-3-7

CONTENTS

PROLOGUE – NO ONE IS COMPLETELY ON YOUR SIDE 5

PART ONE – THE OPENING 6

PART TWO – THE MIDDLEGAME 146

PART THREE – THE ENDGAME 224

EPILOGUE – ICH BIN EIN BERLINER..............................287

To my mother and father, Sylvia and Laurie,
who encouraged my love of chess, the game of Kings

PROLOGUE

NO ONE IS COMPLETELY ON YOUR SIDE

Schönefeld Airport, September 1986

Breathe slowly, he told himself. Hold your nerve.

Taking his seat towards the rear of the plane, Lothar Hartmann did his best to stay composed. The security at check-in had been tight, even by East German standards. The guards had rifled through his luggage, searched his jacket and his trouser pockets, and examined the insides of his shoes. What they thought they were looking for, heaven only knew. Mystified by the pages of obscure typescript and symbols, they had also wanted to confiscate his notebooks, until he pointed out that the books contained his secret analysis, the product of all that hard work at home, and he would be unable to compete without them. Of all people, it took Neuer, the head of their group, to intervene on his behalf.

As the plane charged down the runway, his mind raced and he thought again about the possibilities that lay ahead. It would be dangerous, that was true. But what other course of action did he have? Clutching onto the armrest until his fingers began to ache, he steeled his resolve. To his left sat his teammates, their heads down, immersed in their books and pocket sets. Behind him were the Stasi men, grey and impervious, watching every move, even in this tiny tin box. Of course if they had known what was going to happen next, they would never have allowed him to leave East Germany. But not even the Stasi, all-seeing, all-knowing, can read minds.

PART ONE – THE OPENING

CHAPTER ONE

Bobby Fischer versus the World

When reason fails, the devil helps.
Fyodor Dostoevsky, *Crime and Punishment*

East Berlin, 1967

It was the year they took away his uncle.

Sitting cross-legged in the centre of the living room, Lothar stared at the pieces of the puzzle scattered on the wooden floorboards in front of him. To the untrained eye, the jigsaw was a jumbled mess of jagged edges and unexplained curves. That was what he liked about it. First you looked for the corners, then the straight lines. You put the pieces together, one by one, until you had created order and harmony. Reaching across for a piece of concrete grey – a dark cloud, perhaps – he heard the voices from the kitchen again. Keeping still, holding his breath for as long as he dared, he tried to make sense of the conversation.

'Sack you? They can't do that, can they?' His father's voice sounded tired and strained, heavier than normal.

'They just did.' It was Uncle Leon. Lothar loved his parents, but Leon – with his ready good humour, his words of encouragement, a smile for all occasions – held hero status for him. He wanted to run through to the kitchen and see his uncle, throw his arms around him, his usual greeting.

This time, though, was different. His mother had shut the living room door firmly behind her. 'Stay here, Lothar, until I come and get you.' By the age of eight he knew better than to disobey her.

Lothar shuffled quietly across the floor and put his ear against the crack in the door. 'Who did it?' he heard his father ask.

'Who sacked me?'

'No. Who informed on you?' There was a pause. 'I assume that's what must have happened. You wouldn't have lost your job otherwise.'

Now a woman's voice. Lothar recognised the soft, sympathetic tone of his aunt, Deborah. She sounded like she had been crying. 'We think it was the neighbours. But who can be certain?' There was another pause. Lothar imagined his aunt dabbing the tears from her eyes with a handkerchief. The voices resumed. 'How do we pay the rent? No income, no savings. We'll be out on the street before we know it.'

That evening, Lothar's father pulled his grey toolbox from the cupboard by the front door. Taking a hammer, some nails and a piece of old plywood which he had found discarded in the courtyard below the flats, he fixed up a partition in the main bedroom so that one room became two. 'I told you I should have been a carpenter,' he said, allowing himself a smile for the first time that day and wiping his hands against his overall like a blacksmith. 'A job well done, if I say so myself.'

Leon and Deborah moved in soon after. Lothar was relieved his parents had not made him give up his box room. Situated next to the kitchen, it occupied the best spot in the flat, perfectly placed for those times when, waking early, he wanted to sneak out before dawn and examine the bin for scraps of uneaten food.

On Lothar's ninth birthday, Leon took him fishing. Awake and changed soon after six, filled with expectation for the day ahead, Lothar spent the morning sitting on a kitchen stool in his raincoat, practising his grip on his small home-made fishing rod. By the time they left home, shortly before eleven, he already felt himself a proficient fisherman. Of course, they had little success. But just being with his uncle, enjoying the gentle ripples of the stream, the quiet contemplation, Leon's hug of congratulation when he finally caught a small carp, was enough. Spending these moments with his uncle was so relaxing, so different from the turbulence of the city, with its sad, scowling faces, black briefcases and brown overcoats. He couldn't remember a time when he had felt so happy.

As they walked along the pathway by the river, back towards the town, with its dirty chimneys and prefabricated flats, he fixed his eyes on the grey factory smoke, heavy in the air like a fog, which cast a filthy pallor over them. Reaching a gate, Leon took his nephew by the hand, helping him to clamber over the wooden stile and through to the other side. 'You know, Lothar, this walk holds fond memories for me.'

Lothar looked up at his uncle enquiringly.

'It was the year I met your aunt,' he said, smiling. 'I took her fishing, the same spot we've been today. On the way back, I asked her to marry me.'

'What year was that?' Lothar asked, trying to do the maths in his head, a little embarrassed that he had no idea how old his uncle was.

'1953, Lothar. A good time it was, too. The war was behind us, the Berlin Wall wasn't even a glimmer in Walter Ulbricht's eye.' Leon stubbed his cigarette out on the ground. 'We thought that if we challenged the state, the politicians would listen. We were wrong.'

Leon loved football, and every other Saturday he took Lothar to watch Union Berlin. A poor team, forever at the foot of the table, Union were overshadowed in every respect by their illustrious neighbours, Dynamo Berlin. Dynamo had the famous players, the larger stadium. 'Even the soldiers at Dynamo are more professional,' said Leon sardonically, as they watched a young lad in military uniform, standing just behind the Union goal, fiddle awkwardly with his rifle before slipping over on the wet turf.

'Did you ever think of supporting Dynamo?' Lothar asked, conscious that he was the only boy in his class who followed Union.

'Think of it? I did follow them.' Leon shook his head at the memory of it. 'But then corruption took hold, they became the government-sponsored team. I wanted nothing to do with them after that.' Leon gripped Lothar's shoulder. 'A lesson in life. It's easy to follow the crowd. Much harder to be your own man, to support the underdog.'

At that moment, as he looked up at his uncle, with his broad shoulders, his Roman nose, his dignity, his conviction, Lothar decided what he wanted to do with his life. He would find something that he was good at – a sport perhaps, or a field of science – and he would practise, he would work harder than anyone else. He would succeed on his own merits. He would be the best at what he did, and he would make his uncle proud.

One bleak winter's day, the rain lashing down on him until he was soaked through to the skin, Lothar ran home from school, overwhelmed by dark feelings. Inside the flat, he found his aunt at the kitchen table crying, his mother by her side. His father was pacing up and down the hall, muttering to himself, occasionally punching his hand against the wall.

'What's happened, Dad? Where's Uncle Leon?'

Collecting himself, Lothar's father led him into the living room, sitting next to the boy on the sofa.

'Two policemen came around, Lothar. Members of the Stasi. They've arrested Leon.'

'Why?'

'They had a warrant. They searched the flat and found some of his writing. They claim it's anti-government.'

'What do we do now?'

His father put a hand on his shoulder. 'I'm not sure we can do anything, other than wait.'

That night, Lothar slept badly, tossing and turning as he worried about his uncle. When he did drift off to sleep, his dreams were troubled. He imagined a dark figure in a long cloak standing at the end of his bed, and when he awoke, he was in a cold sweat, petrified that demons had come to take him away too.

Leon was in jail for six months. Shortly after his release, Lothar's uncle and aunt escaped the country, hiding in the boot of a West German friend's car as he crossed the border. Too young to understand what had happened, Lothar missed his uncle and aunt more than he could say. He felt lost without their laughter and smiles, he mourned the loss of the afternoons spent fishing or watching football. More than anything, he worried about what would happen to them in the West. How would they survive? Would they find work? Where would they get money from?

Before he left, Leon had taught Lothar to play chess. 'A game for champions,' he said, as he gave Lothar a battered old chess set, which he himself had owned since he was a boy. A tangible memory of his uncle, it became Lothar's most treasured possession. He loved the way that the wooden pieces, long since shorn of their varnish, danced across the board in their own magical ballet. One day, he told himself, they would dance to his tune.

July 1972

The broadcaster straightened his narrow grey tie and looked intently through his thick box glasses, square into the camera. 'Today, in the second game of the World Chess Championship between Boris Spassky and challenger Bobby Fischer, the American failed to show. Fischer was defaulted, and the Russian now leads by two games to zero. In the battle of East and West, the East is on the verge of victory.'

Failed to show? What on earth was Bobby Fischer thinking? The greatest talent the game had known, a giant amongst men, Fischer had effortlessly dispatched world-class player after world-class player on his way to the title match.

Now, with the championship within his grasp, Fischer had blundered and lost the first game of his match with Boris Spassky. In game two of what should be a twenty-four game marathon, he had not shown up. Lothar felt cheated. Hurrying home from school to watch the game on the family's newly acquired black and white television, he had been anticipating a Fischer comeback, a chance to avenge his first-round defeat. In a country that had gone chess mad – wall-to-wall coverage in the newspapers and on television, a table and board on the pavement outside every café – Lothar had caught the bug. He had been looking forward to the live evening broadcast, even with its anti-West slant, all day. With Fischer's no-show, all he had in front of him was an empty chessboard. Was the match already over?

Tiring of the news, Lothar switched off the television and went outside to play football in the concrete courtyard below the flat with a group of kids from the neighbouring block. His friend Bernd was amongst them. At fourteen, Bernd was already a head taller than Lothar. He was a strong chess player, too, twice the school champion, and Lothar had never yet beaten him in a game.

'Who won?' asked Bernd.

Lothar explained about the no-show. 'Damn,' said Bernd. 'Looks like Fischer's blown it.'

'Are you supporting the Westerner?' asked Troeller, a small, thin boy from a neighbouring flat, with a nasal voice, whose father, it was rumoured, worked for the Stasi.

'I'm no friend of the West,' Lothar replied, 'but I do appreciate genius.'

'Genius?' Troeller scrunched up his face and sniffed. He reminded Lothar of a weasel. 'There's no such thing. Hard work, maybe. But this concept of the superman, it's nonsense. Bobby Fischer, George Best, Muhammad Ali: not an ounce of talent between them. When the West collapses, you'll see your so-called heroes for what they are.'

'When did you turn into Karl Marx?' asked Lothar.

Ignoring Bernd and Lothar, Troeller accelerated away, running the length of the courtyard and smashing the ball between what passed for goalposts – some tired chalk lines marked against the wall – for a magnificent goal. 'Yes! One-nil to East Germany.' There would be no shutting him up now.

Later that evening, Lothar asked his father why people hated the West. Looking across at him, his father put down his pipe. A man of few words, he was happiest when sitting quietly at home, listening to classical music on the radio, while his wife stood nearby, ironing handkerchiefs and shirts and folding linen. 'Best ask your Uncle Leon that,' he replied.

'I don't get it.'

'Lothar, in this country it's not safe to say what you really believe. Not unless you want to get locked up.'

It was the first time in his life that he heard his father say anything political. At the time, he didn't understand what he meant.

Calling for quiet, the Principal took two pawns – one white, one black – and clenched them in his fists. Lothar felt strange and uncomfortable butterflies and a tension in his stomach. He had never played in front of a crowd before, and the twenty-odd classmates who were crowded around the table may as well have been spectators watching Bobby Fischer in his epic victory over Boris Spassky. Pausing, Lothar selected the left hand, drawing the white pawn, and the advantage of the first move.

'Let the final commence,' announced the Principal, and the room fell into a hush. Shaking Bernd's hand warmly, Lothar pushed forward his King's pawn two squares. Inspecting each of the eight pawns in front of him in turn, Bernd chose to push his Queen's pawn two squares. This was a move Lothar had never seen his friend play before. As Lothar sat hunched over the board, evaluating the possibilities, his schoolmate leaned back in his chair, stretching his arms out behind him.

After a moment's thought, Lothar reached out his hand and captured Bernd's pawn with his own. His friend quickly recaptured the pawn with his Queen, and eyes turned back to Lothar. It seemed to him that Bernd's Queen, in the centre of the board, was exposed. Bringing out his Knight, Lothar attacked the errant dame. In reply, Bernd moved his Queen again. His friend appeared confident, but after he developed his remaining pieces, Lothar had suddenly opened up a powerful attack.

It was Bernd's turn now to think. While Lothar sat back, arms folded, his opponent bent forward over the board, holding his chin in his hands. After his longest think of the game, Bernd haltingly pushed a lone pawn forwards one square.

Lothar stared at the humble black pawn, puzzled. What did the move signify? Was there a hidden trap? Surely he could continue to move his pieces forward, threatening his opponent's King? Eventually, feeling the tension grow in his stomach, he made a decision. Picking up his Bishop with his right hand, he slid it delicately across the board, until it stood opposite the lone black King. '*Check*,' he said, softly. Staring at the board, no matter how many times he looked, Lothar couldn't see a single defence for Bernd.

As the crowd around the board gathered closer, pushing against the table until they were almost upon the two boys, Bernd shook his head repeatedly. Lothar's heart was beating faster, his pulse racing. The unthinkable was about to happen. With a despairing gesture, Bernd tipped over his King and offered Lothar his hand. He had won. In his happiness, his breath short, feeling dazed, confused, his eyes beginning to water, it was all Lothar could do to stop himself from crying.

'Congratulations, Lothar. School Champion!' announced the Principal.

Regaining his composure, Bernd stood up, walked around to Lothar's side of the table and hugged him. 'Bobby Fischer watch out,' his friend said. 'There's a new kid in town.'

On a freezing cold, snow-bitten morning, Lothar and Bernd stood at East Berlin railway station, suitcases in hand, hugging their parents goodbye. The National Junior Championship in Halle awaited. As they were too young to travel on their own, Rolf Lehmann, their German Literature teacher and, so he claimed, a chess enthusiast, would be accompanying them. Barely more than thirty years old, medium height, with the squashed nose of a boxer, an ill-fitting suede jacket and a deep, baritone voice, Lehmann was something of a mystery. There were rumours that he had been in trouble with the police the previous year – indeed, he had disappeared from school for six weeks at one stage, reappearing looking considerably more fragile and battle-scarred than when they had last seen him –

but the boys had no idea of the substance behind these stories. Perhaps they would find out during the trip.

As early as the first stop of their journey, when Bernd pulled out his pocket set and their teacher made his excuses and headed down the train, they realised that Lehmann had little interest in chess. After some time, he returned with a sly smile on his face. Sitting back down, he looked around him, as furtive as a squirrel, before opening his jacket to show them a quarter litre of vodka, wrapped in brown paper, hidden inside his pocket.

'I met a soldier travelling home to Halle. He sold me this.' Lehmann tapped his nose like a chess master. 'I got a good price too.' He pulled out the bottle, unscrewed the cap, took a quick swig, and placed the bottle back in his pocket. The whole movement took him about four seconds. 'That hit the spot,' he said. 'Got any food?'

Lothar had nothing. Bernd was better prepared. 'My mother gave me some supplies for the journey,' he said, unhooking his battered suitcase and pulling a headscarf from the top of the case. Lehmann and Lothar watched as Bernd unfolded the headscarf and laid it out on the table in front of them. Inside were two dried sausages and a chunk of black bread. Bernd pushed the food in their direction. 'We could split the sausages into three,' he suggested.

'I had a big breakfast, thanks,' Lothar said. It wasn't true, but he was struggling to keep the image of the headscarf out of his mind. Lehmann, on the other hand, was already tucking in, having grabbed a piece of bread as well, to which he added a dab of vodka, 'for flavour'.

As he savoured the dried sausage, their teacher shared with them his philosophy on the world. 'Enjoy your lives, lads. Eat, drink and be merry. We are only here for a short time on this earth. Make the most of it.'

'Is that why you are a teacher, sir?' asked Bernd, his lips betraying the hint of a smile.

Lehmann pulled a map out of his bag and laid it flat on the table in front of them. 'The truth, is boys, I'd like to travel. Look at the world. It's a large place.'

'Will the government allow you, sir?'

Lehmann stroked his lip. A conductor was approaching. 'Oh, I'd only want to travel in the communist bloc. Who would be interested in the West?'

The man had now reached their table. 'Tickets and identification papers please.'

'Here you go,' said Lehmann, handing across all three tickets along with the special identification papers the school had obtained for the trip. 'What a glorious winter's day it is. The boys and I were just saying how lucky we are to live in this fine country.'

The conductor smiled and clipped their tickets. As he moved on down the carriage, Lehmann put the map away. 'Dreams, eh?' he said, shaking his head wistfully.

Arriving in Halle, they caught a bus to the outskirts of town, where the tournament was to be played in a regional 'Pioneers' Palace', a concrete monolith which looked from the outside like a cross between a hospital and a factory, but actually served as a local youth club. A mural of Karl Marx adorned the front of the building. Inside, over five hundred chessboards and pieces were set up in a vast hall. Paint was coming off the walls, bare electric cables hung from the ceiling and there was a smell of damp throughout. Lehmann took one look at the hall and swore.

'Christ. Good luck being stuck here for a week, lads. Only in communist Europe could something like this be called a palace.' Bernd and Lothar stared at their teacher in amazement. 'You'd better forget I said that,' he continued. 'I'm sure you'll have a great time here.'

'Are you staying, sir?' Lothar asked. 'We need to register for the tournament.'

'No, I'm heading back into town, lads. It's time for a beer. You'll be OK. Have fun and I'll see you later.'

With that, their teacher was gone. Overwhelmed at the size of the venue, they made their way nervously to the front of the hall where a fat, balding man sat in front of a desk with a typed list of tournament entrants in front of him. He was wearing a brown suit and tie, and had a badge reading 'Chief Organiser' pinned to his lapel.

'Name?' the Chief Organiser barked.

'Lothar Hartmann,' he stuttered.

'Identity papers,' the Chief Organiser shouted at him, his voice as loud as a buzz saw.

Lothar wondered from the tone of his voice if he was a military man. Digging into his jacket, he pulled out his papers. The man peered at them as if with a magnifying glass, checked his name against the one he had just written down, and handed the papers back to him. 'Section?' he continued.

'Section?' Lothar repeated, not understanding what he meant.

'What tournament are you in? What age group?' The Chief Organiser looked at Lothar with wide eyes, as though he couldn't quite believe what such a specimen was doing in his playing hall.

'Oh. I'm fourteen years old,' he replied.

The man sighed. 'We will put you in the under-fifteen event then,' he said. 'Unless you fancy taking on the eighteen-year-olds?'

'No, that's fine. Under fifteens it is.'

'Me too, please,' said Bernd.

'Did I ask you?' said the man curtly.

After registering, they explored the venue. Aside from a decrepit games room with a broken table tennis table, they found little to amuse themselves. Few other players had arrived yet, but in the corner of the main hall a crowd of youths had gathered around a chessboard. A large, overweight boy with greasy hair, seated at the board, appeared to be the centre of attention. The boy waved a Bishop in the air, glanced at the two boys, and turned back to the admiring group.

'At this point, I played Bishop takes Rook, and slammed down the clock. Weber was so surprised by my move, he nearly slipped off his chair.' The overweight boy gave a mock shriek and fell back in his seat like a rag doll. The crowd laughed and the boy pulled himself back up. 'Of course, from that moment on,' he said, 'the outcome was never in doubt. At the risk of sounding arrogant, I'm a very good front runner.'

'Wonderful, Sebastian,' said a fair-haired boy with a loud voice, bursting into an impromptu round of applause. 'You're such a strong player.'

'Thank you, Paul,' said Sebastian. 'It was a nice win, but let's not get carried away. Now, who wants to see my game against Schwarz?' Sebastian rubbed his hands together. 'Just wait till I show you how I mangled him with my pawns.'

Lothar and Bernd walked away. 'Who was that?' Lothar asked.

'That was Sebastian Bahl, the top junior in the country.'

'He seemed like a character.'

'You'll find out,' said Bernd. 'Fancy a game of table tennis before we go?'

The organisers had booked them places in a youth hostel a short walk from the Pioneers' Palace. There were twenty boys to a room and the building smelled of old socks and unwashed feet. Lehmann, meanwhile, making full use of the school's spending money, had negotiated himself a room at a boarding house nearby. The boys hoped that he might invite them to dinner, but they found a note from their teacher at reception advising that he had already gone out for the evening. The hostel had little to offer except stale bread, mouldy cheese and thick black soup of an unspecified flavour. At a loss as to what else to do, Lothar and Bernd played some practice games until lights out at ten o'clock. A boy in a neighbouring bunk, who had taken part in the tournament the previous year, told them that this would be the routine every night. It was not an auspicious beginning.

Arriving early at the Pioneers' Palace the following morning, they found their seats. Bernd was up against another player from Berlin and Lothar faced a local lad from Halle. After a series of speeches from politicians and dignitaries, a seven-minute rendition of the national anthem, and a sworn allegiance to Erich Honecker, play finally got underway at half past nine.

Lothar's opponent was an athletic-looking fellow with dark hair and a confident handshake. He was hardly an archetypal chess player. Lothar pushed his King's pawn forward two squares, and his opponent replied with the most aggressive of chess openings, the Sicilian Defence, equally quickly. Soon the other boy had built up a dangerous attack. Lothar was no match for him, and when his opponent swept his Rook almost the length of the board, snapping a white Knight off as he did so, Lothar resigned, humiliated, rather than face the inevitable checkmate.

Bernd had fared no better, losing his game after a grim struggle which took just over three hours. Lehmann, who had appeared shortly before they finished their games, had already disappeared again, heading into town to find a new bar.

Over the next week, no matter how hard they tried, neither boy was able to make any mark on the tournament. After the eleventh and final round, they were both placed around the halfway point in the field, well below their expectations. Putting the pieces back in their box after a final-round loss, Lothar trudged across the hall where he found his teacher and Bernd. He felt sad and defeated. The tournament, and so it seemed to him, his chess dreams, were over.

'What will we tell the Principal?' he asked Lehmann. 'He was expecting one of us to bring back the trophy.'

'Don't worry, lads. We'll tell him you just missed out,' said their teacher. 'I'm proud of your performance, but we need more funding next year. A few good meals out would have helped you both. Not that it's easy to find decent food in this town.'

On the evidence of what he had seen of Lehmann, Lothar very much doubted that a few late evenings with their teacher would have made any difference. Tired, hungry and missing home, he had rarely felt so dejected. He had entered the tournament with so many hopes. He understood now that he had work to do, an enormous amount, if he was to get good at the game.

'Shall we head off, sir? I don't feel like staying for the prize giving.'

'Stay positive, lads. We'll catch the seven o'clock train,' said Lehmann. 'There's someone I'd like you both to meet first.'

'Who's that?'

'An old friend of mine, the man who taught me chess, in fact. A chap called Hans Adler. He arrived here today.'

'Hans Adler? The chess coach?'

'Yes, that's the one. You've heard of him?'

Lothar and Bernd looked at each other with wide eyes.

'He's the most famous coach in East Germany,' Lothar said. 'All the kids here talk about him. If Adler selects you as his pupil, you're almost guaranteed to become a Grandmaster.' Suddenly he felt enthused again. His result had been a terrible disappointment, but there was still a chance to take something away from the week. An opportunity to meet with the great Hans Adler himself, to study, to learn, to improve.

'Perhaps I should have listened more carefully when Hans taught me,' said Lehmann. 'Come this way. Hans is setting up a coaching session in one of the back rooms and you've both got a place in the audience.'

Reinvigorated, they followed their teacher down the length of the hall to a back room on the left. The dishevelled grey man with the moustache, cap and hunched shoulders, busying himself setting up a demonstration board, was not what they had expected.

'Hans, here are the two lads I told you about: Lothar and Bernd.'

The man turned around, shuffled over and shook their hands. 'How did you do in the tournament?' he asked.

'Badly,' said Lothar.

Adler frowned. 'Pay attention to my lecture and you'll do better next year,' he said dryly, motioning to them to take seats in the front row. Adler nodded at Lehmann and went back to his demonstration board, where he continued to place large metallic chess pieces on their starting squares. Their teacher departed and, on cue, a group of ten other children marched into the room. Lothar spotted amongst them Sebastian Bahl, who had finished first in the eighteen and under tournament. Bahl was now proceeding to tell everyone in great detail about his victory. Alongside him was Konrad Welde, the winner of the tournament they had played in, a small, nervous boy with a gap-toothed smile and thick glasses.

Bernd leaned across and whispered, 'Everyone else here is a prize-winner. I feel like an imposter.'

After twenty minutes, Lothar was beginning to wonder if Bernd had been right. Much of what Adler said went over his head, and he seemed to have little to offer, especially in comparison with Bahl and Welde, who solved most of the puzzles set by Adler before he had even got to grips with the question.

When Bahl came up with yet another rapid-fire solution, Adler pondered for a moment. 'Right, time for something more difficult.' Clearing the pieces off the demonstration board, the coach set up a new puzzle. White had a strong attack, with all his pieces in menacing positions. Black's King seemed secure though, protected in the corner.

'This is a game played by two British amateurs, Donovan and Howell,' said Adler. 'From this position, White gave checkmate in nine moves. I was coaching in Moscow last week and showed it to ten Grandmasters, including Vasily Smirov, the Soviet Union's newest star. Do you know how many solved it?'

'Checkmate? It looks impossible,' said Welde.

'There may be a solution,' said Bahl, running his left hand through his hair knowingly like a young professor, 'although frankly, if White had any sense, he would have won this game long ago.' The bespectacled Welde laughed and the two friends exchanged sly Cheshire cat grins.

Adler remained stony-faced. 'There is a solution, and only one person found it. Smirov came up with the right answer. Everybody else gave up. This is a true test of ability. Solve this puzzle and you'll be a Grandmaster one day.'

There was silence as they stared at the board. Bahl made as if to say something a couple of times and then fell quiet again. Bernd sat beside him staring forlornly at the position. Shutting his eyes and clearing his mind of other thoughts, Lothar visualised the chess pieces. The white Knight approaching the black King;

the white Queen ready to swing into action; the Bishop which would be so dangerous if only it could get into play. Suddenly, inspiration struck him. Ignoring the tight feeling in his chest, conscious that he was risking ridicule, Lothar opened his eyes again, stood up and took a step towards Adler. 'White must move his Bishop,' he said, 'attacking the black King.'

Bahl smiled sympathetically, aware of his responsibilities as the new champion. 'An interesting idea,' he said, 'which I considered briefly myself. The problem is that Black can simply play Queen takes Rook with check. Game over.' Bahl crossed his arms with an air of finality, while Welde raised his eyebrows and even Bernd looked at him curiously. Only Adler remained straight-faced.

'Gentlemen, let's not dismiss the idea out of hand. We have a proposal to move the white Bishop. Sorry, what was your name again?'

'Lothar.'

'Lothar suggests White launches an immediate attack.' Adler slid the Bishop diagonally across the demonstration board. 'Sebastian Bahl is countering with his Queen. What do you do then, Lothar?'

'I move my King,' he replied, 'intending a Queen move, check and mate.'

'Very good, Lothar,' said Adler. 'Please, come up to the board and show us yourself.'

Lothar stood up and played the move, nervous, but proud too that he had at least got one thing right. Bahl still looked sceptical. 'Surely Black can defend,' he said.

Hardly drawing breath, Lothar slid the white Bishop diagonally towards the black King. Bahl's face had gone red. Lothar felt he saw a flicker of pain in the other boy's eyes. 'I parry like so,' he said, rising to stand by him, tentatively moving the black Queen two squares to the right. His voice was cracked and unconvincing. The two players made the next few moves in rapid fire. Lothar pushed forward a Bishop and Bahl brought back his Rook. With a flourish, Lothar picked up his Knight and snatched a black pawn off the board.

'Check and mate in four moves,' he announced.

'Bravo,' said Adler, giving a small clap of his hands. 'That is the solution.'

Bahl was open-mouthed. 'Who are you again?' he asked.

'Lothar Hartmann,' he said. 'Champion of Geisler College, East Berlin.'

As Bahl sat shaking his head in bewilderment, Lothar returned to his seat with a quiet satisfaction. His adventures in tournament chess had begun.

CHAPTER TWO

The Coach

Balancing on an old three-legged wooden stool, one hand resting on the door frame, Lothar pinned the final piece of tinsel above the living room door. His father, meanwhile, was putting the finishing touches to the Christmas tree, hanging little wooden angels and glass balls on the top. From the kitchen, where his mother was busying herself at the stove, he could smell Vienna sausage and potato salad. Christmas Eve. His favourite night of the year.

The doorbell rang shortly after they had sat down at the dining table. Cursing, his father put down his knife and fork and, rising stiffly, left the table to answer the door. He walked back into the living room, face gaunt, eyes glazed. In his hands he held a telegram. 'It's Leon,' he said. 'A heart attack. He's in intensive care.' He sat back down and rested his hands on the table, staring blankly at his family.

Lothar looked up at his parents. 'We have to get down to Checkpoint Charlie, don't we, and ask for an emergency exit stamp?'

Lothar's mother put her arm around his shoulder. 'Sweetheart, they don't let people through the border. Not without a lot of paperwork.'

Lothar let out a cry of anguish. 'He's family. They have to let us through.'

Shortly afterwards, Lothar and his mother stood, wrapped in thick winter coats, scarves and woollen hats, watching from the other side of the road as Herr Hartmann pleaded with the border guards, gesticulating, waving his arms in the air and stamping his feet in the snow. Presently, Lothar's father turned and walked back towards them, shaking his head.

'We have to report to the Security and Borders office.'

'Can we do that now?' Lothar asked.

'It's not open until January.'

Lothar let out a sigh of frustration. 'But that's over a week away.'

'Let's be honest. That's the least of our problems,' said his father.

The call came three days later. His uncle, so the hospital said, had died peacefully in his sleep. The news hit Lothar hard. Over the next month, he dreamed repeatedly of his uncle, waking in a cold sweat when he realised that he was gone. His father too, already a man of few words, retreated into a shell after Leon's death. Looking back, it seemed to Lothar that his father was never the same after that day.

In the spring, Rolf Lehmann entered the school into a local league. Once a week, Lothar and Bernd clambered onto the tram with their teacher, their destination the East Berlin Central Chess Club. For a chess enthusiast, it was Paradise. Entering a huge building shaped like a library, inside they found room after room containing tables, boards and chess sets. At every board, grown men in grey suits sat hunched in concentration, looking up occasionally to take a drag from their cigarettes and frown at the newcomers at the door, before returning their focus to the wooden pieces in front of them.

Lothar and Bernd frequently found themselves paired against adults, and the competition was tough. Nevertheless, they won more games than they lost, while Lehmann watched them proudly, a stein of beer always in his hand. On the way back, his tongue loosened by the alcohol, Lehmann would whisper sly remarks about the other passengers — laughing at their polyester suits, their briefcases, their conformity — while pretending to analyse with the boys on the pocket set, the beer on his breath drowning out the smell of burnt electrics from the tram.

At the end of the season, Lehmann spent the entire evening in a local bar while the boys played chess. 'How many do you think he's had?' asked Bernd as they watched their teacher peer at the timetable, trying to make sense of the jumble of numbers in front of him, as they waited for the tram home.

'No point asking,' said Lothar. 'He usually loses count after two glasses.'

However much he had drunk, any discretion their teacher normally had seemed now to have vanished. As they sat on the tram, Lehmann began telling jokes. Not this time in his customary whisper, but out loud, so that anybody who strained their ears could hear.

'Here's a good one,' said their teacher, nudging Lothar and Bernd in the ribs. 'Why do Stasi officers make such good taxi drivers?'

'I don't know, sir,' said Bernd. Lothar sat passively, keeping his face blank.

'You get in the car and they already know your name and where you live,' said Lehmann, chortling to himself.

Bernd smiled weakly, and a man opposite in a beige overcoat and glasses glanced up and stared. Encouraged by his audience, Lehmann continued. 'Here's another one, boys. You'll like this. Why do the Stasi work in groups of three?'

Bernd shook his head. 'Because,' said Lehmann, pausing for effect, 'you need one who can read, one who can write, and a third to keep an eye on the two intellectuals.'

Lothar saw the man opposite take a notebook out of the pocket of his jacket before scribbling something on a piece of paper. Nodding at Bernd, Lothar heaved Lehmann up from his seat. 'Time to get off the tram, sir. This is our stop.'

Lehmann looked puzzled. 'Really? But we've only just got on.'

'We'll walk the last bit,' said Bernd, supporting Lehmann from the other side and leading him off the tram. 'The fresh air will do us all good.'

As Lehmann continued to shake his head, the two boys guided him down the road and away from trouble. The next morning, he would remember nothing about what had happened or the danger he had put himself in. That was the trouble with drunks, thought Lothar. If they didn't recall their mistakes, how could they learn from them?

The following week the club held a special rapid tournament, ten seconds a move. Lothar was one of the first to put his name down. He loved speed chess. The quick pace suited him, and he found that he had a surprising aptitude for problem solving. Shutting his eyes, and picturing the board and pieces, he seemed to be able to find the best move in almost any situation. He didn't know where this talent came from. In some ways it almost scared him, this strange intuition. As he learned to control his new power, however, it added immeasurably to his game, and he began to win game after game.

At the end of the evening, Lothar found himself in a contest for the bronze medal, a performance way above anyone's expectations. Although he lost that final game to one of the top players in the country, Lazlo Vogel, he acquitted himself well, forcing his opponent to work to the end to prove the win.

As he shook hands with his opponent, a man in a cap reached across his shoulder and started resetting the pieces, until they arrived at the position that they had on the board some twenty moves previously. 'At this point,' the man said to him, picking up a black Rook and thrusting it into the heart of Vogel's defences like a Japanese knife, 'you could have sacrificed your piece – like this – to win the game.'

Lothar and Vogel looked at this new possibility. The man was correct. His voice sounded familiar. Lothar turned around to get a proper look at him. With a start, he realised that it was the coach, Hans Adler.

'Thank you, Herr Adler. I didn't see that move,' he said.

'Of course you didn't see it,' said Adler. 'If you had seen the move, you would have played it. You missed lots of other good moves too.'

'Oh.' He didn't know how to respond to that.

'You do, however, have some potential.' Adler handed him a card. 'Here is my address. I'll expect you next Thursday. If you do well next week, the club will pay for a year's coaching. I will see you at five o'clock. Don't be late.'

With that, Adler was gone.

A week later, hurrying home from school, Lothar threw his school bag into the corner of his room, changed out of his uniform and, grabbing a slice of bread, was out of the door again within ten minutes. Running to catch the Number Two tram to Leninplatz, he found the last free seat. Opposite him sat a man in a grey raincoat, about fifty years old, clutching a leather briefcase to his lap. The man's left hand was bandaged, and he stared straight ahead, vacantly. On either side of him sat two elderly men wearing fur hats. None of them smiled. Lothar wondered what the man with the briefcase had done today. His good hand, the one without the bandage, looked well manicured, and he guessed that his was an office job, rather than a manual one. A government official perhaps? But how to explain the bandage? He looked at the man's downturned expression again. His wasn't a life that he wanted, or one that he was going to settle for either.

When they reached Leninplatz, Lothar jumped off the tram, stopping to gaze at the sixty-foot statue in the centre of the square. Determined, purposeful, the hint of a scowl, and yet still benevolent and wise, his left arm outstretched, reaching to his people, here was Vladimir Ilyich Ulyanov, the man who had started it all. Lothar wondered what Lenin would think of the world he had created. Was this the society he had dreamed of?

He stared at the statue for some five minutes before, with a start, he remembered that he had business to attend to. Turning left, he climbed up the steep hill which led away from the city. It had snowed the day before, and the snow was turning to mush under his feet. He wished he had worn his wellingtons. A sea of grey prefabricated concrete flats stood on either side of the road. In the snow they must have looked pretty. Now the snow had melted, their beauty had faded too.

At the top of the hill he stopped to regain his breath. The slush was seeping into his shoes, and just when he thought his feet might fall off from the cold, he found Adler's block, number seventeen, indistinguishable from those which surrounded it except by its number. A sign on the door told him that the lift was out of order. Brushing his feet on the carpet inside the main entrance, he steeled himself for the stairs. Adler was on the top floor, and by the time he made it there, he was clutching on to the handrail for dear life.

'Physical fitness is important,' said Adler, opening his front door and, seeing his heavy panting, ushering him inside with a frown. A small man, his back stooped, his shirt was creased and his trousers were gravy-stained. He was holding a cigarette in one hand and a Russian chess magazine in the other. 'You have the build of a footballer. On a good day, you could even pass for Franz Beckenbauer. But you'll never be a champion if you can't walk up a few flights of stairs.'

'Stop teasing the boy,' said a slim woman with short brown hair, in her early thirties, emerging from the kitchen area to shake his hand. She was wearing a blue apron and had flour on her hands. Her palms were soft, kindly. 'You're hardly one to talk about physical fitness, are you Hans? My name is Freya,' she continued, turning to him and smiling. 'You'll have to excuse my husband. He has no manners.'

'You'll have to excuse my wife,' said Adler. 'She has no idea what it takes to become a champion.' Where others might have said this with a twinkle in their eye, Adler looked deadly serious, stubbing out his cigarette on an ashtray by the front door for emphasis, his moustache bristling.

Adler's flat reminded him of home. The front door led straight into a living room that had just enough space for a shabby sofa, a dining table and a black and white television in the corner. The wallpaper was a fashionable bright yellow, and the carpet a thick deep red. Lothar took his shoes off and went to say hello to two young children, a boy and a girl, no more than five years old, who were playing with an iron construction kit on the floor. It looked like they were building a Soviet tank. To the left was a tiny kitchen with a stove and a sink. The smell of bratwurst was competing valiantly against the odour of tobacco. Lothar made it a score draw. To the right, a narrow hallway led to two bedrooms and a study. He stopped to play with the children, accidentally knocking an ashtray from the table as he did so. Freya appeared with a dustpan within seconds.

Crestfallen at his clumsiness, Lothar went to apologise. 'Don't worry, Lothar,' she said with a smile. 'Hans does that all the time.'

Adler motioned Lothar to follow him into his study. Inside was a row of shelves full of old chess books and magazines. A coffee table and two folding chairs stood in the centre of the room. On top of the table was a wooden chess set, a clock and an overflowing ashtray. A pile of Russian magazines lay at the side of the board, alongside a pack of cigarettes. If he was to spend any time with Hans Adler, Lothar thought to himself, the path of least resistance would be to take up smoking.

Adler pulled out a chair for him. Sitting down opposite, he reached for a thick black book from the shelf behind him. 'The games of Mikhail Voronin,' he said. 'One of our brightest stars. Let's teach you some proper chess.'

For the rest of the evening, they worked their way through some of the great games of the Latvian Mikhail Voronin, World Champion in the early 1960s. Drinker, smoker, fearless adventurer, the magician from Riga was the player that every young enthusiast wanted to emulate. His sacrificial attacks were the stuff of legend, as was his hypnotic stare. Shortly before the Latvian became World Champion, one opponent, the American Grandmaster Kertesz, himself an émigré from communist Hungary, arrived at the board wearing an enormous pair of sunglasses, designed to counteract Voronin. Ever the wit, Voronin had his coach run to the nearest store, returning with an even larger pair of shades, which he wore for the rest of the game. Needless to say, Voronin won.

Impressed as he was, Lothar found himself cursing that Adler had chosen the Latvian wizard for that evening's coaching session. Voronin's play was inventive and surprising and he managed to guess only a few of his moves. Even where he did, it was more by luck than judgement. He wished that Adler had opted for a positional player like Vartanian. He might have made a better impression that way.

When Adler set up a particularly complex position, with pieces seemingly strewn all over the sixty-four squares at random, he was at a loss, staring at the board, unable to make any sense of it. 'Who is winning?' he asked.

'Hah!' said Adler. 'That is the point. Nobody knows who is winning. The play starts from here. Which is where a genius like Voronin is in his element.'

'I could look at this for a week and I don't think I'd solve its mysteries,' he said.

'Precisely,' replied Adler, grinding his cigarette into the ashtray for emphasis. 'Show me a player who thinks he has mastered the game and I will show you a fool.'

At nine o'clock, Freya knocked at the study door. 'It's getting late, Lothar. School tomorrow. Time to be getting home.'

Adler looked up at his wife. 'School won't teach Lothar about Mikhail Voronin. It's more important for the boy that he stays and learns.'

Freya walked across and put her arm on her husband's shoulder. 'Half an hour, my dear.' For the first time since he had met him, Adler smiled. Lothar suspected that Adler loved Mikhail Voronin almost as much as his wife.

At half past nine, the time came to say goodnight. As they shook hands at the door, Adler looked at him intently. 'You have a lot of work to do, Lothar, if you want to make it to Grandmaster. You have a modicum of talent, but you'll never get anywhere unless you start to put the effort in.' His heart sank. So this was to be their only coaching session? Adler stubbed out his cigarette in an ashtray by the front door. The man had nearly as many ashtrays as chess books. 'Which means,' the coach continued, stroking his moustache, 'we had better book you in for a weekly session. I will see you same time next week.'

Only when he reached the tram stop did he realise that he had no money for a return ticket. No matter. The snow had thawed and he didn't mind the forty minutes' walk home. In his excitement, he could have flown.

At school the next day Lothar told his classmates about his adventures.

'The country's finest coach and he's living in squalor,' said Troeller.

'Squalor's not the right word. Hans and his wife just don't place much importance on material possessions,' he replied.

'*Hans* is it now?' said Troeller, putting on his poshest voice. 'Good luck with the coaching. Perhaps one day you'll be as good as *Hans* and you can share his flat.'

'Don't listen to him,' said Bernd as they walked away. 'He's the only guy in school whose ambition is to become a member of the Stasi.'

Over the coming months, Lothar visited Hans Adler's flat religiously every Thursday evening. Hans liked to study the classics, and they began to work their way through the collected games of the Masters: Dasaev, Aleinikov, Weber, Spassky and the great Fischer. For variety, they discussed opening and endgame strategies, and Hans gave him more puzzles to solve, like the one he had showed their coaching group in Halle.

Hans was a hard man to please. He gave praise rarely, continuing to stress how much work Lothar had to do. Nevertheless, he felt his game improve as chess became an obsession. Hunched over the sixty-four squares at home, he abandoned the nightly football in the courtyard below their flat. On weekends, while friends went out on their bikes or hung around the market square or the park, he stayed indoors with his battered copy of Bobby Fischer's *My 60 Memorable Games.*

Once a month Lothar put his newfound abilities to the test at the East Berlin Congress, where the top local players competed for what was, by East German standards, a generous first prize. It was here that Lothar met his first Grandmaster opponent, the great man of East German chess, and many times national champion, Thomas Jensen. In his late thirties, Jensen was one of his heroes, a superb competitor who held his own against the top players in the world. It was rare to see him at a local event, but word had it that after some recent poor results, he was seeking a return to form in humbler surroundings.

Lothar's opportunity to take on the Grandmaster came as early as the second round. He had played so few games up until that point in his life that his ranking – known as a *chess rating* – was one of the lowest in the tournament. As Jensen was to find out, Lothar's real strength was far ahead of his rating. The Grandmaster beat him eventually, but only after three hours of considerable exertion. At the end of the game, the grey-haired Jensen, with his glasses resting on the end of his nose and his tie askew, for all the world looking more like a professor than a sportsman, shook his hand warmly. 'You will be a strong player one day, son.'

Walking home that evening, Lothar was torn between pride – the great Jensen himself had praised him – and deep frustration. He had been so close to a result against the Grandmaster, and he had blown it. What a fool he was! How could he expect to become a world-class player himself if he made such stupid mistakes?

Gradually, his annoyance at his missed opportunity wore off, and by the following Thursday he felt ready to show Hans his

game against the Grandmaster, as well as a victory in the last
round over a local man called Zeeler. At the mention of Zeeler's
name, Hans stubbed out his cigarette in disgust, his moustache
bristling. 'You beat that piece of work? Good thing too.'

'What's Zeeler done to you?'

'Never mind what he's done to me. It's what he stands for.'

'What does he stand for?'

Hans spat into his ashtray. 'He's Stasi. A spy, a member of
the secret police. He tells tales on his own people, his friends,
his family, his colleagues. He'll snitch on you too if you get to
know him.'

'I've got nothing to hide.'

'Fine. Invite him round to your flat. Let him report back on
what you ate for dinner. If that's the world you want to live in,
good luck to you.'

'How do you know he works for the Stasi?'

'I know,' said Hans, raising his voice with emphasis. 'Trust
me.'

For some reason, this explanation wasn't enough for Lothar.
'How do you know, Hans?'

Hans frowned and lit another cigarette, saying nothing,
waiting for him to speak again. Lothar held his ground, staring
back impassively. Eventually, Hans rose and stood by the
window, with his back to him.

'How do I know that Zeeler works for the Stasi? I know,
Lothar, because of what happened to me. Ten years ago, ten
years this month, I had a job, a good job, as a teacher in a
college. Chess was a sideline for me, a lucrative and enjoyable
one, but just a hobby.'

It had grown dark outside. His coach closed the window
and drew the curtains shut. 'Zeeler was a teacher at the same
college. During the lunch breaks we would play chess. We got

on well, or so I thought.' Hans turned around and sat back down opposite him. He lowered his voice to a hush. 'Did I ever tell you that I had a brother?' Lothar shook his head. 'Oskar. He was a writer. Two years younger than me. A sensitive man, a good man too.'

'What happened to him?'

'He was arrested for writing anti-government propaganda.'

Lothar felt the lump in his throat. 'Was he convicted?'

'The case never went to trial. He hanged himself with a rope the day before he was due to go to court.'

'Goodness, I'm so sorry, Hans.' He felt lost for words, unsure what else he should say.

Hans pulled out a handkerchief, which he dabbed against his eyes. 'It was my fault. I made a mistake. I showed Zeeler an article Oskar had written, a critique of the government. Oskar had sent it to the West, anonymously. I thought Zeeler was on our side. Two days later, there was a knock on Oskar's door. He was taken by the police to an interrogation centre.'

'Zeeler was at the interrogation centre?'

'Oh no, the Stasi are subtler than that. Zeeler was nowhere to be seen.'

'How do you know Zeeler was involved then?'

'One of the guards made a mistake. He mentioned Zeeler to my brother. He laughed too, said he was going to tell Zeeler all about the beating they had given him. When Oskar got home, it was the first thing he told me. Of course, I confronted Zeeler immediately. By the afternoon, they had removed me from the college. I've never taught in a school since.'

While he had been talking, Hans had been emptying the board of chessmen, until just a solitary black pawn remained. He drummed the pawn down hard on the board, until Lothar thought it would make a dent.

'The so-called Shield and Sword of the Party? The Stasi are more like a poison, Lothar. They destroy lives, families, whole communities. They bug flats and houses, they falsely imprison, they use torture to extract confessions, genuine or otherwise. I'll tell you another thing. They will try to enlist you too. They like chess players: the analytical skills, the socially awkward disposition. Makes for an ideal recruit.'

'I'm never going to join the Stasi, Hans. I believe in freedom.'

His coach frowned. 'You want to be careful who you say that to.'

'I've heard you talk about freedom enough times. I understand what you mean.'

'The Stasi can no longer touch me. I'm too well known. A young lad like you needs to watch out. Make your reputation first, and then you can talk freely.'

Lothar nodded wisely, like a sage young Buddha. At that age, though, he had no real idea how difficult it could be to escape the clutches of the Stasi.

CHAPTER THREE

The East German Mick Jagger

It rained incessantly for five days. In the midst of the thunder and gloom, two policemen visited Lothar's school. They questioned the pupils about their studies, their teachers; what they were learning. They even asked about their homework assignments. The men spoke to Lothar at length about Rolf Lehmann and he told them that he had great respect for his teacher.

The next day, Lehmann did not come into school and a supply teacher covered his lessons. When Lothar asked where Lehmann was, the supply teacher glared at him and ignored the question. When Lehmann didn't appear the following day either, Lothar began to imagine the worst. What had happened to their teacher? Where had he gone? None of the scenarios he envisaged were good ones.

During the lunch break, he sat with Bernd in the corner of the cafeteria, speculating as to what could have happened to Lehmann.

'Perhaps he's done a bunk,' said Bernd.

'Done a bunk?'

'Made it across the border, escaped to the West.' Bernd looked out of the window and rubbed his hands together. 'Ran to freedom, like a spy in the movies.'

'How would he manage that? Escape, I mean.'

Bernd screwed up his face. 'I suppose he could have dressed up as a solider and pretended he was on border patrol.'

'You believe that?' Lothar did his best not to be dismissive, but the chances of Lehmann fooling anybody sufficiently to make it across the border seemed decidedly remote.

Bernd stroked his chin. 'I guess it is far-fetched.'

'Bernd, I'm worried. It's not like Lehmann to miss school. He came in before Christmas even when he had flu, and the Principal had to send him home. He hasn't missed a day since...'

Bernd finished the sentence for him. 'Since he was arrested a couple of years back.'

'We should go round to his flat. Knock on his door. Check he's alright.'

Bernd nodded. 'After school. We'll go there this evening. Find out for sure.'

The hours dragged by. At four o'clock the bell went, and Lothar ran out of his history class, down to the school gate. Bernd was already waiting for him, his arms behind his back, kicking at a piece of grass by the side of the road. As Lothar approached, his friend turned around hesitantly.

'What's wrong?' Lothar asked.

Bernd stubbed his shoe on the ground again. 'I don't know, Lothar. Finding out what's up with Lehmann seemed so urgent this morning. Now that we can actually go and see him, and his house is only ten minutes' walk away, I don't feel so sure. I mean, supposing it's just a cold. He's only taken a couple of days off. Won't he think it's odd, us visiting?'

Lothar took his friend firmly by the arm. 'Bernd, we need to find out what's happened. This way.'

The boys had been to Lehmann's flat twice before. A single man, he kept his place sparsely decorated, but he was also tidy and clean. The few books he had were stacked neatly in the bookcase in the corner. A plant stood on top of the mantelpiece, its leaves pristine green. When they had dinner, he'd washed and put away the plates as soon as they had eaten.

Now, as they looked through Lehmann's ground-floor window, Lothar didn't recognise what he saw. Papers strewn across the floor; the plant knocked from its vase, lying on its side; books all over the table, covers open, some of them torn. The flat looked like it had been hit by a tornado.

'Do you think we should break in?' said Bernd. 'Perhaps he's asleep, and didn't hear us when we knocked?'

Lothar looked at the window frame. It was old and rotting. A couple of shoves and they could prise it open. His chest trembled though at what they might find in there. Lehmann unconscious on his bed, maybe worse, the alcohol finally having done for him?

'It looks like someone has already broken in,' Lothar said.

'Well then there's no reason to hesitate,' replied his friend.

Lothar felt the base of the window. It was as loose as he had expected. Then, behind them, footsteps. A voice.

'Can I help you, lads?'

Turning around, Lothar saw a man in his sixties, in a thick grey coat, a moustache and a cap. He recognised him as Lehmann's neighbour and, so their teacher had told them, his sometime drinking buddy.

'We're looking for Herr Lehmann. He's our teacher, and we're worried about him.'

The man nodded. 'Yes, I recognise you. I'm afraid you won't find Rolf in.'

'Where is he? Do you know?' asked Bernd.

The man sighed. 'They took him,' he said.

'Who?'

'The Stasi. They came yesterday morning. Six o'clock. Woke me up.' The man looked down at the ground and spat. 'Banging. Lots of noise. Shouting too.'

'When will Herr Lehmann – Rolf – be back?'

'I'm sorry, lads, but that I don't know. If he does come back, I'll tell him you called.'

With that, the man turned and walked off.

'Did you hear that?' asked Bernd.

'*If he does come back*? Yes, I caught that.'

The two boys walked home feeling sombre, saying little, taking the back entrance to avoid the evening football game.

The following week, Lothar's father found out from a friend at work that the police had arrested Lehmann and charged him with subversion against the state. Putting his arm around Lothar's shoulder, his father pulled him close. 'There's no point sugar-coating it, Lothar. Rolf Lehmann won't return to the school after this. He's already had one chance, which is more than most people get.'

'What's going to happen to him?' Lothar asked, feeling a tension in his chest and a throbbing in his head.

'I don't know. Maybe a spell in prison.'

'But what for? He's not done anything.'

Of course his father couldn't answer that. There were no answers. Lothar knew though that he would miss Lehmann. He had taught him nothing about chess, but he was an unusual man with an alternative outlook on life. The school, their lives, would be the poorer for his loss.

The National Junior Championships. How far he had come since his debut at the age of fourteen. When the clock struck midnight, with sleep still eluding him, Lothar rose, put on his dressing grown and walked down the corridor into the kitchen. His coach sat hunched over the dining table with a glass in one hand, a cigarette in the other, and a board in front of him.

'Can't sleep?' Hans asked.

'I'm worked up about tomorrow,' he said.

'If it's any consolation, Konrad Welde will be feeling the same way. The title of East German junior champion isn't one to sniff at. Luckily for us, I have a ready-made solution.'

Without asking, Hans pulled a glass from the cabinet and poured a large measure of vodka, which he put in front of Lothar. 'Drink this and you won't need to worry about getting to sleep.'

Lothar took a sip of the vodka. It was sharp and bitter and he clenched his teeth. 'People drink this for pleasure?'

Hans scratched his chin and considered. 'Hmm, I'm not sure pleasure is the right word.'

'Why do they drink then?'

'Any number of reasons, Lothar. To help raise their spirits, to be sociable, to pass the time, sometimes to forget. Yes, people drink to forget.'

'I like that idea,' Lothar said. 'I'm going to forget about the game. I'll wake up early tomorrow and then I will be ready for battle.'

Hans raised his glass. 'Spoken like a true East German.'

The next day he went for a gentle jog to run off any excess effects of the drink. By the time the game started, he was fresh and alert. Welde, in contrast, looked tired and nervous, his usual gap-toothed grin nowhere to be seen, his eyes, even hidden behind his thick glasses, fearful.

Having drawn the white pieces, Lothar ventured the Queen's Gambit for the first time in his life. Confused by this cautious choice – it was not an opening he had prepared for – Welde stared long and hard at the board, pondering each move with great care. By move twenty, Lothar was an hour ahead on the clock. He had also built up a dangerous attack. He had learned by now to take nothing for granted, but as he watched his opponent fiddle nervously with his watch, his eyes fixated on his vulnerable King, he had an overwhelming feeling that the Championship was within his grasp. The familiar butterflies were rumbling in his stomach. The expectation, the tension, the certain knowledge that one move could ruin all that hard work. Equally, every move was an opportunity to prove himself, to demonstrate his mastery of the game. Was this about to be his moment?

After a further prolonged think – Welde now had only five minutes left for all his moves – his opponent shook his head, and picking up his Bishop, swept it the length of the board until it stood alongside Lothar's King. Check!

Lothar took a deep breath and rubbed his hands across his brow. That wasn't a move he had foreseen. Surely he could just capture the piece? He looked again. He couldn't see what Welde's plan was. Hovering his hand above the black Bishop, he went to pick it up, to remove it from the board. Then he looked for a third time. Could there be a hidden trap? Sitting back in his chair, withdrawing his hand, he closed his eyes, allowed his mind to go blank and visualised the pieces. His breathing slowed and his heart grew calm. All that remained was the chessboard and pieces. Suddenly he understood. If he captured the Bishop, Welde could give a further check, sacrifice his Rook, and win Lothar's Queen. It was a devilishly clever idea, and he felt a whole new level of respect for Welde. Sinking into deep thought, he eventually settled on a calmer and safer move.

With his unexpected ploy, Welde had taken the initiative, but he was now desperately short of time, having to make his remaining moves nearly instantly. Tempting as it was to reply equally quickly, Lothar slowed his own play down, torturing Welde with the fact that he would have to react as soon as he did move.

In these circumstances, it was nearly impossible for Welde to defend, and Lothar's position was already strong when Welde left a Knight *en prise*. Lothar captured the undefended piece, and then tried to maintain his composure as Welde sat with his head in his hands. As his clock ticked down towards zero, his opponent stretched out his right hand.

'Congratulations, Lothar,' he said, with a dignified smile. 'I resign the game.'

National junior champion; this was payback on many hours of hard work. As he staggered up from the board, unsteady on his feet, he felt a wave of emotion sweep through him: joy, exuberance, and tremendous pride in what he had achieved. Gradually becoming conscious of the crowd around him, as if awakening from a dream, he reached across to find Hans, who for the first time that week was smiling. 'I'm proud of you, Lothar,' his coach said. 'If you keep playing like this, you might achieve something one day.'

Back at home, Lothar showed his parents the gleaming silver trophy which he had brought back with him. His father examined the inscriptions on the base. 'There are some famous names here. Thomas Jensen, Rainer Müller, Lazlo Vogel. They are all Grandmasters now, aren't they?'

Lothar breathed in deeply. 'How would you feel if I followed in their footsteps?'

'You have, Lothar. You're East German junior champion, just like they were.'

'I mean become a Grandmaster.'

His father whistled. He held the trophy up to the light. 'Lothar, this trophy was first fought for in 1950. Twenty-three boys have won it in the intervening years. How many of those have gone on to become Grandmasters?'

'The three you mentioned: Jensen, Müller and Vogel.'

'What happened to the other twenty?'

'I get your point, Dad. Chess is a tough game. Lots of young players have dreams which they don't achieve.' Lothar took the trophy back from his father. 'The thing is, I feel alive when I'm at the board. In the final round, when the trophy was on the line, my heart was pounding, my pulse racing a hundred beats to the minute. I decided then what I wanted to do with my life.' Lothar paused and looked out of the window. A soldier stood below holding a rifle. The road was otherwise empty. 'I'd like to try and become a Grandmaster, play in the Olympiad, maybe even compete for the World Championship. I want to make chess my life. I know I can do it too.'

His mother, who had been silent up till this point, put her arm on his shoulder. 'Lothar, there's something we need to tell you.' Her voice was sombre and dry.

Lothar looked up and met his mother's eyes. 'What's up mum? Are you OK?'

Her face creased. 'Not really, no...'

As his mother's voice tailed off, his father took over. 'We had visitors, Lothar. While you were away in Halle.'

'Visitors? Who?'

'The Stasi. Two officials. Men in grey suits. They looked ordinary, like somebody you'd see on a tram or at a bus stop.'

'But they weren't ordinary?'

'Bloody extraordinary, that's what they were, if you'll excuse my language.' Lothar's father stamped his foot on the floor as he said this.

'What did they want?'

'They spent three hours questioning us. They kept asking about your aunt.'

'But she's in the West.' Lothar felt confused and alarmed too.

'They accused us of making plans to escape,' his father said, shaking his head. 'God knows where they got that idea from. It's a ludicrous suggestion. I'm far too old now to move. They are watching us, though. Any sign of misbehaviour and they will stop you playing chess.'

Lothar's mother began to cry. Lothar put his arm around her shoulder, and she looked up at him. 'It's a cruel and difficult world we live in, Lothar. Your father and I will always support you, whatever you do. But it's best not to make too many plans. The powers that be can destroy them, just like that, if they feel like it.'

Lothar hugged his parents. 'Mum, Dad, it's OK. You don't need to worry. Nobody can stop me playing chess. I'm going to be too good for that. When you're a top player, the state has to look after you and your family, everyone knows that.'

That night in bed, Lothar reflected on the conversation. If only he was as confident about his chess prowess as he had sounded. It was, he realised, up to him to protect his family now. That meant behaving, following the party line. It also meant becoming a world-class chess player. No matter how hard he had worked before, he would need a Herculean effort from here on.

Bernd's family had moved to a neighbouring district in East Berlin during the summer, and Lothar had seen little of him since. Bernd had found himself a girlfriend at his new college, and shortly after his seventeenth birthday, Lothar made the trip to Bernd's new house to see his friend and his new girl.

Christiane was a slim girl with long, dark hair and bloodshot eyes, dressed all in black. She had a cousin in West Berlin who would occasionally visit her, smuggling Western goods with him. Bernd was especially excited about the latest gift from the West.

'Just look at the cover. Blond hair, green and blue suit, guitar. This guy is the definition of cool.'

Lothar picked up the record. '*Ziggy Stardust and the Spiders from Mars.* I like the title. Who is David Bowie? And who's Ziggy?'

'It's a concept album.'

'A what?'

'A concept. David Bowie has invented an alter ego called Ziggy Stardust. When you listen to the record, you have to imagine that Ziggy is singing.'

'OK.' He was confused, not that he wanted to admit it.

Bernd put the record on the turntable. 'Let me play you the first track,' he said. 'It's called "Five Years".'

Lothar closed his eyes. Drumbeat. Guitar. A man with a strange androgynous voice sang of how the world was dying. Newsreaders wept, mothers sighed, while the singer gazed at his ex-love in an ice-cream parlour. It was a thing of wonder. In four and a half minutes, Bowie – or Ziggy, he still wasn't sure which – had created another world.

The record ended. He opened his eyes again.

'Wow. That is like nothing I've heard before. Think he'll ever come to Berlin?'

Bernd smiled. 'Not East Berlin, that's for sure. I tell you what, though, Lothar. If we can't see Bowie, then Christiane and I have got the next best alternative for you.'

'What's that?'

'The Karl Rauser Combo. You know Karl Rauser? They call him the East German Mick Jagger. He's the bad boy of East German pop.'

Lothar had heard of Karl Rauser. His version of 'Let's Spend the Night Together' was anarchic, shocking and amusing in equal measure. Long-haired, tattooed, openly dismissive of authority, practically unemployable, Rauser was the antithesis of the model citizen. His records were banned, and it was a mystery why he wasn't locked up. One rumour was that he held secret information about Honecker, and the Stasi allowed him to remain at large provided he kept his mouth shut.

'Is Karl Rauser playing again?' he asked.

'Not officially, no. You won't find this one advertised anywhere. But word is he'll be playing at the old theatre – you know, the disused one, behind the factory on Alexander Street – on Saturday evening. Do you fancy joining us? It should be a riot.'

'It will be loads of fun,' added Christiane. She raised her fist in the air like a young Che Guevara. 'We'll stand in the front row and shout *down with Honecker*!'

Lothar thought for a moment. Shouting anti-Honecker slogans wasn't necessarily the best career move for a budding professional chess player in East Germany. Against that, Bernd was his oldest friend, and he didn't get to see him often these days. How risky could it be to attend one concert? Surely the Stasi couldn't find out about that. Besides, he didn't have to stand in the front row. If things got too lively, he could hide at the back of the hall, ready to make a quick exit. He smiled at Christiane. 'Of course, I'd love to go.'

'Great,' said Bernd. 'You won't regret it.'

Putting on his smartest blue trousers and a dark green shirt, on Saturday evening Lothar met his friends by the clock tower, a few minutes' walk from the old theatre. Christiane had adorned her face with heavy eye shadow and black lipstick. Bernd, who had grown his hair long, had tied it back and secured it with a bandana. His shirt was bright yellow and his jeans were flared.

Bernd led them down a side alley through to the back of the theatre, where a group of youths, dressed just like Bernd and Christiane, with long hair, piercings and flared trousers, had gathered. Bernd had brought three bottles of beer with him, which they drank while they waited to get into the hall. So far, all seemed peaceful and calm.

Presently, a scruffy man with long hair and a moustache made his way through the crowd, opening the back doors of the theatre and ushering them in. Inside, they found a dimly lit hall, no windows, wooden flooring and a musty, unwashed smell. At the front was a stage, on which stood a drum kit, three microphones and an amplifier. Above was a placard reading simply '*Revolution*'. The room was gradually filling up. Lothar guessed it had capacity for around two hundred people, and was already half full.

'Come on,' said Bernd, 'let's make our way forward. We'll get a better view from there.'

Lothar followed Bernd and Christiane, apologising to people in the crowd as they pushed their way through, until they were just a few feet from the front. He had never been to a concert before, and he loved the way that he could feel the anticipation and excitement growing, while they waited for Karl Rauser to appear on stage. The hall was now full and the crowd had begun to chant for their hero.

After a short while, the lights dimmed, and in the gloom, he saw four members of the band come on stage, taking their positions behind the drums and microphones. Then the lights came back on, and with a wild cry, somewhere between a screech and a scream, the great man himself, Karl Rauser, entered. Bearded, with long hair tied back like Bernd's, with what Lothar now realised were the obligatory flared trousers, a guitar in one hand, a cigarette in the other, Rauser waved to the crowd. 'Good evening, my friends. It is time for...'

'Revolution!' shouted the crowd, in unison.

Rauser raised his fist in a clench, and the band launched into the opening bars of 'Won't Be Fooled Again', by The Who. Lothar knew the song – Bernd had played it to him the week before, explaining its anarchist subtext – and when Rauser sang '*the change it had to come*' he shouted along, with the rest of the crowd.

Over the following two hours, Rauser sang a succession of rock classics, some of which Lothar was familiar with, some of which were new to him, but all of which he loved. The common theme seemed to be *revolution*, which Rauser worked into every song, crying the word pleadingly, excitedly or aggressively, depending on how the mood took him. Being more familiar with Rauser's repertoire than Lothar was, Christiane and Bernd joined in repeatedly, shouting out for revolution at the top of their voices whenever the singer commanded.

The constant jumping up and down, shouting and raising of fists in the air was surprisingly tiring, and after a couple of hours, Lothar felt in need of a break. Making his way through the crowd, he found his way to the washrooms at the rear of the hall, where he ran water over his face and rubbed the smoke from his eyes. Heading back out of the washroom, some sixth sense made him stop. From his vantage point, he could see Rauser leading the crowd in the familiar calls to overthrow Honecker. But what was that? It was difficult to see in the gloom, the room filled with smoke, bodies everywhere, but weren't those men pushing through the middle of the crowd, dressed in green... police officers?

With a start, he realised what had happened. A police raid, the very thing he had feared but had assumed so unlikely. A few seconds later, the lights went on and the music stopped, as the police pushed through to the front of the crowd, randomly hitting out with batons as they did so. Rauser and his band had already left the stage, and around him the crowd were running for the entrance. 'The show is over!' shouted an officer with a loudhailer. 'Everybody out, now. Move. Leave the building.'

The blood rushing to his head, Lothar acted on raw instinct. Turning on his heels, he followed the hordes of people running out of the building screaming, as fast as his legs would take him, only stopping for breath when he reached the clock tower where he had met Bernd and Christiane earlier that evening. Their pre-arranged meeting point should anything go wrong. He sat down on the kerb, stretched out his legs, lit a cigarette and tried to recover his breath.

An hour later, when he had finally regained some sort of composure, he felt a tap on his shoulder. Just when he had begun to give up on them, there stood his friends. They were a sorry sight. Bernd's shirt was ripped, his bandana had bloodstains on it, and Christiane was crying.

'Goodness, what happened?'

His friends sat down next to him and he offered them both cigarettes. Bernd took one but seemed too stunned to talk. It was Christiane who spoke first. 'The police,' she said. 'They are scum. We did what they told us, and they still hit us.' Rolling up her sleeve, she showed him a newly bruised arm.

'Pushed us in a van,' said Bernd, shaking his head. His voice sounded cracked and broken. 'Thought we'd go to jail.'

Christiane put her arm around her boyfriend. 'Eventually they let us out,' she said. 'They took our names. We have to report back to the station on Monday.'

'What's going to happen? Will they charge you?' His heart was beating rapidly again, concerned for his friends.

'Who knows?' said Christiane. 'They think that a few beatings will stop us. Well, they are wrong.' She spat on the ground.

Bernd took a drag of his cigarette and blew out a smoke ring. 'Down with Honecker,' he said, but under his breath, so that no passer-by could hear.

For another hour, until the clock struck midnight, Lothar sat there with his friends, shivering in the cold, with blue melancholy in his heart. He was worried for them. But if he was honest, he was also relieved at his lucky escape. He could so easily have been arrested himself. His guilt mingled with relief until he could no longer think straight. What world was this they had found themselves in?

CHAPTER FOUR

The Death Strip

As the tension between East and West increased, it became increasingly difficult to travel outside the Eastern bloc. Even opportunities to leave the country were hard to come by. When Poland hosted the 1976 European Junior Championships in Krakow, Lothar leapt at the opportunity to represent his country. To secure his place, he attended several events arranged by the youth wing of the Socialist Unity Party. Excruciating affairs where the young Party members marched on the parade ground and watched films about Lenin, he made sure to conceal what he was doing from Hans.

Lothar had expected that he and his compatriot Sebastian Bahl would work together to prepare for their opponents, but events didn't turn out that way. After a quick victory in the first game, he found himself in a tough match in the second round against the scruffily dressed English player Jon Forester, his beard, jeans and T-shirt contrasting with Lothar's suit and tie. Seated next to him, Bahl won quickly. Rather than leave the tournament area, his countryman reset the pieces and loudly discussed the key moments of his game with his opponent. Lothar motioned to Bahl to be quiet, but entranced by the analysis, and oblivious to him, his neighbour merely flicked his hand through his hair and carried on talking. Against a fearsome opponent, with his clock ticking, Lothar was finding it difficult to think. It was his own compatriot who was distracting him.

Somehow, he managed to draw the game with Forester, although only after coming perilously close to defeat. As he left the playing hall, he bumped into Bahl and their trainer, Georg Schneider, in the lobby. A contemporary of Hans Adler, Schneider was a tiny man, a schoolteacher by trade, barely more than five feet in height, with a high-pitched voice and the confidence of one who spent his days lecturing others. They made a comic couple, the portly Bahl, six feet tall, alongside the diminutive coach.

'How did you get on, Hartmann?' asked Schneider, fiddling with the buttons of his waistcoat.

'I held the draw,' he replied, with a modicum of pride.

'You only drew? I thought you were going to win that,' said Bahl, shaking his head in surprise. 'What went wrong?'

Lothar shrugged his shoulders and walked off. As he headed down the corridor, he heard Bahl say to Schneider, 'I have a lot of time for Lothar, but I'm still not convinced about his play. I'm sure Konrad Welde would have won from that position.'

That evening at dinner Bahl pushed his pocket set in front of him.

'Lothar, I wondered if you would show us today's game?' Bahl looked across at Schneider. 'We know how keen you are to improve. Perhaps the two of us can help you?'

Lothar was feeling exhausted after a long and tough game, and listening to Bahl's advice, well-meaning or not, was the last thing he wanted to do. Realising that Schneider would frown on him if he said no, he pulled his score sheet out of his wallet and began to play through the game on Bahl's set with a heavy heart. As they reached the seventh move, Bahl rested his stubby fingers on Lothar's.

'Ah, a moment there, Lothar. Stop please!' Bahl peered down at the pocket-size pieces. 'I wonder if, instead of moving your Knight, you could have played here, with your Queen.'

'Well, yes, I...'

'Or, yet another idea,' Bahl interrupted him, picking up the Bishop, 'you could perhaps have tried this.' Bahl shook his head. 'Such a shame, Lothar.'

'The fact is, Sebastian, I moved the Knight. To get back to the game, my opponent pushed his pawn and then...'

'Ah, Lothar. Stop again please. I see here a very interesting idea. Instead of the move you played, did you consider this pawn thrust?'

Lothar sighed. This was going to be a long evening. Bahl would not let a single move of his pass without comment or criticism. Eventually, he snapped. 'Come on, Sebastian, you can't seriously question that move. It's an obvious capture.'

Bahl shook his head at him. 'I'm afraid, Lothar, that *obvious* moves, as you call them, are just not good enough. You are representing the people of East Germany, after all. They deserve better than the *obvious*.'

'Sebastian, you don't need to worry about me. I play just fine.'

'But *fine* isn't good enough either, Lothar. This is a serious tournament, with world-class competitors. You need to raise the bar, Lothar, or you will never make it.'

'Stop lecturing me, Sebastian. You're not my coach.' To his surprise, Bahl had jumped back in shock when he raised his voice. Red mist was descending in front of his eyes. He was conscious that he was losing control, but he could do nothing to stop it.

Bahl looked across at Schneider. 'What do you think, Georg?'

Schneider clasped his fingers together and took a deep breath. 'Bahl has a lot of experience, Hartmann. You should listen to him.'

Lothar felt like shouting out in anger but, from somewhere, he found sufficient self-restraint to keep quiet. 'Thanks, Georg, yes, of course.'

That evening, he took a stroll into the old town, walking off his frustration. Arriving at Krakow's main square he sat on the steps of the Town Hall and surveyed the view. In front of him was the Church of St Adalbert. Just think, this tiny, white stone structure, with its green domed roof, had stood for over a thousand years. To his left were the twin Gothic Towers of St Mary's Basilica, rebuilt in the fourteenth century, and still standing proud over six hundred years later. He thought about the history of this wonderful city, and of the numerous attacks that it had suffered through the ages. A town that could survive medieval invasions, Hitler, Brezhnev too, deserved much admiration. Thinking about what the people of Krakow had been through helped give him perspective and he decided that from that point on he would focus purely on his own tournament. He would not allow Bahl or Schneider to distract him.

The following round, reinvigorated, Lothar beat a French player followed by another Englishman and two Hungarians. In round eight, his Scottish opponent was clearly inebriated and he won that too. With one game to go, he was in second place in the tournament, half a point ahead of Bahl in third.

In the final round, he would be facing the Soviet player Lev Ivanov. Born in the same year as him, Ivanov was a world away in his chess education. Originally from the Ukraine, Ivanov had been playing full time since the age of five. At seven, his family relocated to Moscow, after the Soviet authorities identified the youngster as a potential World Champion. Lothar had been studying Ivanov's games closely throughout the tournament. Some of his moves he understood, some he did not, but Ivanov had won every match. Lothar had never before come across anyone who appeared to have so much talent for the game. If he beat Ivanov, he would finish the tournament equal first, and would enter a play-off for the title of European Junior Champion. A draw would leave him in second place, with a guaranteed silver medal, a fine achievement in such a field.

The night before the game, Ivanov knocked on his door, shortly after dinner. A thin man with round glasses, he was shy and spoke only broken German. 'Lothar, I congratulate you on your great performance in this tournament. Out of respect to you and your country, I would like to propose a draw tomorrow.'

'Lev, I will need to think about it. Can I let you know in the morning?'

Ivanov gave a small bow. 'Of course, Lothar. I look forward to hearing from you.'

Closing the door behind him, Ivanov departed, and Lothar sat back down on his bed. Lev Ivanov, potential future World Champion, had just offered him a draw. Accept his offer, and he would finish second in the European Junior Championships. The honour, the prestige! It was in his gift now. He could accept Ivanov's proposal, knowing that a great prize would be his. How tempted he was.

Against that, what Ivanov had proposed was unlawful. The two of them would be breaking the rules. They would not just be cheating themselves, either. They would be cheating other people too. There were the spectators, of course. Then, most important of all, their fellow competitors. Could he live with that? Was his conscience able to stand the thought that he had lied, dissembled, won a medal without earning it?

Lothar spent the rest of the evening pondering what to do. The angel on one shoulder kept telling him to be a man and play the game properly. Meanwhile, the shiny red devil on the other whispered continuously into his ear about prizes, glory. 'It's what all sportsmen do,' Beelzebub said. 'You'll never amount to anything if you're not prepared to bend the rules a little.'

Eventually, his head throbbing, he collected his spare coins and made his way downstairs where he picked up the pay phone in the corner of the hotel lobby and dialled Hans' number. Before Hans answered, he heard a click on the line. Hans had told him long ago that his phone was bugged, and Lothar wondered why his coach had installed such a luxury in the first place.

'How many times in your life will you get a chance to play for a European championship, Lothar?'

'That's difficult to say. Maybe just the one.'

'Precisely. This may be your one opportunity. Why would you throw that away with a short draw? If you have any respect for yourself, and for the game of chess, then you must play for the win.'

In his heart, Lothar knew that Hans was right. Ivanov was a strong player, however, much more experienced than him, and he was afraid of him. What if Ivanov beat him easily? How foolish he would look then. Worse, he might end up outside the medals completely, going home empty-handed.

The next morning, he rose early and went for breakfast with Georg Schneider. While Lothar explained his dilemma, the coach played with the black bread in front of him, inspecting it from all sides before breaking it with his hands into tiny pieces, which he ate slowly, one by one.

Lothar came to the end of the story and paused. Schneider pushed his plate to one side and wiped his hands on his trousers. 'Thank you, Hartmann, for talking to me, for asking for my view. You have done the right thing.'

'What is your advice?'

'Let me put it this way, Hartmann.' Schneider paused and looked at him, resting his chin in his hand. 'Over there. The Russian delegation.' Schneider pointed his hand towards Ivanov and his team – coaches, trainers and even a physio – seated on the other side of the breakfast hall. 'Look at the size of their party. What conclusion do you draw?'

'That the Russians are a powerful nation?' said Lothar.

'Indeed they are powerful. It's not just the size of their group either. See the food they are eating? It's a feast. They even get cheese with their bread. When did we ever get cheese?'

Lothar looked enviously at the banquet on the Russian table. 'Never.'

'Precisely. But one more thing. The Russians are not just a powerful group, they are our allies too. Do you think it wise to take on our friends in hand-to-hand combat?'

Lothar shook his head. Schneider was right. He made a decision. 'No, Georg. Taking on the Russians would not be wise.'

Schneider put his hand on his shoulder. 'I'm glad you see sense, Hartmann. Now here is what we are going to do...'

That afternoon, Lothar sat down opposite Lev Ivanov, and with a furrowed brow, determinedly pushed his King's pawn forward two squares, punching down the clock as he did so. When Ivanov ventured a Sicilian Defence, Lothar sacrificed first a Knight and then a Rook for a raging attack. Just when it looked as though Ivanov's defences were about to crumble, the hardy Siberian found a defence where none appeared possible and Lothar had to settle for a perpetual check and a draw, with neither player able to break the series of checks which his Queen gave to Ivanov's King. The spectators applauded and shouted 'bravo'. Lothar had finished second in the tournament, winning the silver medal in the process.

After shaking hands with Ivanov, he made his way over to Schneider, who hugged him. 'Congratulations, Hartmann,' he said. 'You've done your country proud today.'

Lothar smiled for Schneider and the cameras, but inside he felt an uncomfortable pressure against his chest. Even from the other side of the room, he could see Sebastian Bahl glaring at him, his expression a mixture of anger, contempt and jealousy. Bahl had spotted something that had passed others by. The game, awarded a special prize for its brilliancy by the organisers, had been a sham, invented beforehand with Ivanov purely to please the spectators, with not a single genuine move played over the board.

Later, when he got back home, he thought more about what had just happened. Against Hans' advice, and against his own better instinct, he had cheated. True, Bahl aside, he seemed to have got away with it, to have prospered in fact. Schneider was pleased with him, and had promised to look after him. To his peers, he was now recognised as an expert player, a champion in the making.

Falling out with Bahl he could live with. But what about his own conscience? He had achieved an ambition. But he had got there by illicit means. The longer Lothar reflected, the harder it was to dispel the feeling. No matter what others might think of his achievement, he had not yet proved himself. What's more, no matter what else he achieved in his career, he would always know that he had broken the laws of the game. He had won his first international medal on a lie. It was an uncomfortable feeling, and not one that he imagined he would be able to shake off lightly.

High Hall, so called because at twenty-two stories it was one of the tallest buildings in East Berlin, was a true monstrosity. Shabby and grey, the building dominated the local skyline, an unsightly landmark in a city which was already full of gloomy high-rise blocks. Inside, it smelled of smoke and unwashed bodies. Rumour had it that when it was constructed, the budget extended to either fire extinguishers or carpets. Unable to make a choice, the university officials opted for neither. On a clear day, from the top floor Lothar could see over the Berlin Wall and into the West. When he felt low, depressed by his tiny box room, with space for only a single bed, desk and chair, he used to stand on the top floor gazing across to West Berlin, wondering what life would be like on the other side.

At least he had his studies to distract him. Arriving early for the first lecture of the new term, he marvelled at the huge amphitheatre, with its high ceilings and a row of desks stretching back as far as the eye could see. The stage could comfortably have held a brass band. As for the lectern, it would not have embarrassed Honecker himself. Taking his seat towards the back of the room, however, he began to see the signs of neglect. The desks were scratched with graffiti – including the impossibly brave inscription 'Down with the Wall' – and the posters celebrating the history of the GDR were faded and torn.

At nine o'clock, a bell rang and an earnest, bearded professor in a brown suit and polyester tie entered the room, holding a clipboard in his hand. Taking their names on a register, marking carefully where they were seated, the lecturer put down his clipboard, crossed his arms and paused.

'Students, before we begin: a warning!' said the lecturer, taking off his jacket, throwing it to one side, and holding one hand in the air like a conductor. 'Our history has been fraught with challenges. Enemies of the state, those who seek to undermine us, are everywhere. In this course, you will learn about the fascists, the capitalists and the bourgeoisie who have sought to deny us a true socialist paradise.'

While his fellow students were scribbling frantically on their pads, Lothar's notebook remained closed. He had heard nothing yet which he wanted to transcribe to paper.

'In June 1953,' continued the lecturer, 'a group of renegade construction workers went on strike. The government tried to talk with the workers – not an unreasonable approach – but the rebels were having none of it. Within days, what had started as an isolated incident had spread. Tram drivers, printers, even shop workers, were threatening to come out in sympathy. None of them had any just cause, of course. But pollution spreads, like a cancer.'

The lecturer paused, and put down his pen. His voice had begun to crack and Lothar thought he saw a tear forming in his eye. He was some actor. 'Students, the study of such material will not be easy.'

Leaving his lectern, the lecturer walked across to the side of the room to collect a glass of water. Lothar picked up his pen to make a note, and then put it back down again. His uncle had taken part in the 1953 Workers' Uprising and he knew full well that he was not an agent of the enemy. He also knew about the role of Soviet troops in aggressively putting down what had been a peaceful protest.

He wondered about challenging the lecturer but, thinking better of it, opened his pad and began to doodle, so that he would at least give the impression of paying some interest. Two rows in front of him, he saw that a long-haired student with a beard had raised his hand. The lecturer signalled for the student to speak.

'If the revolutionaries were standing up for workers' rights,' said the student, 'doesn't that make them socialists?'

The lecturer picked up his register and inspected it. He looked back up at the student. 'You are Krabbe?' he asked. The student nodded. 'Thank you,' said the lecturer, making a note against the register. 'That they were socialists is, of course, exactly what the revolutionaries would want you to think.' The lecturer had raised his voice, and a girl next to Krabbe, who had nodded off, awoke with a start. 'The reality, is of course, entirely different.'

Krabbe looked dissatisfied and went to say something more, but the lecturer gestured for him to be quiet. Lothar breathed a sigh of relief that he had not chosen to share his own thoughts.

The following day, Krabbe asked another awkward question. On the third day he asked a further question, and the lecturer asked to see him afterwards. On the fourth, Krabbe was gone. They didn't see him in their class again. East Berlin University, it quickly became apparent, was not a place where it was wise to engage in debate, or the exchange of ideas, especially when studying political history.

'What made you choose politics anyway, for goodness' sake? Anybody could have told you what you were letting yourself in for.' Lothar's flatmate Max Schuster took another swig from his beer and threw the empty bottle into a stash in the corner of the room.

'Go easy on the drink, Max. You must be approaching double figures by now.'

'You only turn twenty once, Lothar.' Max stood up, stretched his six-foot frame and looked out of Lothar's window into the courtyard below. 'How did you get such a good room by the way? A window, a view, even a rug. Are you connected?'

'Tell me more about this new girlfriend. Where did you meet her? And it's political history, by the way, not politics. There is a difference.' Anything to change the subject. The last thing Lothar wanted was to be questioned about the deal he had cut with Schneider.

Max opened the window and leaned out. He waved at a girl opposite. 'It's what university is about, isn't it? Meeting new people. I don't think Stella would want me to describe her as my girlfriend. She's nice though. Very smart. Would you believe I met her in the library?'

'What were you doing there?'

'I know. Crazy isn't it? Only time I've been in the library since we started. She helped me find a book on Mechanical Engineering.'

'But you're not studying Engineering.'

'Take every chance you can, Lothar. That's my motto.'

That Friday, as Lothar and Max walked back to High Hall, they spotted an older woman lying on the ground sobbing. A border guard, clad in a long green jacket, rifle in hand, stood motionless, watching the woman. Emboldened by an evening drinking beer, Lothar approached him to ask what had happened.

'Her son tried to scale the Wall,' the guard said, pointing behind him to the narrow space of land between the Wall and the West German border on the other side, known as the Death Strip. 'The soldiers in the watchtower shot him.'

With a jolt, Lothar imagined the shot. A man falling. The cry of agony. The dull thud as his body hit the ground. 'Where is her son now?' he asked.

'The ambulance took him away.'

'Will he live?'

The guard shrugged and looked down at his boots. 'Depends on how quickly they can get him to hospital, I would say. The last one didn't make it.'

'The last one?'

'A student tried the same thing two weeks ago.' The guard gestured up towards the watchtower. 'They are trained marksmen up there. They don't often miss.'

Lothar looked back at the woman. She was lying still on the ground, her head buried in the earth. There were no words he could say, but he felt he had to do something. Walking over to her, he knelt down beside her and held her hand. Above, the full moon shone down, lighting up the factories, the blocks of flats, the Death Strip. Just another night in East Berlin.

The following summer, in 1977, Lothar's father suffered a massive heart attack while he was at work. His colleagues rushed him to hospital but he died before he got there. His mother took the news hard. They had been together nearly thirty years, and had barely had an argument or a fight in that time. Breaking up from university early, Lothar helped with the arrangements for the funeral, contacting their small number of remaining relatives, and sorting through his father's papers and belongings. In the bottom drawer of his bedside cabinet he found a collection of old love letters between his mother and father. He didn't read them, but he gave them to his mother, and they made her cry. He also found a photo of himself, playing chess with his uncle, shortly before Leon fled the country. His father was stood behind him with his arm on his shoulder. Over the next few weeks he found his own eyes watering at the most unexpected times. His uncle and his father both gone, way too soon.

A few weeks later, Lothar caught a flight with Sebastian Bahl, Konrad Welde and another teammate Erno Dreher to Lvov in the Ukraine for the European Student Team Championships. Still distraught after his father's death, he was worried about leaving his mother on her own. Lacking focus, he really wanted to drop out of the team. Eventually though, when the coach, Georg Schneider, in a meeting at the East Berlin Central Chess Club, implored him otherwise, he was reluctantly persuaded. 'Come now, Hartmann, this is far too good an opportunity to miss. Besides which, if you turn down your country this time, you might find that this is the last invitation you get for a little while.'

Coming from East Germany, Lothar was used to poor living conditions, but the standards of habitation in Lvov surprised even him. A minibus took them directly from the airport to their hotel, an imposing seven-storey block of grey concrete that overlooked a construction site. The driver advised the team not to leave the hotel for the duration of their stay. 'The Ukraine is not safe,' he said dryly.

'Not safe for tourists?' asked Schneider.

'Not safe for anyone,' said the driver, running his hand across his throat in a disturbing way.

Inside, the hotel was as uninviting as it had appeared from the outside. Lothar's room, on the fifth floor, had space for a single bed, a bedside table and a sink. The basin was cracked and the water a suspicious-looking brown colour. A tiny mat, barely large enough to stand on, lay on the concrete floor. He tried opening the window to drown out the aroma of cheap cigarettes but the noise from the construction work below was deafening. Hanging up his coat on the solitary hook on the wall, Lothar left his suitcase unpacked and wandered down the corridor until he found Dreher's room at the other end of the hallway. Dreher, who was sitting morosely on his bed, looked up at him. 'Rough, isn't it?'

'If we'd known it was going to be like this,' said Lothar, 'we could have stayed at home and phoned in our moves.'

That evening they dined in the hotel. Dinner consisted of a ration of dry vegetables, a strange yellow mash and a type of meat they could not identify. The following morning the hotel served the same vegetables and mash for breakfast. At lunch, it was the same again.

It was a relief when the chess began. On paper, East Germany were one of the stronger teams, and Schneider set them an ambitious target to finish second, behind the Soviets. In a field of twenty teams, this certainly should have been possible. Lothar didn't feel remotely match-fit, or ready for action, but perhaps, he reflected, he could play himself into form during the week.

The team won their first match after a struggle. In the second round, things began to go seriously awry. Sitting down and shaking the hand of his Hungarian opponent, an earnest-looking fellow with a beard, Lothar played a prepared attack against his Sicilian Defence. His opponent sunk into deep thought, and as Lothar waited for him to move, he strolled around the hall confidently, watching the other games.

Returning to the board, he saw that the Hungarian had moved his Queen to a spot where he could take it. How odd! With little thought, he captured the Queen with his Bishop. Jumping energetically out of his seat the moment Lothar made his move, his opponent picked up his Knight and thrust it forward. It was check, and to Lothar's astonishment, checkmate in two further moves. His position was now completely lost.

Lothar was so bemused by the turn of events that he almost forgot to be upset. But when he saw Sebastian Bahl, seated next to him, laughing slyly to himself at his misfortune, he began to realise what he had done. More importantly, as a result of his defeat the team lost too. The round after, they were beaten again. They had barely begun the competition, and already a medal was out of the question.

That evening, over dinner, Bahl explained to Lothar where he was going wrong.

'Lothar, if I may speak frankly, you are far too risk-averse.' Bahl took a large meatball from his plate and stuffed it into his mouth, whole. 'I've rarely seen you make a sacrifice,' he continued, 'and you always seem to choose the cautious route. I'm saying this because I want to help you, you understand.'

Still shocked by how badly he had played that day, the last thing Lothar wanted was a lecture from Bahl. Before he could stop himself, he found himself snapping back at his teammate. 'Sebastian, I sacrificed two pieces yesterday and won with a crushing attack.'

Bahl looked at Lothar and stroked his chin. His huge bulk filled the table opposite. 'You call that a sacrifice? A child would have seen that combination.' Lothar tried to turn away, and Bahl put his paw on his arm. 'The other thing, and I mean this respectfully, is that I don't see you as a team player.' Bahl ran his left hand through his hair as he said this and then inspected the last remaining meatball on his plate with his fingers.

'In what way am I not a team player?'

'If you were truly concerned for the team, you would help the rest of us with our preparation, and take more interest in our games. All you seem to care about is yourself.'

'That's pot and kettle, Sebastian.' Lothar turned up his nose dismissively.

Bahl turned red. 'What do you mean?'

'I mean you're in no place to lecture me about putting others first.'

The rest of the table looked on, not saying a word. 'Lothar, that's very upsetting,' said Bahl. 'Do you realise how hurtful you are being?'

'Sebastian, if you're going to give it, you have to be prepared to take it.'

To Lothar's surprise, Bahl looked genuinely troubled at his remarks, and for once his teammate was lost for words. Before he could reply, Lothar walked off, heading back to his room, where he spent the rest of the evening on his own staring into space, feeling despondent about the world and wondering why he had allowed himself to be talked into coming on this ill-fated trip. Things continued in the same vein throughout the tournament, the team rife with tension and a succession of poor results sending them spiralling down the standings.

The lowest point came in the match against the English. Lothar was once again paired against the talented mathematician Jon Forester. One of the strongest players in England, Forester was on the verge of the title of Grandmaster, and was also a respected chess writer. On the morning of the game, Lothar considered preparing by looking at some of Forester's recent articles. It would have been his father's birthday, and all the gloom and despondency that he had felt over recent weeks came flooding back to hit him in one go. His head throbbed, his mind was in turmoil; it was an effort even getting out of bed. Turning back the alarm clock two hours, he pulled up the covers and went back to sleep. At the board, he lost easily and Forester spent little time on the game.

Afterwards, the friendly Englishman shook his head in bewilderment. 'Haven't you seen my recent piece on the Sicilian? I've already analysed our entire game through to checkmate.'

Seated next to him, Bahl struggled to hide his amusement, a smirk playing across his lips as he watched Lothar and Forester replay the final moves. His turn was to follow, though, when the English Master Tony Marlowe ground him down in a seven-hour marathon. Easily beaten by the English, they lost in the following rounds to the Dutch and the French. After a last-round defeat, they even managed to finish behind the Welsh team, an unparalleled embarrassment. The only redeeming feature was that they had not had to face their arch-rivals West Germany. They would certainly have lost that match too, given their form.

Their performance had been disgraceful and not even Schneider, their trainer, could do anything to bring the group together. Only Erno Dreher showed any verve, winning the gold medal on the bottom board. On the flight home, Lothar buried himself in a book, not talking to anybody, still desperately depressed about his father, and unable to process what had happened in the chess. Bahl meanwhile made pointed remarks to Schneider about the weak opposition which Lothar and Dreher had faced.

Dreher took him aside when they arrived back at Berlin airport. 'I'm sorry, Lothar,' he said, 'but I've had enough.'

'Enough of what?'

'Of Bahl, his arrogance, his aggression, his rudeness. Schneider's hopeless too. He does nothing to stop Bahl.' Dreher shook his head. 'I quit, Lothar. That's it. No more chess.'

It was a sad moment, but things were about to get worse. No doubt because of his contacts in the Socialist Unity Party, Bahl escaped censure, but the press was highly critical of Lothar. The papers said that his play was superficial and lacked depth. He had not prepared properly and worse, on the one evening he had spent in the bar, he had been spotted drinking after hours.

Hans advised him to issue a public apology. 'Show some contrition, Lothar. Admit you've been in the wrong, and commit yourself to working harder next year. Do the decent thing, and you'll be let off with a warning.'

Strong-willed as he was, and certain that Bahl was behind the allegations, Lothar was too hot-headed to follow his coach's advice. He might have saved himself with an apology, but when he said nothing, Georg Schneider convened a special meeting of the East German Chess Federation Disciplinary Committee. In front of five other senior officials, Schneider asked him what he had learned from the experience in Lvov.

'What have I learned? That to succeed, the whole team needs to work together for a common purpose.'

Schneider leaned forward and peered at him through his square, black glasses. Lothar noticed that he had a new polyester suit on. Was that a new waistcoat as well? The light grey matched the wall behind him.

'You don't feel that happened on this occasion, Hartmann?'

'No.'

Schneider frowned and played with his wristwatch. 'May I ask why not?'

'Because certain members of the team were allowed by you to get away with bullying and unpleasant behaviour. It was impossible for the rest of us to concentrate.'

Schneider opened his mouth to reply, but he could find no words. Shaking his head, he turned to his colleagues, at a loss as to how to continue. Lothar had criticised his leadership in public, an unforgiveable sin.

After a prolonged silence, Schneider asked him to leave the room while the officials considered his case. He sat in the corridor outside on a small wooden stool, grimly contemplating his fate. Half an hour later, a secretary called him back in. A sombre man in yet another grey polyester suit administered the verdict.

'Lothar Hartmann, you are guilty of disrespect to your teammates, to your coach, and worst of all, to the GDR. In our utopian society, we cannot tolerate such behaviour. You are henceforth banned from all tournament and match chess for twelve months.'

Twelve months? He had known that a ban was a possibility, but a whole year? Such a thing had never featured in even his darkest imaginings. How would he cope, away from the board, for such a long time? Chess was what had made him tick, had motivated and inspired him. The thought of being without the game was too much.

Returning to university, he found that, as a further indignity, the authorities had halved his student grant. He had also lost his place at High Hall, and would need to find his own digs for his second year. Never miss an opportunity to kick a man when he is down. That was what the authorities seemed to be saying to him.

In the years since he had started playing competitively, this was his first serious reverse, and it was a painful one. Was there, he asked himself, still a place for him in East German chess? Could his career be over almost before it had begun?

CHAPTER FIVE

Joker

Summer passed and autumn began to cast its spell. The skies were overcast, leaves fell and the nights drew in. Banned from chess, Lothar's mood matched the autumnal gloom. His spirits were low and not even the prospect of returning to college cheered him. For all its shabbiness, he felt sorry to be leaving High Hall. Uncertain where he would live, or who with, he was glad when, in a spirit of solidarity, Max offered to move out with him. After a couple of days of fruitless searching, they found two spare rooms in a flat less than a kilometre from campus. The accommodation had its own unique charm. Like High Hall, the stairwells had a permanent aroma of stale cigarette smoke, and the carpets, a sticky dark brown, looked like they had not been cleaned since the 1950s. Their new flatmates seemed pleasant though. A girl in her early twenties, with a ponytail and wearing an artist's smock, greeted them with a warm smile at the door and introduced herself as Beth.

'The whole place was institutional white when we moved in,' she said. 'I couldn't stand it. Then it struck me. The solution was to cover the walls with these large red and blue abstracts.'

'You painted these yourself?' Lothar asked. 'Rothko would be proud of them.'

'That may be an exaggeration, but thank you. Yes, I did them all myself in a week! I can get quite enthusiastic when I put my mind to it. Do either of you paint?'

Max and Lothar shook their heads. 'Lothar plays chess,' said Max, 'which is about as creative as either of us gets.'

'Chess?' said a tall, balding man with glasses, emerging from one of the bedrooms. 'Does someone want a game?'

Lothar did not know the full name of Beth's friend and their other new flatmate, but everybody called him Joker, a nickname which he also quickly adopted.

Joker was a physicist, but for a man of science it seemed to Lothar that he had some remarkably strange theories. His nickname, Lothar soon realised, was ironic. A more sombre fellow he did not believe he had ever met. With his goatee beard, a little overweight, a year or two older than him, Joker was shy and otherworldly. Once they got to know each other, Lothar found it impossible to stop Joker's wild conjectures and theories.

In September, the flatmates went to the student union bar. On the television, East Germany were playing football against Czechoslovakia, one of the strongest teams in Europe. East Germany were winning the match by two goals to one.

Precariously balancing a round of coffees on the table, Joker eased himself into the seat next to Lothar. 'I see they have been at it again,' Joker said.

'What do you mean?'

'The East German team cheating. It wouldn't be the first time.'

Beth sighed. She was obviously used to this by now. 'Where is your evidence, Joker?' she asked.

Joker looked at Beth calmly. 'Fact: Czechoslovakia have by far best team. There is no way that we could beat them, not without money changing hands.'

'So Czechoslovakia have the best team on paper. The underdog can often win.'

'Fact number two,' continued Joker. 'The Czechoslovakian players were seen laughing and joking when they arrived at the airport. Why would anyone smile when they came to this country, unless they knew they were in for a pay-off?'

'All conjecture,' said Beth. 'Come back with some solid evidence and we might believe you.'

'I know a man,' said Joker. 'I'm not at liberty to say any more than that.'

Beth tutted. '*You know a man.* How can we argue with you when you make claims like that?'

Joker smiled. 'You're not supposed to argue with me, Beth. Take my word on trust.'

When East Germany duly won the match, Joker saw this as proof that he had been correct. Intrigued to hear more bizarre theories, Lothar and Max spent their time egging him on. Joker did not need much encouragement. The next night he told them how the Soviets had fixed the Olympics in favour of Nadia Comaneci and Nellie Kim.

'Wasn't Nadia Comaneci Romanian?' Lothar asked.

'Yes, of course. The Soviets don't distinguish. It's all Eastern bloc, a chance to show their superiority against the West. Just like they tried to fix Boris Spassky's match with Bobby Fischer. You should know that as a chess player.'

'But Fischer won.'

'I didn't say that they were infallible, did I?'

Over recent weeks, one man had dominated the news. Niclas Herig, the East German cosmonaut who had become the first German to go into space, had returned triumphantly to East Berlin. When the government decided to mark Herig's achievement with a procession, the route went right past the University, and Lothar had a bird's eye view from the library window.

'How was it?' asked Beth that evening, as they sat in the student union bar.

'Oh, pretty low-key,' said Lothar. 'Tanks, a marching band of four hundred odd, and an armed guard to lead Herig through the city. I think I spotted Honecker there too, alongside him.'

'Perhaps we could draw a mural?' said Beth. 'It would look good on our living room wall.'

Joker sniffed dismissively. 'The next person who mentions that fraudster Herig is going to get a piece of my mind.' Beth and Lothar looked blankly at Joker. 'It's the cheek of the man. Pretending he's been into space. Nonsense.'

'What do you mean, Joker?' said Beth. 'You think the space mission was made up? You'll be telling us the moon landings are fake next.'

'The lunar landings. Now don't get me started,' said Joker.

Lothar took a sip from his coffee, looked at Joker, and raised his eyebrows. 'The moon landings fake? Even by your standards, that's stretching it, isn't it?'

Joker put down his cigarette and stubbed it out in the ashtray next to him. Leaning towards his friends, he lowered his voice to a hush. 'You mean you've not heard of the lunar conspiracy?'

They shook their heads.

'So you've not heard about the photographs produced by NASA? How the same backdrop appears in multiple shots, often miles apart?'

'No. I've not heard that,' said Lothar. Beth, meanwhile, had already made an excuse and wandered over to the other side of the bar to speak to some friends. Joker was not deterred.

'You haven't wondered why there are no stars in the photos?'

'No.' Lothar shook his head again and shrugged his shoulders. As usual, he had no idea what to make of Joker. Behind him, a couple sat holding hands, gazing into each other's eyes. The man was whispering what he assumed were sweet nothings into his girlfriend's ear. Lothar felt confident the man was not talking to her about the lunar conspiracy.

'Lothar, pay attention! This is important.' Joker waved his hand in front of Lothar's face.

'Sorry, Joker, I was distracted. What were you saying?'

'The shadows in the photos. Ever wondered about their positioning?'

'No, I've never thought about that.'

'OK, how about man's ability to travel four hundred thousand kilometres into space, passing through a level of radiation that would have cooked the astronauts?'

Lothar looked blankly at Joker. His friend sipped at his coffee, pulling a face at the bitter taste. 'Take it from me, Lothar, none of it adds up. It does not make sense. The authorities are lying to us. It's the biggest conspiracy pulled on mankind for two thousand years, and billions around the globe are still being fooled by it.'

'I'm no scientist, Joker, but so many questions come to mind. To pull a stunt like this, the Americans would have had to go to enormous trouble. Heavens, half of NASA would have to be in on the conspiracy. Never mind the Soviets. Wouldn't they have said something?'

Joker stroked his goatee beard. 'It was a tense time, Lothar. The Americans wanted to demonstrate that they were leading the science race.'

'What about the Soviets?'

'They couldn't say anything, for fear the Americans would reveal the truth about Yuri Gagarin. Of course you know he didn't go into space either. The whole of the Eastern bloc is at it now. This absurd story about Niclas Herig. Don't believe a word.'

Lothar shook his head. 'Has there ever been any genuine space travel?'

Joker put down his mug and pondered. 'Possibly not, no. Word is, by the way, that the film of Neil Armstrong was shot by Stanley Kubrick in the Nevada desert.'

'Stanley Kubrick? Now you really are pulling my leg, Joker.'

Lothar smiled but Joker remained stony-faced. 'It's no laughing matter,' he said, stuffing his mouth full of bread while he spoke.

Lothar wasn't sure what to think about Joker. Genius or madman, who could be sure? What he did know was that he found Joker's company amusing. His view on life was completely different to anybody else's that he had met. In a society where everybody was potentially a secret agent for the Stasi, it was extraordinary to meet someone who gave their ideas so freely. Secretly, he wished that he had the courage to be like Joker, to say what he really thought about politics, about nationhood, about East Germany's place in the world. He also knew, of course, that speaking openly was unlikely to end well. Look at what had happened to his uncle for expressing his views. There was Krabbe, the student in his first lecture. Rolf Lehmann too. He had never seen or even heard of him again after he left their school. Finally, Hans' brother, Oskar. The same pattern every time. You didn't need to be a Grandmaster to see it.

As the new term began, Beth was the first to notice that all was not well with Joker. 'I know that he is a sombre fellow at the best of times,' she said to Lothar, when the two of them were alone one evening in the kitchen, 'but have you spotted how gloomy and despondent he's become? He couldn't raise a smile yesterday, even after several glasses of beer. When Max tried to chat up the barmaid, that would normally have raised a chuckle. But I didn't see any reaction from him.'

'Now that you mention it, he hasn't seemed too bright. I told him about my ban being lifted early, and all he could talk about was Soviet plots to conquer the West.'

'We need to keep an eye on him.'

The following evening, while Beth and Max stayed late in the library working on their dissertations, Lothar and Joker went for a drink in the student union bar. It was a bitterly cold night – Lothar was wearing two woollen pullovers, as well as a thick scarf, even indoors – and the bar was unusually quiet. Two students in leather jackets sat smoking roll-ups while mournful rock music played in the background. Finding a table in the corner, they ordered two beers, and Joker told him what was troubling him.

'It's the Soviets, Lothar.'

'The Soviets?'

'To be more precise, the Russians. Never mind this nonsense about a Soviet empire. We all know that power rests with the Russians.'

'Stalin wasn't from Russia. He was from Georgia.'

'Look how that turned out,' replied Joker. 'My point is this. The Russians set the agenda for the whole of the Soviet Union. In turn, the Soviet Union determines the fate of Hungary, Poland, Czechoslovakia, and East Germany too. We are all puppets, answerable to the whims of our Russian paymasters.'

A barmaid passed by their table collecting empty glasses. 'Keep your voice down,' Lothar said. 'You never know who could be listening.'

Joker ignored him. 'Who do you think,' he continued, 'is in charge of this kleptocracy?'

'Leonid Brezhnev of course.'

Joker slammed down his glass on the table and raised his voice. If she hadn't been listening before, the barmaid was certainly paying attention now. 'That's what the Russians want you to think. It's what they need you to believe. The reality is different.'

Lothar lit a cigarette and offered one to his friend. There was no stopping Joker when he was on a roll.

'What I'm about to tell you,' said Joker, 'may blow your mind. It's so secret that if I tell you, your life may be in danger.'

Lothar leaned in. 'In that case, do you think you should lower your voice a little?'

Joker looked up and surveyed the room. The barmaid, who had been busying herself at the next table, turned a shade of red and returned to the bar. On the other side, the students had left, their place taken by a couple who sat holding hands. They appeared disinterested, but who could be sure?

'OK,' said Joker, now talking in a hushed whisper. 'The truth is this. Leonid Brezhnev died last winter of a heart attack. The Russians haven't been able to identify a successor, so they are pretending he is still alive.'

'But didn't he visit East Germany earlier this year?'

'Did you see him?'

'No, it was a VIP-only event. I would never make that type of guest list.'

'Do you know anyone who saw Brezhnev?'

'Not directly, no.' Lothar shook his head in bewilderment.

'Then how do you know it was really him?' Joker banged his fist on the table emphatically as he said this, and then scooped a handful of black bread into his mouth.

'I keep meaning to ask you, Joker. Where did you get that bread?'

Joker pulled a rotten-looking hunk of bread out of his pocket. 'This? I've had it for a couple of weeks. I bought it off a peasant when I visited Halle. Like a piece?'

'Err, no thanks.' Lothar's stomach had turned queasy just thinking about the bread.

'Right you are. Anyway, as I was saying, how do you know it was Brezhnev?'

'What about the Soviet military parade? That was broadcast all over Eastern Europe.'

'What did you actually see?'

'Brezhnev giving a salute. The pictures made the front pages of all the newspapers.'

Joker leaned in closer, until Lothar could feel his breath against his neck. 'That's not Brezhnev at all. It's a body double,' Joker whispered, so quietly he could hardly hear him. 'The Soviets wheel out the double for big occasions such as parades, and manipulate him like a puppet.'

'Oh that's ridiculous. Who told you this garbage?'

'I know a man,' said Joker.

'You know a man...' Lothar gave up and took another sip of beer. There was no arguing with Joker in this mood.

Well before he reached the flat, Lothar could hear the music blaring from Max's stereo. At least it was David Bowie. That was something. If you were going to disturb the neighbours in your final year at university, you might as well put some decent music on. But whose idea had it been to arrange a New Year's Eve party? Such a thing could only end in chaos. Spend a few days away from the flat, back at his mother's, and look what had happened.

Opening the front door, still only eight in the evening, Lothar found the party already in full swing. Beth and Max were handing out wine glasses to anyone who would take them, and twenty or so of their friends were dancing in the centre of the lounge. Only one person was missing.

'Where's Joker?' he mouthed to Beth.

Beth shook her head. 'In the kitchen.'

'What's up?'

'You'd better go and see for yourself.'

Lothar wandered through to the kitchen. Joker sat at their dining table with three earnest-looking students. Two of them he didn't recognise. The third was Troeller, his old schoolmate. Lothar's heart sank. He had consciously made a habit of avoiding Troeller, who with his suit and side parting had morphed into a senior figure in the Students' Socialist Unity Party. As he entered the room, Troeller was talking.

'Tell me again, Joker, of your theories about Erich Honecker and the Soviet Union. My friends would like to hear what you have to say.'

Lothar groaned to himself. It looked like his worst fears were about to be realised. Troeller was renowned as a snitch. People said he had betrayed his best friend to the Stasi while still at school. When his widowed mother threw him out of the house, he informed on her too and she was now in jail for conspiracy. Lothar didn't know how Troeller came to be at their party and the best outcome, to his mind, would be if they could arrange his quick exit.

'Troeller,' he interrupted. 'Nice to see you. Can I get you and your friends another drink? Perhaps a bite to eat before you go?' He waved a stale piece of bread in front of Troeller, and the young socialist shook his head. Lothar turned to Joker. 'Beth was after a word with you, Joker,' he said. 'She's in the other room.'

Troeller put his arm down firmly on top of Joker's. 'Joker was just going to finish our conversation first, if that's alright with you, Lothar?'

Lothar thought about protesting but he wasn't sure it would help. For the first time since he had met him, Joker appeared to have lost his usual confidence.

'I'm afraid I'm not sure what you mean, Troeller,' said Joker. 'I don't have any views on Honecker or the Soviets.'

Troeller leaned towards Joker and put an arm around his shoulder. 'But Joker, you were overheard, yesterday, in the bar. You told the barman that our society is built on a lie.' Troeller pinched Joker's cheek. 'Isn't that what you said, Joker? Or are you calling the barman a liar?'

'I don't know. I'm afraid I was... I was very drunk, Troeller. I really am not sure what I said.'

'So you don't remember? Well I'll tell you then.' Troeller paused, looked up at Lothar and smiled malevolently before turning back to Joker. 'You said that Honecker isn't a great leader. He's a Soviet puppet. What's more, you said that we are not a great nation. We are the plaything of the Soviet empire. All our sporting successes, we owe to the goodwill and patronage of the Soviet Union.' Troeller leaned in even closer. 'Do you remember now, Joker?'

Joker stammered and looked towards Lothar. 'Well, perhaps I was thinking of the chess world, when I was talking about sporting success. No disrespect, Lothar, but your so-called Grandmaster friends, none of them earned their titles legitimately. They all cheated.' Joker breathed a huge sigh of relief. 'That was it, Troeller, I was thinking of chess.'

Troeller looked across at Lothar. There was a pause, and then, thank goodness, Troeller laughed. 'Indeed, chess players. All the same, aren't they? You'd better watch this one, Joker. He'll rob you of your beer money if you're not careful.'

As Joker and Troeller chuckled, Lothar grabbed a bottle of vodka and returned to the living room. With no idea how to rescue his flatmate from Troeller, the only thing for it was to see in the new year by getting spectacularly drunk.

Later that evening Troeller and his friends left the party, Max put on some cheesy Eurovision music, and a group of them danced the remainder of the year away. Joker rejoined his friends and started downing concoctions of beer, blackcurrant and vodka in one.

Max had invited his younger sister Anna to join them that evening. A studious-looking girl, with glasses, long dark hair which she tied in a ponytail, and dressed all in denim, there was something about her which intrigued Lothar. He had little idea how to strike up a conversation – even when Anna was standing on her own in the corner, he didn't manage to pluck up the courage to talk to her – but when Max put Iggy Pop on the record player, Anna joined him in the centre of the room. They danced deliriously while everyone else looked on mystified.

'What is this strange music?' asked Joker.

'This is Iggy Pop, the Godfather of Punk,' said Anna. Her voice was soft, melodic, like a bell.

'Iggy's an anarchist, Joker. He should be right up your street,' said Lothar.

'I have to say it's rather good,' said Joker, jumping up and down pogo-style, shaking his head wildly and singing tunelessly, '*Oh the passenger. I ride and I ride. I am a passenger, a passenger.*'

Anna fell to the floor, laughing. 'Joker, you're magnificent. If you grew your hair long, you would even look like Iggy.'

While Joker continued to pogo, oblivious to the world, Lothar bent down to pick up Anna. She squeezed his hand as she stood, clutching on to his fingers as they walked across to the corner of the room.

The alcohol was beginning to take effect. Previously tongue-tied, he suddenly found his voice. 'Max never told me he had such an attractive sister,' he said

Anna smiled. 'My mother told me to be wary of men like you. *Charmer.*'

Lothar puffed out his chest and did his best to look like David Bowie. 'I save my flattery for people I like.'

Anna groaned. She was still holding his hand. 'Very smooth,' she said. 'I hear you are a chess player too.'

'I play a bit, yes. It's not something I normally tell women about though.'

'Why not?'

'They usually laugh.'

'Not me,' said Anna. 'I like guys with brains.'

Lothar did his best to look composed and confident. Inside, his heart was pounding. 'It doesn't necessarily follow that chess players are bright.'

'Modest too. Do you have any flaws?'

'Loads,' he said. 'But I'm good at keeping them hidden, at least until you get to know me better.'

As the clock struck twelve, ringing in the new year, Anna pulled him back to the dance floor by the arm. 'It looks like Joker is preoccupied right now,' she said, 'so you'll have to be my Iggy Pop.' Lothar drew Anna towards him and they kissed briefly before a scrum of their friends landed on top of them.

'Happy New Year!'

Everybody cheered and they were all happy. Even Joker seemed at peace.

Good times, Lothar thought to himself. The question was, how long would they last?

CHAPTER SIX

Innocent in a Land of Thieves

The winter was as harsh as any Lothar could remember. The wind was biting and temperatures fell below zero. They had little heating in the flat and he started wearing gloves and a scarf indoors. In the middle of the month, it snowed heavily and lectures were suspended. When the snow was at its height, and the roads were almost impassable, Lothar and his friends went tobogganing in Friedrich Park before returning home where they built a snowman in the courtyard. Anna had covered her slender frame in a light blue ski-jacket and thick winter boots. He thought she looked beautiful and he wanted to wrap his arms around her and protect her from any passing blizzards. After the others went indoors, the two of them had a snowball fight and they kissed for the second time.

Later that week Anna took him to see a Bertolt Brecht play. He stayed the night at her house, lying on her bed, just talking. 'I enjoyed the show,' he said. 'Thank you for taking me. I've not seen much Brecht before.'

'But he's Germany's greatest playwright.'

'I've led a sheltered life.'

Lothar pretended to look sad, and Anna pinched him on the arm. 'You've missed out. He was a genius: a dramatist, a poet and a philosopher. Truly original as well. Did you know that Kurt Weill used Brecht's poetry in his music?'

'Alabama Song?'

'Very good.'

'Show me the way to the next whisky bar, please,' Lothar sang.

'Now you're showing off,' Anna teased him, running her finger gently down his cheek towards his lips. She was right too. Lothar's cultural education was extremely limited. His uncle used to enjoy Kurt Weill, though, and he remembered enough to be able to quote him. Before he could protest his innocence, Anna rolled over on top of him and they kissed again.

A few days later, the snow having cleared, they took a bus into the country to go hiking. Anna told him that she loved the countryside. Free of factories, of the smoke of the city, and of the feeling that every third person was spying on you, he could understand the appeal.

As they reached the top of a hill, Lothar kicked a piece of moss from beneath his feet and surveyed the city below. In between the row of factories on the left, there was High Hall, towering above the buildings around it, harsh, uninviting and an unwelcome blot on an already bleak landscape. He wondered who had ever thought it would be a good idea to construct such a building. 'I see the American government has just issued an apology to Bertolt Brecht,' he said.

'An apology? What for?'

'They blacklisted him in the fifties for being a communist.'

'Oh.' Anna shrugged her shoulders and turned away.

'What do you think about that?'

'Not much.'

'I thought you'd be pleased he's been cleared.'

Anna looked down at the ground. 'Sorry, Lothar, but I don't talk about politics.'

'Why not?'

'When I know you better, we can talk then.'

They had walked on towards the forest, and the spot was secluded. He pulled Anna towards him, put his hands around the thick winter jacket that smothered her like a blanket, and kissed her. 'Do you know me well enough to tell me now?'

Anna smiled at him, paused and reflected. 'Sorry, but no.'

Lothar pulled her towards him once more and kissed her again, this time passionately. 'Now?'

'Still no!' Suddenly Anna looked serious and pensive, and the smile was gone. They walked silently up the pathway towards the exit.

As they sat on the bus on the way back to town, Anna turned and rested her head on his shoulder, her untied hair brushing against his cheek. He felt the touch of her soft skin against his. 'When you asked about politics...' She paused and turned her head towards the window. 'I'm sorry if I was abrupt. Something bad happened to me once, when someone who I trusted betrayed me. Now I don't talk about politics to anyone. Not until I know them really well.'

Lothar squeezed Anna's hand. 'I hope we get to know each other well. I hope you get to trust me.'

'I hope so too,' she said.

As Lothar's relationship with Anna blossomed, so Joker's behaviour became more and more eccentric. His friend had told him before Christmas that he suspected one of his lecturers was a Stasi agent. At the end of January, he said that he feared all of his tutors were conspiring against him. By February Joker had stopped attending lectures altogether. He slept during the day and rose late in the evening, spending his nights in the library, hidden from the world. Whole days would pass where the household barely saw their flatmate. At best, their paths might cross at breakfast, as Joker retired to bed at the very point when the rest of them were getting up.

In early March, Lothar and Anna bumped into Joker at the student union bar. Joker was dressed in a tight-fitting mauve suit, at least three sizes too small from what Lothar could see, and was reading a Western newspaper.

'Do you think it's wise to draw attention to yourself like that, Joker?' Lothar asked.

'You don't like the colour?' his friend replied, stroking the lapel of his suit.

'I meant the newspaper,' he said. 'It's a bit provocative, isn't it?'

Joker looked at him blankly.

'What Lothar means, Joker,' said Anna, 'is that some people may not take well to you reading a Western newspaper. They might see it as anti-government.'

'I'm reading this newspaper to help with my dissertation,' said Joker. 'We do live in a free country.'

'That's the problem,' replied Anna. 'It's not free at all, is it?'

Lothar rested his arm next to Anna's and she put her hand in his and squeezed. He focused his eyes on her fingernails. A subtle red, she had painted them that morning. He thought about how the colour matched her lips.

Joker took a drag from his roll-up and coughed. 'Interesting point, Anna. Something which I'll be raising with young Troeller when I see him later.'

'You're seeing Troeller?' Lothar asked. Behind him, two students walked into the bar, and he felt a chill as the breeze came through the open door.

'I've been invited to attend a meeting of the Students' Socialist Unity Party's disciplinary committee.'

'Why do they want to see you?'

'A trumped-up charge of behaviour disloyal to the state. I intend to fight with all my will, of course.' Joker thumped his chest emphatically as he said this.

'Do you want help?' Anna asked. 'Can we join you at the meeting?'

'Thanks, Anna, but this is my issue and I don't want to drag you in. I'll be OK.' Joker patted Anna on the shoulder and rose to leave. 'I'd better be going. The meeting started fifteen minutes ago.'

They sat and watched as Joker shambled out of the bar and across the quad in his comical ill-fitting suit. 'Do you think we should have gone with him?' asked Anna.

'The best we can hope is that he goes in and says sorry,' Lothar replied, feeling the same tight knot in his stomach that he was used to whenever a chess game was going badly. 'Even then, I don't fancy his chances.' He looked into Anna's hazel-brown eyes. 'Will you tell me now what happened that time?' he asked. 'Who betrayed you?'

Anna gazed at him silently, staring into his soul. Then she put out her cigarette and rested her elbows on the table, their eyes still fixed on each other. 'What I'm about to tell you is strictly for you. Only my brother knows this. I've not told my parents, not even my best friend.'

'You can trust me.'

Anna took a deep breath. 'It was just over two years ago, shortly after my seventeenth birthday. I was in my final year at school. Two things happened that year. The first was that I became interested in politics. I met some like-minded people at a party, they got talking about society and all the things that are wrong and they invited me to join an underground movement. A group of radicals who believed in true socialism, not this jumped-up totalitarian system that passes for our government.' Anna's voice was calm and quiet. He squeezed her hand again. There was a commotion at the bar as the barmaid dropped a glass. Anna looked over at the bar and then back at him.

'I was just a kid at the time,' she said, 'and I suppose I was playing at politics. The people in the group seemed sincere, well-meaning, and many of them became friends. The second thing that happened was that I fell in love.' Anna dabbed her eyes, which had begun to fill with tears. 'There were lots of good people in the group. One in particular, Lucas, I grew especially close to. He was a few years older than me, confident, a bit of a heart-throb. I guess you could say he was my first love.'

'What happened?'

'Things went horribly wrong. The police found out about the group. They raided one of our meetings. They beat the leaders till they confessed to all manner of crimes. A couple of them are still in jail.'

'What about you?'

'I was the only one who got away scot-free.' Anna's eyes were creased. Lothar gave her his handkerchief to dab her face. How strangely beautiful she appeared when she was sad. 'Lucas looked after me. He protected me. I have to give him credit for that much.'

'How did he manage that?'

Anna paused. Her voice had gone up several notes. 'Because he was undercover. He was working for the police the whole time. He betrayed us. He lied to everyone.' Anna burst into floods of tears and Lothar hugged her close to him as she sobbed.

Later, they walked back to his flat in a sombre mood. It had turned dark outside, and in the final half mile only a solitary car passed them. As they approached the flat, he pulled Anna towards him and they kissed. He told her for the first time that he loved her. 'Those are big words,' she said, holding him tightly. 'You shouldn't use them if you don't mean them.'

The next morning, Lothar left for the university campus early. Joker had been shut in his room all evening and none of the flatmates could get any sense out of their friend. It was time, Lothar decided, to take things into his own hands. Walking past the lecture halls, he headed for the red-brick building at the far end of the campus. The so-called *People's Quarters*, this was where the bureaucrats and administrators were housed. He had been here twice before in his university career: once when he failed an exam; the second time to explain himself when he had been banned from chess. Neither experience held happy memories for him. Now, turning down a narrow corridor, with faded yellow walls and ragged carpet, he walked past the Disciplinary Office, scene of his last two visits, and knocked on the dark green door at the end of the corridor.

'Enter,' came the familiar nasal voice of his old school colleague Troeller. The Chairman of the Students' Socialist Unity Party was sitting at his desk, a row of papers neatly stacked in front of him.

'Membership applications,' said Troeller, pointing to the papers. 'Record levels. The future of the Party looks promising. Have a seat, Lothar.'

Lothar pulled a plastic chair from under Troeller's desk and sat down. It occurred to him that he had never used Troeller's first name. Perhaps now was the time. 'Wilhelm, I've come to you because I need your help.'

Troeller raised his eyebrows. 'What makes you think I would help you, Lothar?'

Lothar looked at Troeller's buttoned-up shirt and brown tie with distaste. He had to overcome his feelings, or at least to hide them. 'It's about Joker, Wilhelm. I know you saw him yesterday.'

Troeller gave a wry smile. 'Come now, Lothar. I can't discuss the meeting with Joker. It's confidential Party business.'

Lothar had anticipated Troeller's response. 'Wilhelm, you and I go back a long way. I'd like to speak off the record. Man to man.'

Troeller sighed and inhaled deeply. Standing up, he walked across to the door, opened it, had a quick look outside to make sure there was no one lurking in the corridor, and then shut the door again firmly behind him. Returning to his desk, he sat back down, laid his hands on his desk, looked at Lothar and sniffed. 'Joker is in a lot of trouble, Lothar. But I guess you know that already.'

'Wilhelm, I'm not sure what Joker said to you when you met him, but he's harmless. Believe me, I know the man, I live with him. He doesn't have a bad bone in his body.'

Troeller shook his head. 'Really? It seems to me that he's an anarchist, Lothar. He doesn't believe in socialism, he's openly dismissive of the Party. Heavens, you should hear the things he says about Honecker.'

'I've heard all those things. I know what it must sound like. Yes, he's eccentric. But it doesn't make him a criminal.'

'Joker is dangerous, Lothar. We can't afford deviants like him in university. The damage he could do is immense.'

Lothar took a deep breath. 'Wilhelm, whatever Joker does from here on, it's on me. I stand for him.'

Troeller paused and rubbed his hand against his nose. He looked up at Lothar and arched his eyebrows. 'You take responsibility for Joker? That's brave, Lothar.'

'Yes, I take responsibility.' Lothar stared at Troeller. 'I cover for him.' Lothar looked at the picture behind Troeller's desk. A life-size portrait of Erich Honecker. Grey suit, grey tie, black glasses. Now he saw who Troeller was modelling himself on. 'So you'll let him off?'

Troeller exhaled deeply once again. 'I'll make some calls. See what I can do. But it may be too late.'

'Wilhelm, I...'

'Enough, Lothar. I said I'd make the calls. Even if I do think your action is extremely foolish, consorting with a known criminal.' Picking up the papers from his desk with one hand, Troeller waved Lothar away with his other. Not even a nasal goodbye, Lothar thought to himself, leaving the room as quickly as he could.

For the rest of the morning, Lothar busied himself in the library, trying to catch up on the work he had fallen behind with over recent weeks. After lunch, he returned to his flat. Inside, he found Beth and Max sitting soberly at the kitchen table. Beth was in tears.

He ran to hug Beth. 'What's up?'

'They came to collect Joker this morning.'

'Who did?'

'Two men in brown suits. Stasi no doubt. They came to the flat before lunch. Knocked on Joker's door, and pulled him out of his room. Then they dragged him into a van, and drove off with him. Two other men came and collected his possessions shortly afterwards.'

'Did Joker struggle?'

'He was too shocked. The Stasi didn't even give us a chance to say goodbye. Made us wait in the living room the whole time.'

'Where have they taken Joker?'

Beth shrugged. 'They refused to say. Joker was such a mystery, we don't have any contact details for him, no next of kin.'

So the visit to Troeller had failed. It wasn't a surprise, but he still felt a sense of shock. That evening, Lothar sat alone in his room staring at the chessboard, the pieces all on their starting squares except for a solitary white pawn, which stood exposed in the middle of the board. Gloom filled his soul and he wondered if he would ever see Joker again. He remembered when Lehmann had disappeared. The chances were that Joker was gone for good. An innocent in a land of thieves. For all his friend's eccentricities, he knew he would miss Joker. Perhaps, he told himself, his flatmate would flee to the West. Wherever he went, he hoped that he would find people who were more sympathetic to him.

CHAPTER SEVEN

Udo

Lothar looked at the telegram again, reading it for the twentieth time. 'Please phone at earliest convenience. Udo Grosz'

Udo Grosz. The President of the East German Chess Federation, no less. A huge bear of a man, with thick black hair and a bulging waistline, Grosz had devoted his life to chess. People said that he was connected within the highest levels of the Socialist Unity Party. Lothar didn't know the truth of this, but he did know that Grosz was the most influential man in the whole of East German chess. One word from Grosz could make or break a career. Lothar had never spoken to Grosz, but he had dreamed of the day when he would.

Taking a deep breath, he pulled together as many coins as he could find in his room, and took the short walk down to the payphone at the end of the road. Dialling Grosz' number, he heard a short click and a deep voice answered. 'Grosz here.'

'Good evening, Herr Grosz. This is Lothar Hartmann.'

'Ah, Lothar, I'm glad you rang. Very pressing business. Very pressing indeed, Comrade.' The voice was confident and assured. It spoke of influence and power.

' How can I help you, Herr Grosz?'

'Call me Udo, dear boy,' boomed Grosz. 'Are you sitting down?'

'Yes, I'm seated,' Lothar fibbed.

'Good, good. I have some exciting news for you, Lothar.'

Lothar's heart skipped several beats. He did his best to remain composed.

'You have heard about this year's Anniversary Tournament?'

Lothar murmured his assent. Heard about the tournament? It was the talk of the chess world. Fourteen top Grandmasters, three former world champions, the pride of Germany taking on the rest of the world. Tickets were already sold out and it was rumoured that Erich Honecker himself would be attending the opening ceremony.

'Comrade,' said Grosz. 'I've just come from a meeting of the organising committee. On the orders of the General Secretary, no less, we have two extra spaces for Germany's most promising new players. Sebastian Bahl has already accepted his invitation. We've been impressed by the way you've buckled down since you started playing again. The second spot is yours for the taking. Will you play, Lothar?'

Lothar paused and then stumbled on his words, hardly able to believe what he was about to say. 'Sorry, Udo, but there is one hitch.'

'A hitch? What do you mean, a *hitch*?' Grosz sounded incredulous.

'I have exams in the middle of the event. It's a really awkward clash, I know, but...'

'Lothar,' Grosz interrupted. 'Don't worry. That will be taken care of.'

'Taken care of?'

Grosz gave a chuckle. 'Comrade, you're in the big league now. There are more important things to worry about than mere exams. I will talk to your tutors tomorrow. Accept the invitation and you will graduate with honours. We will exempt you from your military service as well. That's eighteen months you can spend focusing on your chess.'

There was another pause and then Lothar realised that he had to say something. 'Thank you, Udo. I accept.'

'No need to thank me, Comrade. Just make sure to do the nation proud with your play.'

The final round. At the age of fifteen, when he had first sat down with Hans, they had studied the games of the Latvian genius Mikhail Voronin. Now, by holding Voronin to a draw, he had finished the Anniversary Tournament sixth in the table, gaining a place in the East German team for the European Championships in Amsterdam as a bonus. Shaking hands with Voronin, standing up ready to leave the stage of the Palace of the Republic for the last time, it was difficult even now not to look in awe at the players around him. Grandmasters, World Champions, stars of the game. In this elite company, he had held his own, finishing as the top-performing German. He had exceeded all expectations, including even his own.

As the two players sat in the bar afterwards, Lothar sipped at his drink, still in awe of the great man opposite. 'Do you know, Misha, the very first evening I sat down with Hans, we looked through a book of your best games.'

Voronin smiled and lit a cigarette, his third in an hour. 'It flatters me that you remember this, Lothar,' he said in broken German. 'I hope that my book, it helped you.' A thin man, his voice was high-pitched and nasal.

'At that stage, your play was too complex for me. But it gave me something to aim for.'

'There are times, Lothar, when my own moves, I do not understand,' said Voronin. 'I look to heavens, I see inspiration, and I sacrifice piece.' He smiled and blew a ring of smoke in the air. 'Our fates, Lothar, they lie with the gods. It is your round, yes?'

Lothar waved at the barman. He had barely started his own drink. There was no keeping up with Voronin. 'Misha,' he said, 'how can I improve my play? How do I become a world-class player?'

Voronin scratched his neck. 'In your case, Lothar, the answer, I believe, it is easy.' Leaning towards him, as though imparting a great secret, he whispered, 'You are serious about chess. You treat it like' – Voronin waved his arm in the air dismissively – 'like sport. You do not drink. You go home early. You work at game. Very impressive. But, my friend, in this way, you will not make it to top.'

Lothar frowned, not understanding what Voronin meant.

'Chess is not sport,' said Voronin. 'It is art. You try to be Bjorn Borg. Serious, intense, physically fit. Chess players are not sportsmen. They are artists.' Voronin paused and pointed to a piece of second-rate abstract German art on the wall. 'Not like that. But Picasso, Dali, Jackson Pollock. The great player, he needs inspiration, imagination, flair. To create the unexpected. Ask yourself,' he said rhetorically, 'do you prefer day as lion, or lifetime as mouse?' Voronin looked at him meaningfully. 'A vodka to wash down beer?'

Lothar summoned the waiter and ordered two vodkas. Voronin was a former World Champion, and who was he to argue with him when he said that alcohol would help creativity.

At the prize-giving banquet that evening, he sat next to the long-haired and maverick Englishman Tony Marlowe, who made him laugh incessantly with his eccentric humour. Conscious of their Western visitors, the East German Federation had laid on a feast the like of which he had never seen before. Roast lamb, new potatoes, broccoli, mustard and mint sauce. The alcohol was of an unprecedented quality too. They mixed wine, beer and vodka until Lothar could drink no more, at which point Marlowe began drinking from his neighbour's glass as well.

By eleven, Marlowe had fallen asleep face down, his flowing

locks spread across the table. His English compatriot, the Oxford maths prodigy Jon Forester, was solving quadratic equations in his head. Jensen and Bahl were discussing chess strategy. Bahl was still upset that Lothar had finished ahead of him and could barely look at him. As for Lothar, it had been a long day and he was ready to go home. Udo Grosz, though, had other ideas, intercepting him as he walked across the banquet hall floor, and throwing a bulky arm around him. 'Well done, Comrade! Your play has been wonderful this week.'

'Thank you, Udo, I'm honoured just to be here.'

'Before you go home, Lothar, let's have a drink to celebrate your qualification for the national team. A toast. What will it be?'

'I will have whatever you're drinking, Udo.'

Grosz led him to the bar and snapped his fingers at the barman. 'Two large vodkas please, and make it snappy. This man is the finest young chess player in the country, and he waits for no man.'

The vodkas arrived and Grosz downed his in a single movement, rubbing his large belly as he did so. 'Barman, another!'

Lothar had had too many drinks already to be able to keep up with Grosz, and he sipped slowly at his vodka while the President drank another four rounds. Presently, even Grosz had drunk enough. 'Comrade,' he said, as he stood up to leave, 'I'm proud of the way you played, both today and throughout the tournament. You've done the nation a great service. I will be saying as much when I meet with the General Secretary next week.'

'You mean Erich Honecker?' Lothar tried not to show his surprise. He knew Grosz had connections. But he hadn't realised they were at such an exalted level.

Grosz smiled broadly, revealing rolls of fat under his chin. 'Yes, Erich and I go back a long way. I was his protégé for a while, until' – Grosz bit his lip – 'his progress up the Party hierarchy accelerated, and I didn't manage to keep pace. I will mention your name in dispatches. Keep in with the right people, Lothar, and you will have a bright future ahead of you.'

Lothar shook Grosz' hand warmly. Top East German in the tournament; a place in the national team; the admiration of Udo Grosz, the most powerful man in East German chess. This had been a successful two weeks' work.

'Goodnight, Udo.'

'Goodnight, Lothar. May Lenin be with you.'

Chapter Eight

First Time in the West

He must have packed and repacked his old brown suitcase at least four times. When the zip refused to fasten, he picked through the shirts and sweaters, throwing out the ones he didn't think he needed, until only two remained.

'Don't you at least need a change of clothes?' Anna asked, looking with raised eyebrows at the case crammed full of chess books and journals.

'This is how chess players travel,' said Lothar, holding up one of the books, a Yugoslavian guide to chess openings, its pages full of hieroglyphics a mystery to Anna. 'Information at your fingertips,' he said. 'Besides, I'm hoping to buy some Western clothes while I'm out there. If I get short, I'll wear those.'

At the airport, he met with three teammates – Jensen, Müller and Vogel – and no fewer than five officials who would also be travelling to Amsterdam.

'Who are these people?' he asked Jensen, as the two of them washed their hands in the bathroom.

'The first four are Party officials. Their job is to keep an eye on us, ensure we don't do anything stupid.'

'You mean drink too much?'

'I mean defect to the West.'

'Who is the fifth guy?'

'The balding chap with the glasses? His name is Wolfgang Neuer. He's Stasi.'

'What's his role?'

'Technically, he's the leader of our delegation. In practice, he's here to spy on the Party officials.'

Lothar shook his head in bemusement. 'As long as we are all focused on winning this thing.'

Jensen gave a wry smile. 'I'm not sure that's too high up the agenda, Lothar.'

After a turbulent flight, with two false landings, they eventually disembarked at Schiphol Airport shortly after one o'clock. Jensen had warned Lothar to expect questioning at customs, but even so the experience was an uncomfortable one. The security officers looked at his chess books blankly and he had to rummage through his luggage until he found a pocket set, to prove that he was actually a chess player. Examining his passport, the guards seemed particularly interested in the fact that he had once been to Poland, questioning him for over an hour on what he knew about a recent bombing in Warsaw. It was four o'clock before he made it through to the other side of the airport. His teammates found his misfortune highly amusing. 'We thought you must have defected, you'd been gone that long,' said Jensen. Neuer meanwhile sat stony-faced at the front of the bus, looking at his watch and sighing.

Lothar spent the rest of the journey staring with wonder at the roads full of traffic, the advertising billboards on the sides of the road, and as they came to a halt in a gridlock of cars, at the well-fed and smartly dressed Dutch walking or cycling past.

They were booked in at the Regency Hotel. With its marble floors, ornate staircase and Olympic-size swimming pool, the luxury of the hotel was way beyond his expectations, or any previous experience. Once they had checked in, he amused himself simply walking around the reception in a circle, bemused at the lavish surroundings.

That evening, they dined in the hotel restaurant. Having grown accustomed to the food in Eastern European hotels

– stodgy vegetables, stringy meat and undrinkable wine – it was with some wonder that he tasted the fine soup, the rare and tender steak and the fresh apple pie and cream. Even the Coca-Cola tasted unrecognisable compared to Vita Cola, the bitter substitute for Coke that he was used to. They were under strict curfew – ever since the defection of Viktor Gavrilov from the Soviet Union in 1976, the entire Eastern bloc had become obsessive about avoiding another escape – but Neuer allowed them to stay in the bar until gone eleven, and he enjoyed his first ever taste of whisky. Sharp and sour, with a bitter aftertaste; Lothar wasn't convinced. Hans had told him that whisky was an acquired taste, however, and he was determined to work at it.

Lothar was sharing a twin room with Rainer Müller, a serious and thoughtful man five years older than him. Their plan to spend time each evening discussing their games went awry as early as the second evening when, investigating the sound of heavy metal from down the corridor, they discovered that they were in the next room to the Englishmen Tony Marlowe and Jon Forester, their fellow competitors from the Anniversary Tournament. Marlowe ordered two bottles of wine on room service and they spent the rest of the evening discussing music and culture.

Since returning from Berlin, Marlowe had acquired a stud in his ear, and the Englishman tried unsuccessfully to persuade the two East Germans to get their ears pierced. Several times during the subsequent week, Marlowe and Forester invited them for a drink in the city centre, but Lothar and Rainer were both fearful of being spotted. It was rumoured that Neuer had spies watching the hotel exit. The consequences of being caught fraternising in a bar with Westerners, which as a minimum meant being sent home in disgrace, did not bear thinking about.

Inspired by the lavish surroundings, their team won its first four matches, and he remained undefeated. In the fifth round they lost as expected to the top-seeded Soviets. They had not disgraced themselves though, and Neuer rewarded them the following morning with their first excursion outside the hotel. They must have looked an odd group, Lothar reflected, in their ill-fitting and worn suits, as they walked open-mouthed through Hema, one of the largest and most famous department stores in Amsterdam. Rainer could hardly contain his excitement, running from one part of the store to the next. 'Look, Lothar, blue Levi jeans. Just like on television.' By the time Lothar caught up with him, he had already moved on. 'Over there, look, brown boots, with buckles. Real leather. Goodness, sheepskin coats!'

Neuer had negotiated an allowance for them, and Lothar bought two pairs of jeans, a check shirt and a leather jacket. Rainer came back with a leather wallet and a pair of gold earrings for his wife. Jensen bought chocolate and whisky, plus a carton of John Player cigarettes, which he said tasted much better than the rough Marlboros that they smoked back in East Germany.

On the way back to the hotel, they passed the railway station. A man with one arm, Lothar guessed in his late fifties, sat cross-legged outside the station, with a sign around his neck. His jeans and jacket were torn, and his hands were a filthy grey. Lothar wasn't able to read the sign, but he assumed that the man was a war veteran. As they walked past, the beggar reached out imploringly.

They carried on walking, and Neuer gripped Lothar by the arm. 'Homelessness, Lothar. It's the curse of the West.'

Lothar nodded. Tony Marlowe had told him something similar. For all the grandeur of the hotels, shops and business districts, it seemed that poverty was a feature of Western life.

'One minute, Wolfgang,' he said to Neuer. Turning around, he ran back to the beggar and, reaching into his pocket, handed him five shiny new Dutch coins. It was enough, he figured, for the man to buy himself at least one hot meal, possibly more. The man looked at him and saluted. Lothar returned the greeting before heading back to the side of the road where Neuer and the others stood waiting for him.

The next day, they made a draw with the strong Hungarians. Meanwhile, England defeated the Soviets, with Tony Marlowe beating the former World Champion Mikhail Dasaev. That evening, Lothar and Rainer joined Marlowe for a celebratory drink in his room. On the back of his greatest ever performance, the Englishman insisted that they had to accompany him into town. Despite their resistance, he would not take no for an answer. It was Rainer who gave in first. 'OK, Tony, we'll join you. But the first sign of any trouble and we're heading straight back.'

The Englishman stroked his beard. 'Relax, Rainer. Nobody will see you. There are no spies waiting at the exit. You'll be completely safe with me.'

Lothar wasn't as confident as Marlowe, but having already drunk two beers, his faculties blunted, he found himself agreeing to the scheme. Before he knew it, he was following Tony Marlowe as part of a disparate group of Englishmen, Dutchmen and two East Germans on a tour of Amsterdam. After a bar crawl through the centre of town, they window-shopped in the Red Light District before stopping at Amsterdam's largest nightclub, Bar Red. As they stood outside the club, he watched the crowds milling around in the street. He had never seen so many bars, so many people.

The atmosphere was lively, but tense too, always on the edge of violence. Ahead of them, a group of local lads stood arguing with each other. On the other side of the road, two girls sat by the kerb smoking. One of the lads went and sat with the girls, until they pushed him away. Opposite them, a beggar sat on the side of the road, leaning against a tree, a tin cup by his side. Meanwhile a French tourist cycled down the road waving and shouting, and one of the locals chased after him, trying to push him off his bike. Lothar thought about home, and what would happen to anyone who tried to behave like that in East Berlin.

Turning back to his friends, he found that Marlowe had negotiated a group discount with the huge, shaven-headed bouncer outside Bar Red. Rainer, meanwhile, was having second thoughts. 'We can't go in here, Tony,' he said. 'You know what goes on in this place. We'll be banned from travelling for life if we get caught.'

'Nonsense,' said Marlowe. 'Who's going to see you in here? Besides which, you can always come and live in England.'

Rainer looked pensive but when everybody else entered, he followed. The alternative of walking home on his own was even less appealing than being caught in Bar Red.

Inside, the club was dark and smoke-filled. Disco music played at full volume while scantily clad waitresses mixed cocktails behind the bar. Marlowe found them a table near the stage while Forester went to buy a round of drinks. Settling down to enjoy the show, Lothar was finally beginning to relax when Rainer poked him frantically in the ribs.

'What's up?'

'Over there?'

'What?'

'Look who's sitting over there!' Rainer's voice was shrill and his face betrayed panic.

Lothar looked across to the other side of the stage. 'Oh my God.' With his brown suit, thick black spectacles, and balding pate, Wolfgang Neuer was unmistakable.

'Too late. He's seen us.'

The next few moments passed in slow motion. Neuer stared at them. They looked back at Neuer. Neuer continued to stare at them, open-mouthed. Lothar thought about his career, his ambitions, his place in the national team. He thought about Anna. The looming disgrace, caught red-handed in a Western nightclub, breaking their curfew, mixing with Westerners. The disciplinary panel would make his previous ban look like a picnic.

Lothar wanted to jump up, to run, but his eyes seemed somehow fixed on Neuer, and his feet were made of stone. He assumed the same thoughts were going through Rainer's head as his colleague sat beside him motionless. His teammate had a wife and child to think of too.

Then salvation, of a sort. A brunette dancer in a tight outfit, taking a shine to Neuer, stripped off her dress and threw it over the Stasi man's spectacles, before jumping off the stage and onto his lap. Seizing their moment, with Neuer now smothered and unable to move, the two East Germans leapt out of their seats, giving a hurried apology to Forester at the bar before running out of the club.

Back in their hotel room, having sprinted the entire way, Lothar doubled up in pain on his bed. 'What do we do now, Rainer? Neuer is going to give us hell tomorrow morning. That is, if he doesn't come knocking on our door in the middle of the night.'

Rainer was sitting on his own bed with his head in his hands. 'It's not good, Lothar. I'll admit that. But we do have one saving grace.'

'What's that?'

'If he wants to take any action against us, Neuer will have to explain what he was doing in the club himself. We can plead that we are young and naïve. He doesn't have that excuse.'

Lothar sat back up, walked across to the bathroom and splashed cold water over his face. 'How do we play it from here?'

'We don't say a word,' Rainer replied. 'Keep our heads down, carry on as normal.'

The following morning, Neuer greeted the two of them at breakfast as though nothing had happened. They did the same. As they finished their coffees and rose to leave, Neuer followed them, putting on a surprising sprint and catching them just as they entered the lift.

'How are you feeling, fellows?' he asked.

Lothar looked at his shoes and coughed, unsure what to say. Beside him, Rainer was motionless.

'About last night,' the Stasi man continued. 'It's been a long tournament, and we were all letting our hair down. Does a man good to let loose once in a while.' Neuer chuckled and put an arm on each of their shoulders. 'So we'll say no more about the club. Our little secret, eh, boys?' Rainer nodded and Lothar followed suit. 'Good lads,' said Neuer, as the lift door opened. 'Fourth floor. This is me.'

They watched as Neuer ambled down the corridor. 'Told you,' said Rainer. 'He'd be in as much trouble as us if anyone found out what he was up to last night.' The lift door shut and Rainer turned back to him. 'We caught a lucky break there. If we'd met him in the middle of the street, instead of the club, we'd be toast by now.'

Lothar wasn't entirely sure that he trusted Neuer. Still, they did seem to have survived the incident in one piece. The tournament concluded the following day and they returned to East Germany a contented team. They had won the bronze medal, and Lothar had proved he could compete with the Grandmasters, the very best players in the world. Now it was time to aim for that great honour, the Grandmaster title, himself. He spent the journey home thinking about how proud Anna would be, and his mother too, if he could only make that final leap. With the confidence of youth, he assumed that the hunt for the title would be an easy task. Time would tell if he was right.

CHAPTER NINE

The Yucca Plant

Lothar and Anna had been going out together for nearly a year. What had started as something low-key, with afternoons spent hiking in the woods, or evenings listening to music, had become more serious. They began to see each other most days, and when he wasn't with Anna, Lothar found himself missing her. When he felt down or lacking in confidence, she knew how to find the right words of encouragement. She was his biggest supporter, and his best friend too.

At the end of the month they celebrated their anniversary by booking a weekend in Leipzig. He had not felt as relaxed in months, strolling through the park in the centre of the town, watching the kids playing football, and sipping coffee in a café on the Market Square, allowing the world to go by. On the Sunday they climbed the Panorama Tower and the views of the city were breathtaking. That afternoon they visited the Bach Museum and in the evening they went to a concert in the Town Hall. As they walked back to their hotel, he made a confession.

'Do you know, that's the first classical concert I've been to in my life.' He thought back to the only other live music event he had attended. Karl Rauser. A very different experience.

Anna turned to look at him in surprise. 'Your first classical concert? Is that true? What have you been doing with yourself all these years?'

'Playing chess, mainly. That, and the occasional evening drinking beer.'

She put her arm through Lothar's. 'So what did you make of it? Is it an experiment you are going to repeat?'

'I'm not sure I can explain why, but it really moved me. I'm embarrassed admitting it's my first experience of classical music.'

'The tragedy would be if you didn't want to see any more. Now that you know what you've been missing, we can do something about it.'

Ahead of them, a clock tower struck ten. 'Where do we go from here, Anna?'

'Back to the hotel I guess.'

Lothar pulled his girlfriend towards him. 'I don't mean right now. I mean, in our lives.'

She tugged him back. 'That's a deep question.'

'I'm a chess player. I like to think ahead.'

'That may be true, but from what I've seen, when you chess masters think ahead, your focus is purely on the sixty-four squares.'

'What about the thirty-two pieces?'

'Hah, yes. Those too.' They were passing the canal. Anna pointed to a bench. 'Let's sit down here.'

Taking a seat, they watched as the boats went past. The night was calm and tranquil. He felt secure and at ease. He looked across at his girlfriend. What a picture she was in the moonlight, so beautiful, so enigmatic. 'Move in with me?' he asked.

Anna gave a half smile. 'Maybe, Lothar.'

'What does the maybe depend on?'

'Do you have room for a thirty-third piece in your life?'

He watched as another boat went past, causing a gentle ripple in the waves. 'I only need one piece to make my life complete. You don't need to worry about the other thirty-two.'

Anna took his hand in hers and Lothar squeezed back. His future was with her. He had never felt so certain of anything in his life.

Flats in the centre of town were hard to come by, but Udo Grosz wielded his influence with the Ministry of Housing, and without having to go through the usual rigmaroles – application forms, waiting lists, interviews with government officials, loyalty tests – Lothar and Anna took possession of a two-bedroomed flat in the centre of East Berlin. The previous tenant was a Party official who had fallen out of favour with the government, and now languished in jail awaiting trial for an unknown crime. He had bequeathed them an interior that was monochrome grey. The walls, the carpets, the sofa, even the light bulbs were grey.

They set to work transforming the place, determined to put their own stamp on it. Anna hung pictures of Iggy Pop and David Bowie in their bedroom and Beth's abstract paintings in the hallway. They put the greatest effort into the living room, which became the centre of their home. Lothar bought some overalls, and painted the walls electric blue. Anna's parents gave them an old sofa and armchair, and they covered them with blankets and cushions, giving the room a warm and comfortable feel. They kept the wooden bookcase in the corner, left by the previous tenant, and Anna filled the shelves with her books on poetry and literature. Clambering onto a stepladder, Anna placed a yucca plant on the top of the bookcase, its green blades proudly pointing skywards.

'Do you know what's special about the yucca?' Anna asked. He shook his head. 'It's highly adaptable and can survive in almost any climate. It reminds me of you in some ways.'

He looked up from the chessboard. 'Is that a compliment?'

Anna stepped back down from the ladder and came across and hugged him. She was wearing her red sweater, the one he had given her for Christmas. He was always pleased when she wore it. It made him feel more connected to her, as though she must think of him every time she touched the fabric. 'Yes, it's a compliment. It means you're resilient, that you won't let adversity get the better of you. Just like when you play chess.'

'Thanks. I would say you're pretty tough yourself.'

His girlfriend shook her head. 'Afraid not, Lothar. I'm an idealist. That means I want things to be perfect. If something isn't right, I can't just stand by.' Anna picked up a vase and walked over to the window. The light reflected against her hair, and she smiled sadly. 'It will be my downfall one of these days too. I know it.'

Their flat was situated less than ten minutes' walk from Lothar's mother, and every Sunday, Lothar and Anna would visit her for lunch. Lothar helped with odd jobs around his mother's flat, putting up shelving, fixing leaking taps and changing broken electrical sockets. Anna took her shopping, and the two of them became firm friends, united by their ability to tease and make fun of him. He didn't mind this, pleased that the two of them got along so well.

Three evenings a week, Lothar took the tram to Hans' flat, where they continued their study. Hans had changed little since they had first teamed up. Irascible, sardonic, with a trace of bitterness, he remained a hard man to impress. Lothar knew though that he had his best interests at heart, and they worked well together.

One Wednesday, he arrived at Hans' earlier than normal. Anna's parents were visiting, and he wanted an excuse to escape. Knocking on the door, he found that Hans had company. A tall, thin man with a beard sat earnestly on the sofa, sipping a glass of white wine. The handwritten pages of a manuscript were scattered over the coffee table in front of him. The flat was tidier than usual. The children's toys were stacked neatly at the back of the living room and the chess books and magazines had all been returned to the study. A gramophone played in the background.

'Lothar,' said Hans, 'allow me to introduce my oldest friend, the one and only Daniel Lorenz.'

Daniel Lorenz? Who knew that Hans mixed in such circles? Lothar had never been one to pay attention to literature lessons at school, but even he was aware that Daniel Lorenz was the most famous East German playwright of his generation, a core part of any advanced literature course.

'I'm honoured,' he said.

Daniel Lorenz stood up and shook his hand firmly. He was greying and had a slight stoop, but his eyes were still piercing, and even with his stoop, he towered above Lothar. 'Pleased to meet you,' said Lorenz. 'Hans has told me a lot about you.'

Lothar laughed. 'I'm not sure whether that's good or bad.' He took a deep breath, not quite sure of the etiquette when meeting a famous writer. 'My girlfriend has your collected plays in our bookcase. She is a big fan.'

'Thank you, young man,' said Lorenz. 'I hope that she gets a chance to see my plays performed again one day.'

Lothar was not sure he understood what Lorenz meant, but he smiled warmly. 'I'm sure she will. We both will.'

Daniel Lorenz nodded, gathered the papers from the table and took his leave. 'That was an unexpected surprise,' Lothar said to Hans, when the playwright had gone. 'I'd love to take Anna to see one of Lorenz's plays. Maybe an opening night. Could you help get tickets? We could all go: you, me, Anna and Freya.'

Hans looked at him oddly. 'We'll see,' he said, tidying away the wine glasses and putting the kettle on the stove. 'Let's get a coffee before we start. I need to sober up.'

As the year progressed, Lothar began to meet frequently with Udo Grosz. A man of huge appetites, Grosz enjoyed fine wines and dining, and more often than not they would meet in the restaurant at the top of the Berliner Fernsehturm, a place so expensive that only a senior politician or a member of the Stasi could go there. The food was as good, if not better, than it had been at the Centenary Congress. Waiters were constantly on hand to attend to their needs, and a barmaid refilled their wine as quickly as they drank it. Lothar could never afford to pay for such luxuries himself, and the bill was always on Grosz. Bizarrely, for a man of culinary tastes, Grosz smoked the most appalling fake Cuban cigars – a brand by the name of Bison, with an aroma of pig swill and manure and a picture of Che Guevara on the front of the packet. Rather than inflict the punishment of Grosz' noxious fumes on other guests, the waiters usually showed them to a private room.

Grosz had great faith in Lothar's abilities, and he would mark every dinner with at least one toast to 'the future Grandmaster and great hope of East Germany'. Lothar was embarrassed by the praise, but secretly flattered too. At his best, Grosz was a witty raconteur, with endless stories of bribery, corruption and skulduggery in the chess world. Lothar's eyes were opened by his tales of thrown games, of Grandmaster titles and even national championships won or lost on the exchange of hard cash, and of players who had seemingly based entire careers around cheating.

'Have you heard of the Austrian Grandmaster Schweiger?' began one such tall tale. 'He once travelled to Ireland, where he put on a false beard and glasses, and played in an amateur tournament under the name O'Schweiger. His intention was to win the first prize, something which, as a professional, he would not be eligible for.'

'What happened?'

Grosz took a puff from his cigar, and proceeded to blow smoke all over him. 'Oh, he won the tournament alright. Nobody could match him. People were suspicious, but when they questioned him, he glared back in stony silence.'

'Did he get the prize money?'

'Yes, he did. But when he returned to Austria, and tried to cash the cheque, the authorities confiscated it. You see, there really is an O'Schweiger living in Austria, and the bank believed that the money belonged to him.'

Lothar suspected that Grosz had exaggerated most of the stories, and some he had made up altogether, but he had to admit the man was a good storyteller. As for Grosz' political leanings, Lothar felt on less solid ground. Anna, who had never warmed to Grosz, gave him a hard time over this. 'Are you going drinking with that dreadful man again?' she would ask sardonically, pinching him on his arm. 'You might as well sign up with the Stasi now.'

Although he had his own doubts about Grosz – he had no idea how far his connections with the secret service went – Lothar found himself defending the President in front of Anna. He was, though, becoming increasingly conscious of Grosz' antipathy towards Hans Adler, and it was something which troubled him.

'Tell me, Comrade,' said Grosz, one evening over dinner, 'what openings are you studying? How is Adler helping you improve your attacking game?'

'We don't focus on openings or attacking ploys, Udo. Hans prefers to look at the games of the great masters.'

Grosz stroked his bulging chin. 'How interesting. One might call that approach *unique*, for this day and age.'

'You sound surprised, Udo.'

'I'm not saying there's anything wrong with Adler's training methods, Lothar. You're the expert, not me. As you've described it, though, Adler's style feels amateur and outdated. No structure, no order, no logic, no study plan. You turn up at Adler's house, get out the pieces and start analysing. It's quite charming really. I worry though that such an unsystematic approach will hold you back.'

Lothar lit a cigarette, his fifth that evening. His throat was dry but he still needed the nicotine in his system, prisoner as he was to the poison. 'Hans has made me the player I am today,' he said. He's stuck by me through thick and thin, and he's been there when I've needed him. I'm not sure I would still be playing without him.'

Grosz reached for the red wine and poured two large glasses. 'Admirable loyalty, Comrade. It's one of the qualities I like about you. Please don't think I'm criticising Adler. I have enormous respect for the man.' Grosz lifted his glass and clinked it against Lothar's. Rubbing his belly with his left hand, he hiccupped and took a large gulp of wine. 'To achieve what he's done, from his impoverished background, little schooling or education, is remarkable. But I want what's best for you, Lothar. I want you to become a Grandmaster. I want you to challenge for the World Championship one day. I believe you can do so, and I know you want that success too.'

Lothar lifted his own glass. 'Thank you, Udo. I hope I don't let you down.'

Grosz smiled, a slightly crooked smile, showing the glints of his yellow, uneven teeth. 'To success, Lothar, however it's achieved.'

Pulling his trusty old suitcase from under the bed, Lothar packed the familiar set of chess books and journals, along with two extra sweaters. This was Tallinn he was headed for, after all, and who knew what the weather might do. The event was a strong one, with several players ranked in the top twenty in the world. Play well and it would be an opportunity to secure the title of Grandmaster which he so coveted. Lothar felt confident in his play and his abilities, but almost from the off things did not proceed as planned. The weather was freezing, even by Baltic standards, the bedroom in his boarding house had no heating, and he caught a chill that stayed with him for several days. After somehow drawing his first two games, despite an appalling cold, he proceeded to lose no fewer than three rounds in a row, the first time that had happened in his life. Each successive loss was like a dagger to his chest. After the third defeat, he felt himself almost mortally wounded. Staggering back to his boarding house that evening, he could hardly speak, barely breathe in fact. Nor could he touch the bread and soup that his concerned landlady tried to force upon him.

After a brief respite of two draws, he lost again, this time to the softly spoken Soviet champion Vasily Smirov, in less than twenty moves. The tournament had turned into a disaster, and in his heart he wanted to go home. But there was still one shot at redemption. In the next round he would be facing Sebastian Bahl. His rival was having a very successful tournament, only one point off the lead. This did nothing to cheer Lothar up, but it did give him an opportunity. Beat Bahl, and he could bring his fellow East German back down to size. It wouldn't compensate for all the defeats, but with a victory over his countryman he would certainly feel better about himself.

The evening before the game, Lothar stayed in his room preparing an opening strategy to surprise Bahl. He went to bed early, slept well, and on the following morning, now recovered from his cold, he took a bracing walk through the city centre.

Sitting down at the board, shaking Bahl's hand, Lothar felt focused and alert. Even Bahl's mock sympathy at the start of the game – 'Having a difficult time of it, are we Lothar? Never mind, only another few days, and it will all be over' – didn't bother him. The more irritating Bahl became, questioning whether he had ever finished last in a tournament before, the more determined Lothar became to teach his compatriot a lesson.

Thirty moves into the game, and Lothar's fortunes had finally turned. Sacrificing a pawn, he had developed a strong attack. Bahl's confidence, so evident at the start of the game, had evaporated, and as Lothar sat back in his chair his opponent gnawed at his fingernails, staring all the while at the board in front of him, shaking his head, scarlet-faced.

Eventually, Bahl picked up a Knight, gripped it in his hand for a while, before moving it one square sideways, two squares forwards, towards Lothar's King. He sighed as he did so. Lothar had envisaged this move already, and he had seen at least three different replies which would win him the game. Which to choose? As he reflected, it struck him. This was Sebastian Bahl he was facing. Playing either his Rook or Bishop would win easily. But if he moved his Queen, then he had a chance to sacrifice, to win in spectacular style. That was the aesthetic choice, the move to cause maximum humiliation to Bahl. Smiling to himself, Lothar picked up his Queen, moved it forward three squares and pressed his clock.

Feeling content with life for the first time in several days, Lothar looked up at Bahl. To his surprise, his opponent's face had broken into a disbelieving smirk. Bahl raised his hands in the air, and shaking his head, mouthed the words 'What are you doing?'

Lothar looked back down at the board. Suddenly, he realised. By moving his Queen, he had allowed Bahl to bring his own

Queen crashing down towards his King. It was too awful. He was going to lose the game.

Before he had registered the full horror, Bahl had gripped the black Queen in his hand and played the move with a thump. It would be checkmate in just a few moves. Lothar found himself frozen to the spot, unable to comprehend the turn of events. The other players had begun to crowd round the board. Bahl meanwhile sat with his arms crossed, grinning smugly. Unable to speak, Lothar knocked over his King in resignation, stood, took his coat from the back of his chair, and stumbled past the bemused spectators and out of the hall. Behind him, he thought he heard Bahl chuckle.

For chess players, losing is an occupational hazard, but this was truly his lowest moment. He had lost a game to his bitterest rival, and in truly embarrassing fashion. He felt ashamed of himself, and humiliated too. As he headed back through the narrow streets of Tallinn, it seemed that people passing the other way were laughing at him, as though they could see his misery and were aware of his abject failure. Impossible, he knew, but his brain was so scrambled by the defeat that he was no longer able to distinguish reality. After walking endlessly in a circle for over forty minutes, he could see only one solution. Finding a tiny smoke-filled bar hidden in a side street near the city walls, he took a seat in the corner where he ordered a double shot of Vana Tallinn. Downing the glass in one and slamming it on the table before the barman had even put the bottle back on the shelf, he ordered another round, then a third, then a fourth.

Twenty-two hours later, Vasily Smirov found Lothar slumped in the same spot where he had sat down. Picking him up by his lapels, Smirov poured a glass of water down his throat and dragged him semi-conscious to the tournament hall. With no sleep, no food, and precious little fluid other than alcohol in his system, he felt at death's door, and in no state to play proper chess. Somehow though, he drew that game, as well as the following three. It almost felt as if his opponents were taking pity on him.

After the high hopes he had had going into the event, the overall result was a bitter failure, made worse by the fact that Sebastian Bahl had finished in second place, in the process gaining the Grandmaster title. The journey home was a long and painful one, only made bearable by the bottle of Vana Tallinn that he smuggled through customs.

Back in Berlin, there was going to be a price to pay, both for his drunkenness and for his poor result. Knocking on his coach's door sheepishly, he felt the full force of Hans' anger before he had even sat down.

'Twenty-four-hour drinking. What did you think you were doing? How did you ever imagine you would be able to play after a session like that?'

'To be fair, I drew the remaining games.'

'You drew!' Hans thumped his hand on the table. 'So that's the limit of your ambitions? A draw. You know you only drew because your opponents were paid off by Grosz.'

'Who says?'

'I say. Grosz called in a favour to stop you looking ridiculous. Do you think a man like that gives favours for free, that he won't want anything in return?'

'I don't understand.'

'Grosz is connected, Lothar. He's a member of the Stasi. He's helping you now, but he'll want payback later. Whether it's a share of your prize money, or bringing down a colleague, there's no lengths he won't go to in exploiting you. It wouldn't surprise me if he already has you under surveillance.'

'Hans, I accept I was wrong and I made a mistake. I need to cut down my drinking, I recognise that. As for Udo Grosz, he may be Stasi. Who knows? The fact is, though, I get on well with him, and I can handle him. He's never tried to drag me into any intrigues, and if he does, I'll refuse.'

Hans looked at him soberly and shook his head. 'We will see, Lothar. I just hope you're right. The consequences if you're not don't bear thinking about.'

CHAPTER TEN

Reminiscence of Marie A.

He had enjoyed the concert. He was, he felt, almost becoming an aficionado of classical music. Now, as they walked home, shortly after ten o'clock, the streets deserted, he took Anna by the arm, gently pulling her off the main road and down a side street which would lead them past the factories and the steelworks, through to the back of their flat.

'Why are we going this way?' she asked. 'Isn't it the long route home?'

He pointed back to the main road, towards the Death Strip. Soldiers stood, silhouetted, in the watchtowers above. 'I don't like walking past the Wall at night. I saw a woman there once, kneeling on the ground. Her son had been shot and she was crying. The image has stayed with me.'

She slipped her hand into his. 'I was two years old when they built the Wall,' she said. 'I don't remember anything else.'

'Me neither. My mother still talks about it, though, the time before the Wall was put up. She used to go dancing every Saturday in a club just five minutes from here.' He pointed across the Wall. 'Some of her best friends; she's never seen them since.'

'Do you think the Wall will make it to a quarter of a century?' she asked.

He did the maths in his head. That was just five years away. 'If the Wall comes down in our lifetime,' he said, 'that would be something.'

A man in a dark overcoat was coming the other way, and they both fell silent until he had passed. Anna took his hand again. 'I'm more optimistic than that, Lothar. The Stasi might think they are in control, but the people will rebel eventually. No system can survive forever, especially one as corrupt as this.'

He wondered if she was right. The optimist in him hoped so. The cynic thought that the worse the regime, the longer it was likely to survive. They were back now at the entrance to their flat. Pulling out his keys, he went to open the front door. Something was wrong. What was it? He paused and collected himself. The light was on inside. Surely they hadn't left it switched on all day? It wasn't like either of them to be that careless.

Anna looked up at him, puzzled. 'What's up?'

Putting his finger to his lips, he slid the key into the lock and gently opened the front door, not making a sound. Tiptoeing through the entrance, he inched his way down the hallway, into the bedroom and then the lounge. The flat seemed to be empty, but the lights were on in three separate rooms. In the bedroom, the drawers had been turned inside out, and clothes were scattered across the floor. In the kitchen, plates and glasses had been smashed and rubbish emptied on the floor.

Walking back through to the bedroom, he found Anna sitting on the bed sobbing. She looked up at him, her shoulders shaking. 'My jewellery,' she said, pointing at the empty space on the bedside table where the black jewellery case, which her grandmother had bequeathed, usually stood. He put his arm around her, hugging her tightly, not knowing what to say.

Hearing the noise, their elderly neighbours Benjamin and Elsa knocked on the door, and Elsa comforted Anna while Benjamin called the police. Their neighbours stayed with them until late that evening, Benjamin sitting with him through the police interview while Elsa helped tidy the flat. It was Elsa who found Anna's jewellery box kicked underneath their bed, the contents safely inside.

After the police had gone, while Elsa continued to sit with Anna in the kitchen, Benjamin shut the dining room door behind them and sat back down opposite him. His face was long and drawn. 'Have you ever been in trouble with the authorities, Lothar?'

Lothar gripped tightly onto his chair and tried to steady his voice. He couldn't believe how shaken he was at the intrusion into their flat. He remembered back to his student days, the international ban. 'I got myself into a spot of bother at university. That's all in the past now, though. Why do you ask?'

'Ever been involved in any anti-government demonstrations, any marches?'

A vision of Karl Rauser, the long-haired anarchist with the passion for revolution, came to mind. 'Not since I was a kid,' he said.

'Does anyone have any reason to think you might be anti-government? Any friends in the West or Western sympathies?'

He thought about his Uncle Leon, long deceased. There was Joker too. He had no idea where he was. Of course there was also Anna, but few people, if any, knew about her political allegiances. 'No, Benjamin. Nobody could accuse me of being anti-government.'

Benjamin put his arm on his shoulder. 'I've seen enough crime scenes in my time, Lothar, when I was working as a criminal lawyer. This is no ordinary break-in. Nothing of value taken. The one thing that is worth money – Anna's jewellery – kicked to one side. Plates and glasses smashed, to what purpose? Drawers rummaged through and rifled. It tells me this, Lothar. Somebody thinks you're hiding something in here. Maybe anti-government propaganda, political writings, anti-state material. It doesn't matter what. Someone doesn't trust you, Lothar.'

'Thanks, Benjamin,' he said, doing his best to appear calm. 'I really think this was just a chance attack. Let's see what the police come up with.' Outwardly he may have regained his composure, but inside Lothar was in turmoil. He was sure Benjamin was right. This wasn't random. No, it was a coded message, a warning to be careful, to toe the party line. It was a deeply sobering thought.

Lothar had been aware for some time that Udo Grosz harboured political ambitions. He also knew that, with his connections, Grosz stood a good chance of election to the East German Parliament. But even he was surprised at the scale of Grosz' victory.

'He won ninety-nine per cent of the vote, apparently,' he said to Anna, as they sat in the kitchen eating dinner. Several weeks had passed since the burglary, but when he looked at the new crockery, bought to replace the set that had been smashed to smithereens, a present from his mother, he still felt violated. He also found himself jumping at the slightest sound, waking in the middle of the night in a cold sweat.

'Who were the one per cent who didn't vote for Grosz?' Anna asked.

'They've not made themselves known as yet.'

Anna smiled. 'What's this meeting the old man has asked you to go to?'

'It's the annual Socialist Unity Party conference. Grosz wants me to speak on the role of chess in a rounded education.'

Anna raised her eyebrows. 'Mixing in some exalted circles now, aren't we?'

'I'm not planning to stay long. I'll give the speech and then go.'

His girlfriend smiled again, this time sadly. 'You always say that when you meet Grosz. *I won't be long.* Then eight hours later you re-surface half-cut.'

'He's an important man...'

Anna shook her head, picked up the plates and carried them across to the sink. Lothar made to say something more, but she had turned her back to him. The conversation, it seemed, was over.

As they stood at the bar, Grosz gave him one of his bear hugs, almost squeezing the life out of him. 'Well done, Comrade. You showed yourself to be a true follower of the Party this evening. A wonderful speech. Our nation needs more like you.'

'Thank you, Udo. It was the least I could do.'

Waving at the barman, Grosz ordered two steins of beer. 'You did your career a lot of good tonight, Lothar,' he said. 'These are influential people. Now that they know you're on the right side, they will help you.'

'I've always been on the right side, Udo.'

'Well, people did wonder, what with your association with that maverick, Hans Adler. We all know that his political views are rather extreme.'

Lothar felt an uncomfortable pressure in his chest. Getting dragged into a political discussion with Udo Grosz was the last thing he wanted. There was no way such a conversation could end well. 'Hans and I don't talk about politics. We only play chess.'

Grosz stroked his double chin. 'But in this great nation of ours politics is chess, and chess is politics. Don't you understand that?'

How to change the subject? 'Udo, I'm no politician. But I'm glad I was able to help this evening. The future of East German chess looks bright!'

Grosz slapped him on the back. 'Indeed it does, Comrade. A toast to your future, too. I think you'll find that rewards will come your way, sooner than you expect.'

While Lothar was sipping his drink, Grosz had already finished his own and was waving again to the barman. With his enormous bulk, the man could certainly put away the beer. Just lately, Lothar had begun to feel permanently on edge when he talked to Grosz, as though any slip could be fatal. It was a very fine balance, he reflected, drinking enough alcohol to relax, trying to keep up with Grosz, without losing control and putting himself – or worse, his friends – in trouble.

In early December, Hans turned fifty. He said nothing at their Wednesday night coaching session, but on Thursday an invitation arrived from Hans and Freya, requesting that Lothar and Anna join them at a party at their flat on Saturday night.

Lothar had little idea what to expect. How should he dress for the evening? Who would the other guests be? Did Hans have any friends who were not chess players? It was a leap into the unknown, but Anna selected a smart blue dress, and he settled on a jacket and shirt with no tie. They bought Hans a limited edition of Brecht's collected works. With a yellow, leather-bound cover, and a foreword by Daniel Lorenz, whom he had met the previous year at Hans' flat, it made a beautiful present.

Arriving a few minutes late, they found the flat already full of guests. Lothar made a beeline for the chess contingent gathered in the corner, notable for their ill-fitting jackets, worn trousers and lack of interaction with the rest of the room. Anna, meanwhile, recognised a group of writers, who were friends of Freya. While he talked chess, she was happy discussing literature and art, and the hours passed quickly.

Shortly before midnight, when much wine had flowed and only a handful of guests remained, Freya clapped her hands and Hans rose to his feet. A shy man even after several glasses of wine, Hans' speech was short and modest. The crowd cheered rapturously and drank more toasts.

As Hans sat down, Daniel Lorenz, who had himself arrived not half an hour before, stood up. 'Friends, colleagues, loved ones: I am glad to see you all here tonight, paying tribute to a wonderful man, Hans Adler. Many of you will know that Hans and I go back a long way. We started junior school together. When we were young, we drank beer together and we chased girls, at least that is until Hans met the wonderful Freya.' Everybody laughed. 'After we graduated, we went our separate ways, followed our own professions, but we have stayed friends.' More cheers. 'Over the years, we have seen times good and bad. We grew up when Hitler was in power. We saw evil at first hand. Then the war ended, and things improved, at least for a while. The German Democratic Republic was established in 1949, the year that we both turned eighteen. We had hopes for a better way of life.' Lorenz paused and surveyed the room around him. 'We were, of course, wrong.'

The group was quiet now and all eyes were on Daniel Lorenz.

'Many of you will know that I have not written a play in over three years. Why is this? Is it because I have writer's block? No. Is it because I have become lazy? No!' Lorenz paused again and raised his left arm in the air. 'It is because the state has blacklisted me.' There were boos. Lorenz waved his hand to indicate quiet. 'Enough. Tonight isn't about me. It's about my friend Hans Adler. No matter how difficult things have been over the last three years, when others have crossed the road to avoid me, Hans has stuck with me. He invited me here tonight, when it was dangerous to do so. That is the mark of true friendship. Ladies and gentlemen, a toast to Hans Adler, a great man.'

Hans, tears in his eyes, rose and hugged Daniel Lorenz. Finding his voice again, the coach raised his glass: 'A toast, to a free and united Germany, where artists no longer live in fear of speaking the truth.'

As he raised his own glass, Lothar felt a knot tighten in his stomach. With what they had just said, both men had committed a crime against the state. This was East Germany. He had seen what had happened in the past to Rolf Lehmann, to Joker and to his uncle. His own flat had been burgled too, and he continued to carry the scars from that, waking in the middle of the night, panicking that an intruder was inside. He cared for Hans and he didn't want to see him get into trouble.

Later that evening, back in their flat, he sat with Anna at their kitchen table. As Anna sorted through university papers, he played with the vase of flowers in the centre of the table. 'Anna, why isn't Daniel Lorenz allowed to write any more?' he asked.

Anna looked up at him and raised her eyebrows. 'You haven't heard? He wrote a play, three years ago, *The Republic*.'

He shook his head. 'That's not one I know.'

Anna pushed her papers to one side and put down her pen. 'No, because it didn't make it to opening night. The censors pulled it as soon as they saw it.'

'Why?'

'It was supposedly about corruption in Roman times.'

'What does that have to do with our government?'

'It was a parable about East Germany, an attack on what Daniel Lorenz sees as the denial of free speech. The play was banned and Lorenz hasn't been able to work since.'

He picked at the flowers again. 'Do you think it was wise for Lorenz to make that speech tonight?'

'What do you mean?'

'I thought he was putting himself at risk.'

'The man has been banned from writing. He's no longer able to earn a living. What more is there to risk?'

'What about Hans? He needs to be careful. Otherwise he'll find himself blacklisted too.'

Anna frowned. 'Lothar, are you going to meekly accept everything the authorities tell you to do?'

'I don't like taking orders, Anna. But I will admit I'm scared. Scared of what the state can do to us. I'm a government employee now. I earn a stipend to play chess. The Stasi could take that away from me – from us – at a moment's notice.'

'So what's your point, Lothar?' Anna had raised her voice and was looking at him incredulously.

'I love Hans like a father. By mixing with Lorenz, he's putting his freedom at risk though. Ours too, come to that.'

Picking up a copy of Brecht's collected works, the same book they had just given Hans, Anna threw the heavy volume straight at him. For a small girl, she had more strength than he expected. 'Damn you, Lothar. Read some Brecht, read it properly that is, then we can talk about freedom.' As she stormed out of the apartment, slamming the door behind her, she cursed at him. 'You might have the courage of a lion on the chessboard. But when it comes to real life, you're a mouse.'

Lothar opened the book at the page where it had landed: *Reminiscence of Marie A.* It was one of the few pieces of literature that he recalled from school. The poet looked up as a lone white cloud passed by. When he looked again, the cloud had gone. Just like his love.

Taking a bottle of vodka from the sideboard, he poured himself a large glass, which he downed almost in one. Picking up the bottle and the glass he wandered through to the living room, plumped up a couple of cushions on the sofa and sat for the rest of the evening staring at the television. His feelings were complex and conflicted. He had tried to explain how he felt to Anna, and he realised he had failed. He wanted to be a great chess player, and to maintain his integrity. How to do both, when faced with a surveillance state? That was the question and, at this moment, he had no idea what the answer was.

Several hours later, he awoke with an uncomfortable crick in his neck. Looking up, he realised that he had fallen asleep on the sofa. The bottle of vodka, now empty, lay discarded on the floor. A low buzz emanated from the television, programmes having long since finished for the night. Peeping through the bedroom door, he saw that Anna had returned and was asleep in bed. Taking a blanket from the cupboard in the hallway, he went back to his makeshift bed on the sofa. He could only hope that things would get easier in the morning.

Chapter Eleven

Budapest

The first time he saw a man shot, Lothar was nine years old. The day had started innocently enough. Blue sky, sunshine, a perfect spring afternoon. Uncle Leon had taken him to see Union Berlin's final home game of the season. Walking back, they stopped at a newsagent where Leon bought an evening paper and a pack of cigarettes. While Leon and the shopkeeper bemoaned Union's fortunes, the team having lost yet again, Lothar leafed through the comic strips, imagining what it would be like to be an action hero.

As they opened the door to leave the shop, a young lad, no more than eighteen, with a crew cut and a red T-shirt ran past, chased by three police officers. The youth was fast, too fast for the officers. As they laboured under the weight of their uniforms, he was almost out of sight at the top of the road. Suddenly, Lothar heard a loud explosion, like cannon fire, and the lad stumbled and fell, collapsing in a heap on the road. Turning, he saw one of the officers put his gun back in his holster.

Leon pulled him in the opposite direction. 'What will happen to the boy?' Lothar asked. 'Will he be OK?'

'Yes, he'll be fine,' said Leon. 'They shot him in the leg. You don't die of that.'

'Why did they shoot him?'

Leon shrugged. 'Goodness knows. He upset the police somehow, that's all we can say.'

Lothar fell into silence, thinking about the youth, wondering if he would walk again. When they got home, his parents were still out. His aunt made him a cup of warm milk while he sat with Leon in the dining room.

'We saw a criminal. The police shot him,' he told his aunt when she came back into the room.

Leon put his arm around his shoulder. 'We don't know he was a criminal, Lothar,' he said. 'Sometimes the police make mistakes, or even act out of malice.'

His aunt looked at Leon pointedly, and Leon rested his hand on hers. 'He needs to know these things, Deborah,' he said to her, before turning back to him. 'When I was young, only a few years older than you, the police shot and killed five hundred students in Berlin, because they thought they were revolutionaries.' Leon paused. 'Friends of mine died.'

Lothar sipped at his milk, puzzled. Was life really so unfair? Leon still had his hand on his shoulder. 'Those were difficult years,' he continued. 'In Hungary, over three thousand protestors died in 1956. It's a brutal world, Lothar. Never trust anyone in authority, and keep your head down.'

Time passed, and Lothar's memories of that day began to fade. When, in late 1981, Udo Grosz secured him an invitation to a tournament in Budapest, celebrating the twenty-fifth anniversary of the downfall of the Hungarian Revolution, they came flooding back.

Conflicted, he spoke to Hans about whether he should accept. Hans was bemused that he was even considering the question. 'You know how many people died in 1956 in the name of democracy?' he asked.

Hans was right, of course. The death of thousands of people was hardly a matter to celebrate. But he was a professional; he made his living through the game. A strong tournament such as this one represented a chance to gain the Grandmaster title, something which was essential if he wanted to pursue his further ambitions: a place in the Olympiad, a competitor for the World Championship.

Lothar agonised long and hard, tossed numerous coins, drew straws, decided to say no, then to accept, then again to say no. All the while, Udo Grosz kept phoning him, and Anna too began to ask him what was on his mind. Knowing that his girlfriend's answer would be as unequivocal as Hans', if not more so, he lied and told her that Grosz wanted him to help with a coaching programme for promising junior players.

Eventually, the devil sitting on his shoulder overcame his better instinct, and in a moment of weakness he rang Udo Grosz. Overhearing from the kitchen, Anna came through to the hall and put her arms around him. 'So you've accepted the coaching assignment? I think that's wonderful, Lothar.'

'I forgot to mention,' he said. 'It's in Hungary.'

Anna looked puzzled. 'Why would you go to Hungary to teach East German juniors?'

'We're going to enter them in a tournament. I dare say I'll take part myself, as well. Kill two birds with one stone.'

'OK,' said Anna. 'Make sure you don't lead those youngsters astray, start them smoking or drinking. I know what you chess players are like.'

Lothar still wasn't sure if he'd made the right decision, but he needed to begin planning for the trip. The tournament lasted ten days, and he wanted company, as well as a second to help with his preparation. Given his views on the uprising, he could hardly ask Hans to accompany him. He turned instead to Udo Grosz.

'Tell me again, why won't Adler travel to Hungary?' Grosz asked.

'It's not Hungary that he has the problem with. The issue is the celebration of the end of the students' revolution.'

'Surely Adler doesn't think that those petty criminals, bourgeois enemies of the state, so-called student revolutionaries, should have been allowed to win the day? He must realise the threat that the students represented to society? Not just Hungarian society, the whole of Eastern Europe?' Grosz practically spat with disgust as he said this.

Fearing that he had already said far too much, Lothar did his best to repair the situation. 'Oh, it's nothing like that, Udo. Hans is a loyal Party man. It's simply that he has an aversion to violence. He doesn't want to celebrate an occasion where people died. I understand his view, but it's not one that I share.'

Grosz patted him on the shoulder. 'That's a relief, Comrade. For a moment, I thought you might have gone soft. This is your chance for the Grandmaster title, after all.'

'I know that, Udo. Believe me, I want that title more than anything.'

Grosz stroked his chin. 'More than anything? You'd do whatever it takes to get the title?'

'Yes, Udo. Absolutely.'

Grosz nodded. 'Comrade, don't worry, we'll find you a coach. I know just the man. A good fellow, the right sort, a man who will definitely get results.'

A week later, Lothar took the tram to Alexanderplatz and, getting off at the main square, headed for a grey-fronted café opposite the Tower. Taking a seat at a table by the window, he ordered a drink from a dour-looking waitress in a blue uniform and a cap. The waitress returned shortly afterwards, scowling at him as she threw down his coffee clumsily on the table in front of him, spilling a third of it in the process. He looked around the café. To his left, an elderly man with a moustache sat on his own, staring vacantly into the distance. Behind him, a young couple sat opposite each other, saying nothing. The other tables were empty, even at midday. What a grim place this was.

Dabbing the spilt coffee with his handkerchief, Lothar looked up at the wonder that was the Berliner Fernsehturm. Nearly four hundred metres high, the tower was the tallest structure in the whole of Germany, East or West. He wondered if anybody had ever tried to climb it. You wouldn't want to slip, that was for sure. If they weren't communists, he figured that the government would already have found a way to make money from the tower. A lift, a viewing gallery, postcards for sale. Perhaps he should put his ideas forward as a commercial proposition. Even communist governments needed money, after all.

Presently, an overweight, broad-shouldered man swung open the door of the café and strode towards him, beaming, grabbing Lothar's hand and pumping it up and down vigorously. In his youth, Manfrit Nester had been a celebrated athlete, competing for East Germany in middle-distance running at the Olympics. The years had not perhaps been particularly kind. His hair was greying, and his face was red from the exertion of walking across the square. Nevertheless, as he sat down opposite Lothar, ordering himself a mug of tea and launching into an introduction, it was clear that this was a man who had led an interesting and varied life.

'My highlight, Lothar? That's easy. Rome 1960. Fifteen hundred metres. Fastest in the heats, I should have taken the gold. But the Americans tricked me.'

'How did they do that, Manfrit?'

Nester looked around the café, leaned towards him and lowered his voice. The young couple had paid their bill and left, and the waitress had disappeared into the kitchen. Only the solitary elderly man remained. 'Do you remember Debbie Cornish?' Nester asked.

Lothar shook his head.

'She was the hottest actress of her day. Starred in all the A-list movies, back when we used to be able to see those things. Goodness, she was something.' Nester pulled his handkerchief out of his pocket and wiped his brow. 'Where was I? Oh, yes. Debbie Cornish. The Americans sent her round to my hotel room the night before the final. Let's just say, I was rather preoccupied. Didn't get the sleep I should have, if you get my drift.'

Nester poked him in the ribs and winked. Lothar must have looked alarmed, because the older man continued, 'Don't worry, Lothar. When it comes to chess, I'm very focused. We'll have no distractions during the tournament. I won't hear of it.'

As well as being an Olympic athlete, Nester was also a strong chess player in his own right, having finished near the top of the East German national championships on numerous occasions. Like almost everybody who held a position of influence in East Germany, however, there were innumerable rumours about Nester. It was said that as an athlete he had failed a drugs test, and the government had to pay hush money to cover up the scandal. There were also stories that he had both bought and sold games, winning or losing on demand to suit the circumstance. Lothar did not know how many of these tales were true, and he didn't ask. Nester had agreed to spend nearly two weeks in Hungary with him, and that was enough.

Arriving for round one of the tournament, taking his seat on the stage, smiling for the assorted cameramen, Lothar shook hands with the veteran Italian Grandmaster, Rudolfo Ponzi. A thin, wrinkled man with a crooked smile, Ponzi gave a small bow as he sat down at the board, before waving to the press and spectators. A former Italian champion, word had it that he was a communist sympathiser and had been friends with Udo Grosz since their student days together, years before in Austria.

Lothar and Nester had spent a short amount of time the evening before preparing for the game. Unfortunately, their study was disturbed by the arrival of the Dutch contingent. Their party included the legendary Grandmaster Loek De Jong, one of the greatest players in the world, as well as a renowned party animal. De Jong had become famous in the early seventies for travelling Europe armed with just a toothbrush and a duffel coat, winning tournaments wherever he played, and more often than not sleeping on a spare floor, using his coat as a blanket. Nester and De Jong were old friends, and his coach lost no time in heading down to the hotel bar with the Dutchman.

Lothar resisted the temptation to join them, staying in his room and working. For such an important game he didn't feel entirely ready, and his mood was hardly helped by the chill in the playing hall. Why had he not brought a sweater with him? For the first few moves at least, he found it difficult to find any rhythm, and his thinking was blurred. To his surprise, Ponzi appeared in even worse shape than him. His play was slow and ponderous, he gasped with surprise even at Lothar's most mundane moves, and on move twenty-five, he blundered a whole Rook trying to protect against a harmless Knight sortie.

Lothar was feeling so hesitant and unsure that he spent a good fifteen minutes thinking before he captured the Italian's Rook. As soon as he did, Ponzi stretched out his hand warmly. 'I resign. Many congratulations, Lothar, on a wonderful performance. You played with great brilliance. I feel sure that this tournament will be the one where you become a Grandmaster.'

It was an odd game, and a bizarre reaction from Ponzi. In round two, he did at least arrive at the board feeling properly prepared, although that was wholly down to his own efforts, with no credit due to Nester, who was nowhere to be found all morning. His opponent was a local Grandmaster by the name of Bako. With the black pieces, Lothar played the Sicilian Defence, perhaps the most well-known of all openings. Bako seemed strangely unfamiliar with his strategy, and thought for a long time over even the most obvious moves. On the thirtieth move, Bako exceeded the time limit for the game, and he had secured another victory. Bako didn't seem remotely upset by his misfortune and afterwards he saw him talking happily outside the playing hall to Nester. Lothar asked Nester what the conversation was about, and the older man told him the two of them had been discussing football.

The tournament continued in this vein. Nester contributed little or nothing to his preparation, and Lothar's play was unspectacular at best. Whatever error he made, though, the opponent would make a worse one. He could not remember a tournament where so many strong opponents had played so many bad moves against him. After eight rounds, he had six wins and a draw, and was on the verge of the Grandmaster title. Only the peerless De Jong had beaten him, a game that had caused the Dutchman little trouble, and was evidence if he needed it that he was not in good form.

In the ninth and final round, he was due to face the Polish player Szabo, an experienced and very solid Master. He needed just to avoid defeat, and he would achieve his life's ambition, the Grandmaster title. After all those years of hard work, this was everything that he had striven for. Despite this, Lothar felt oddly flat. He had prepared and played indifferently throughout the tournament. There were no games that he was proud of, and a number of opponents had handed him victories on a plate.

In the morning, by now used to the fact that there would be no sign of Nester before the game, he went for a walk, came back and changed into his suit, and arrived at the board twenty minutes early. As the clock struck half past two, thirty minutes into the game, he made his twelfth move, a careful Knight retreat, before uttering the words, 'Would you like a draw?'

Lothar reflected as he made his offer that chess is the only competitive sport where the two opponents can of their own accord simply abandon a game and call it a draw. It certainly could not happen in tennis or football. In response, Szabo looked at him, scrunched up his nose, paused for a moment, and then reached out to shake his hand, confirming his agreement. Lothar went to say something further but Szabo dismissed him.

'I hope it pleases you to make your title this way.'

'I'm sorry?'

'Titles for sale, for hard cash, it sickens me,' the Pole continued, before getting up from the board, tearing his score sheet into pieces, and walking away with a look of contempt.

He went to follow Szabo, to ask him what he meant, but his opponent was already out of the playing room and halfway down the corridor. Before he could pick up his pace, a delighted Nester had intercepted him and was grabbing him by the lapels. 'Lothar, well done. You've made it. Grandmaster. Look at you, what a champion!'

Lothar pulled Nester into the empty analysis room to the side of the main hall. 'Manfrit, what the hell's been going on?'

'What do you mean, Lothar?'

'Szabo just accused me of buying the title. What have you been doing?'

Nester jumped when he said this. 'Me? Nothing, Lothar. Why would I do a thing like that?'

'I don't believe you. I think you've been paying people off, giving them money to throw games.'

'I would never do that, Lothar. Perhaps it's Udo Grosz?' Nester was struggling to look him in the eye, and his face had turned red.

'What, all the way from Berlin?'

'He has contacts.'

'Yes, precisely. You!'

Lothar walked off, disgusted. All the suspicions he'd had during the tournament, half founded as they were, had proved to be true. There was no way that so many opponents could play that badly against him. He had always dreamed of the Grandmaster title, but he wanted it on his own merits, because he deserved it, not because he was the friend of someone powerful in East Berlin who had money and influence.

That evening he had to suffer at the closing ceremony, pretending to be happy, revelling in his achievement, while everybody in the room, including the organisers, would know by now that his success had been a farce. For a fleeting moment, he even contemplated denouncing Nester in front of the room, but he had no actual proof it was him and, in his experience, trying to act the hero in Eastern Europe never ended well. No, the deed was done. He thought back to his conversation with Udo Grosz, where he had said that he would do whatever it took to become a Grandmaster. Cheating was not what he had meant.

Two weeks after he returned home, he had still not heard from Hans. On Saturday morning, plucking up his courage, and fighting through a hangover, he rose early. Taking the tram to

Leninplatz, he walked up the familiar hill, through pouring rain, up the nine flights of stairs, until he reached Hans' flat. His coach greeted him coolly, and Lothar had to ask to be let in, taking off his drenched coat and shoes as he entered.

Lothar took a seat at the living room table. It was scattered with Western newspapers and old chess magazines. A half-eaten plate of toast stood balanced precariously on one corner of the table, a cup of coffee on the other. He assumed, given the mess, that Freya must have taken the children away for the holidays. Hans sat down opposite him. He had not yet offered him a drink. In fact, he had hardly said hello.

Lighting a cigarette, Lothar held one out for Hans, which his coach for once declined.

'I guess you heard what happened then?' he said.

Without speaking, Hans stood up, walked across to his sideboard, and opened the top drawer. He pulled out a battered envelope that he placed on the table in front of him. 'Read it,' he said. 'He thought I should know what sort of player I have trained.'

Lothar opened the letter. It was from the Pole, Szabo. It was all there. How Nester had paid him and others to play badly against Lothar. How Udo Grosz and the East German Federation had funded the whole affair. Szabo had refused to comply at first, before being threatened with violence. It seemed that, of the nine games in the tournament, the only genuine one had been the one he lost, against De Jong.

'My aim was to help you become a great player, Lothar. To help you win by fair means, to get the Grandmaster title because you deserved it.' Hans had turned red and clenched his fists.

'Hans, you have to believe me. I knew nothing of this. Not until the last round, when it was too late. I'm an innocent victim.'

His coach swore, and with a sharp tilt of his hand knocked over the chair next to him. 'There are millions of innocent victims in this country, Lothar. Trust me, you're not one of them. I advised you not to go to Budapest in the first place. I also told you to be careful of Grosz. You ignored me both times.'

'Hans...' He tried to speak, but his coach interrupted him before he could get the words out.

'Don't try and explain yourself, Lothar. Allowing yourself to be duped by Grosz and Nester is bad enough. Doing so with your eyes wide open is far worse.'

Lothar put his head in his hands. He didn't know what to say, or how to defend himself. In the uncomfortable silence that followed, he could feel Hans' eyes staring into him, to the depths of his soul. Eventually, Hans broke the silence. 'Our time is up, Lothar. Now get out of my flat. From this day on, I'm no longer your coach.'

Lothar rose from the table slowly, chilled to the bone by Hans' words. His now former coach turned his back, refusing even to acknowledge his presence. Gathering his things, he took his exit, picking up Szabo's letter from the table before he left, steeling himself for the long and painful journey home.

PART TWO – THE MIDDLEGAME

CHAPTER TWELVE

A New Beginning

The next year, the next day, the next hour are lying ready for you, as perfect, as unspoiled, as if you had never wasted or misapplied a single moment in all your life.
Arnold Bennett

In becoming a Grandmaster, Lothar had achieved a lifetime ambition, and yet all was far from well. The letter from the Pole, Szabo, which sat uncomfortably locked in his top drawer, contained the dirty secret that he kept hidden from Anna. He was a Grandmaster fraud and he had lost his coach, his friend, one of the few stable influences in his life, in the process.

Since his return, he had done his best to avoid Udo Grosz. He hadn't visited the headquarters of the Federation, nor had he played in any events at the Central Chess Club, where Grosz could often be found. The President of the Federation had left several phone messages with Anna which he had not returned, and two postcards lay on his kitchen worktop urging him to call Grosz at his earliest convenience. Never a fan of Grosz, Anna wasn't worried in the least by Lothar's failure to respond. Indeed, she encouraged it, telling him repeatedly that he had to find his own way in life.

Try as he might, however, Grosz was not the type of man that one could escape from forever. One Wednesday afternoon, as Lothar sat in the dining room studying an intricate variation of the Sicilian Defence, he was disturbed by an insistent ringing of the front door bell.

Opening the door, he found Grosz, wrapped in a thick winter coat, a fur hat and leather gloves. 'Comrade,' Grosz boomed, throwing his arms around him. 'How glad I am that you are in. It is positively arctic outside. Never have I felt in such need of a vodka!'

Before he could speak, Grosz had shut the front door behind him, guiding him into his kitchen with one hand, throwing his coat off with the other. Offering him one of his own chairs, Grosz grabbed two glasses from the cupboard, along with a bottle of vodka from the sideboard.

'My dear Lothar, my long-standing friend, I have the perfect opportunity for you.'

Lothar sat down at the table. What a force of nature Grosz was. Like a hurricane, and capable of doing as much damage. 'Opportunity?'

Grosz sat down opposite him. 'A world-class tournament. It starts in ten days' time. It's tailor-made for you.'

'What is the tournament, Udo?'

'The European Championships in Warsaw, Lothar. I need one word from you. Just one word. Tell me, Lothar, that you will play.'

Grosz had hardly given him time to draw breath.

'Udo,' he said hesitating, 'I don't know.'

'You don't know!' boomed Grosz. 'Comrade, what don't you know? Why won't you play?' Grosz pushed at his ribs with a large, fat finger. 'I demand, my dear fellow, that you play. Your nation expects it.'

Lothar sat with his arms crossed, and when Grosz poked at him, he leaned away. He was conscious of how defensive he must look.

'Udo, I have a problem.'

'Problem? What problem? Let me know, and I will help.'

'It's Nester. I know he cheated. He bought me the title. I can't cope with it, Udo. The corruption. It's not how I want things to be.'

Grosz looked at him with wide eyes and paused for a moment, seemingly lost for words. 'Nester cheated? No! Say it isn't so, Lothar.'

'I'm afraid so, Udo. He paid everybody off. I do mean everybody, too. That includes the organisers. It's totally unacceptable.' Lothar put his glass down on the table. 'Udo, I'm sorry. I have to ask you. Did you know what Nester was up to?'

Grosz breathed out deeply and shook his head. 'Comrade,' he said softly, 'I give you my word, on my mother's life, I knew nothing of this outrage. I am truly sorry for all you have been through.'

Lothar didn't trust Grosz, but it was certainly a convincing act. He uncrossed his arms. 'No more help from the likes of Nester. From now on, Udo, I succeed or fail at the board on my own.'

Grosz downed his vodka and poured himself another glass. 'Lothar, I understand, and I agree. Damn that rascal Nester. I should never have trusted him. What an unscrupulous individual. I am so sorry that this has happened to you. Believe me, all will be different from here. Let's raise a glass. Goodbye to the scoundrel Nester, and hello to your future success, legitimately earned. May Lenin be with you.'

Over the next week, Grosz rang Lothar daily, sometimes hourly, in his bid to persuade him to play in Warsaw. With his unique blend of begging and cajoling, mixed in with the occasional threat – if he said no to the tournament, there would be no more invitations for a long time, or perhaps ever – eventually the President of the Federation began to wear him down. Finding it difficult to explain the situation to Anna – she disliked Grosz enough already; throw in a story about Budapest and she would never forgive Lothar if he saw the man again – he asked his mother for her view.

Life on her own was not proving easy for Frau Hartmann. Following her husband's death, the state had granted her a small widow's pension. It was barely enough to pay the gas bill and put food on the table, and when he visited, Lothar often found his mother sitting in the cold and dark, with the heating switched off and just a candle for light. He told her off for her frugality, but she wouldn't listen or accept his offers of money. He had tried asking Udo Grosz if he could arrange an increase in her widow's pension, but Grosz had shaken his head. 'I'm sorry, Lothar, but my influence doesn't extend to finances. Ask me something else, and I'll see if I can help. The truth is, though, it's a difficult time at the moment. We are all having to tighten our belts.' At a loss as to what else to do, he began to find more surreptitious ways to help his mother, visiting her increasingly frequently and leaving groceries or small jars of Spreewald gherkins in the kitchen, or packs of sliced ham in the fridge.

For once, when Lothar knocked on his mother's door that Thursday evening, he found her in good spirits. She had spent the afternoon with neighbours, two flats down, and they had reminisced about life in Berlin before the Wall. 'They weren't easy days, Lothar,' she said. 'We had no more money then than we have now. Post-war, food was still short, and there was precious little in the shops. But at least we could sing and dance. Oh, how I used to love those evenings at the music hall, your father with a glass of beer in his hand. It brings a smile to my face now, just thinking about it.'

Lothar sipped his black coffee. He wished he had brought some powdered milk with him. 'What do you think about Poland, mother? I've got an opportunity to play chess in Warsaw.'

'Poland? It will be cold there. Take an extra jumper. A scarf too.'

'The thing is, it's become political.'

'Political?' His mother rested her cup on the coffee table next to her and clenched her hands together. 'That doesn't sound good.'

'The President of the Chess Federation wants me to play. But I've got evidence he's corrupt. He's been paying people to throw games.'

'Is he asking you to cheat?'

'No, but he's threatened that if I don't play in Warsaw, I won't get selected for any more events.'

His mother leant across and put her arm around him. 'Oh, Lothar, didn't I tell you this would happen? Years ago, I said that the Stasi would find a way to interfere in your chess, to mess up your plans.'

'I know, Mum, you did say that, and I ignored you. I was wrong. But we are where we are. The question is what to do next.'

Frau Hartmann sighed. 'This is East Germany, Lothar. I don't think you have a choice. Go to Poland, play, do your best, and if you can, keep your integrity. It's going to be difficult, but I don't see any other option.'

Lothar hugged his mother. Even in her impoverished state, she was a fount of wisdom and strength. He wished he could do more to support her.

The following week, Lothar took the tram to East Berlin station, where he met his fellow Berliner, Johan Martins. Unkempt, unshaven and invariably dressed in the same faded grey shirt and worn trousers, Martins had a dishevelled look which stood out even amongst chess players, a group hardly noted for their sartorial elegance. After the traditional evening's warm-up in a local bar, they met the following lunchtime. Always a cheery soul, Martins appeared especially full of life that day.

'Hey, Lothar, I've just remembered I still owe you for those beers last night. Can I buy you something from the kiosk?'

Lothar looked over at the small wooden hut to the left of the platform. An elderly woman dressed in a brown shawl stood hunched behind the counter. In front of her was a row of steaming cabbages and a pot of tea. 'Thanks, Johan. Just a black tea please.'

'No food? That cabbage looks good.' Martins stubbed out his roll-up and immediately lit another, offering him one too.

'Just the tea would be great, thanks, Johan,' he said, turning down the cigarette and the cabbage.

As they were talking, a peasant arrived at the station and laid down a blanket in front of him, on top of which he placed a row of shiny bottles of beer. 'Make it a lager, if you like,' said Martins. 'It's gone midday, after all.'

'Why not? Thanks, Johan.'

'Leave it with me, Lothar.' Martins paused, as if a thought had just struck him. 'Just one thing, Lothar.' Martins looked at him plaintively. He had taken off his old winter jacket and Lothar noticed that there was a hole the size of a tennis ball in his woollen cardigan.

'What's that, Johan?'

'I'm still a bit short of readies. You couldn't lend me ten Marks, could you?'

Such incidents were typical. Martins was long on promise and short on delivery. As his friend, Lothar tolerated his idiosyncrasies, a rare example of a nonconformist who had somehow managed to survive in regimented East German society. In all the time he had known him, Martins never had any money, never appeared to eat, and lived it seemed off a diet of cigarettes and alcohol. Lothar couldn't have lived his life the way Martins did, but secretly he admired his refusal to fit into the established order.

Martins' play was a revelation at Warsaw, Lothar's compatriot winning many games in fine style. With a round to go, he was near the top of the field. A victory would give him not just the tournament but also the Grandmaster title. Unfortunately, the night before the final round, someone spiked Martins' drinks. Suffering from a terrible hangover, he arrived for the critical round over an hour late, and was defaulted without making a move. For a player of great promise, such strange events had been common in Martins' career.

On the last night, while Martins slept off his hangover and the disappointment of his defeat, Lothar sat in the bar of the hotel with Tony Marlowe, the winner of the tournament. Since Lothar had first met him, the Englishman had taken his career from strength to strength, and he was now ranked one of the top five players in the world. Only two years older than him, Marlowe seemed to have done and achieved so much more.

'You want to know how I've improved, Lothar?'

He nodded, eager for any alchemy, anything that would bring him closer to the top of the game.

'Three things.' Marlowe paused and then held up the cigarette in his left hand. 'See this? The cigarette? I'm allowing myself a fag now, at the end of the tournament. But tomorrow, I'll cut out the tobacco again, till the end of the next event.'

Lothar glanced at his own nicotine-stained fingers. He could not imagine going more than a couple of hours without a cigarette.

Marlowe raised his right hand. 'See this glass of lager? There's nothing like a good beer. As an Englishman, sitting with a German, in a bar, what else would we drink? I admit I love a drink. But I've cut down, and if you notice, you didn't see me in the bar at all during the tournament.'

This seemed impressive dedication. Lothar thought back to the evening he had spent with Mikhail Voronin. The Latvian genius wouldn't approve of such abstinence, and he was a former World Champion. 'What's the third secret?' he asked.

'State funding,' said Marlowe, enjoying the bemused look on Lothar's face. 'I know what you're thinking, Lothar. In the communist bloc, you get all this special training and support, lots of coaching when you're young, the state pays you a salary, all you have to do is turn up and play chess. Life is easy, right? Well the truth is, Lothar, all that mollycoddling makes you lazy. Us Brits, we get no help from the state, no funding whatsoever. When I was growing up, I never had a coach, always had to survive on my own. It's dog eat dog, survival of the fittest.' As the Englishman put out his cigarette, a barman came past and Marlowe ordered another round of beers, taking out a wad of crisp new notes from his wallet to pay for them. 'But of course, the great thing is, when I win, the money is all mine.' At this point, a gleam came into his eyes. 'You should try it, Lothar. Come and join me in the West.'

'Defect, you mean?'

'Yes, come and live in England. I'll get you a place in the national team. We can train together. Now that Bobby Fischer's retired, you and me, we could be the two strongest players in the free world.' Marlowe put his arm around him conspiratorially. 'It would be us against the commies. Think about that.'

'What if I believe in communism?'

'You're joking, surely, Lothar? Look at this place, Warsaw. A grey monstrosity, a concrete jungle. The women all look haggard and miserable, the men are browbeaten. Nobody is having any fun. If you make a joke they're liable to call the police. As for the food... God, the food. Stodgy mash, awful processed meat – heaven knows where it's from, not beef, lamb or any respectable animal, that's for sure – and that terrible ground powder you call coffee. Lothar, you've been to the West. We met in Amsterdam. You know how much better life can be.'

Marlowe was an affable, good-natured man, and yet also a determined and successful player. A sharp contrast to Sebastian Bahl, he was proof that decent people could win at chess. His suggestion to move to the West needed serious consideration. There was certainly merit in what Marlowe had said about living standards in the East. Lothar thought back to the stew he'd eaten earlier that evening. He did not like to think what animal it was either. Nor could he claim that conditions were any better in Berlin. Poverty and hardship abounded. On the debit side, however, were a number of issues. Firstly, as a chess player, people treated him with respect in East Germany. In Udo Grosz, he had an important supporter, even if he was uneasy about Grosz' links with the Stasi. In relative terms, he was well placed in East German society. He was not sure that would be the case in England. Secondly, what about the poverty he had seen in Amsterdam? Beggars, homeless people, the unemployed. How did these fit into Marlowe's Western utopia? Third and finally, one factor loomed above everything else. He could try to defect, but what if he got caught? He would be disgraced. As a minimum he would be banned from playing chess. Possibly jail would await too. If he somehow made it to safety, then what about the friends and family he left behind? What about Anna? The state would make them pay for his crimes, of that he was clear. No, the dangers were insurmountable. He was an East German born and bred and that was how he would stay.

That summer, Lothar and Anna took a break on the Baltic coast. It was almost unprecedented to take a holiday outside East Germany, and such a trip wouldn't have been possible without Udo Grosz' help. Their chalet overlooked the beach, and they spent the mornings swimming or playing with a football on the sand. In the afternoons, Anna lazed on their veranda reading, protecting her pale skin under a sun umbrella. They took long walks along the coast, and in the second week hired a couple of pushbikes to explore the local area. In the evenings, they talked about films and books and drank beer at a bar that overlooked the sea. How happy he was, just sitting with his girlfriend, idling away his time, relaxing. As they talked, he found himself gazing at her soft lips, at her long dark hair, the way she played with the fringe with her fingers. He marvelled at the fact that he found her as attractive now, if not more so, than the evening they first met.

On the final night, Lothar booked a table at a fish restaurant. After a candlelit dinner, and two glasses of wine, he pulled a box from his pocket that he handed to his girlfriend.

Anna opened the box. Inside was a diamond-encrusted ring. 'What's this for, Lothar?'

'It's for you, Anna. I know we've been through difficult times lately, but I wanted to tell you that I love you. I want to spend the rest of my life with you. Anna, will you marry me?'

Anna burst into tears. 'Lothar, that's so sweet. I've been wondering whether you would do this.'

'So the answer is?'

Anna paused. 'The answer is... not yet.'

'Not yet? What does that mean?'

'It means I love you. But there are some things I need you to do before we can marry.'

'Which are?' He tried to disguise it, but his voice was cracked and dry.

'Lothar, I don't care whether you make a success of your chess career.' Anna toyed with the vase of flowers in the middle of the table. Behind her, a waiter hovered, wondering whether to approach them. Catching Lothar's eye, the waiter backed away. 'I don't mind whether you bring home a secure income,' she said. 'What does matter to me is that you are your own man. I want you to succeed, or fail, on your own, not because the state is helping you. We live in a bad place. I can't marry someone who is complicit in what is happening.'

Lothar reached out to take Anna's hand. Outwardly he did his best to appear calm, but inside his stomach was churning and his heart was in turmoil. 'Trust me, Anna, that is exactly what I intend to do. I will be a success, and I'll make it on my own too. You just need to give me time. I'll get there, I promise.'

On their return from the Baltic coast, Lothar began his preparations for the national championships in Dresden. It was now nearly six months since he had seen Hans. For the first time, he felt that he could manage successfully without a coach. Tony Marlowe had shown him some interesting opening ideas when they were in Warsaw, and he had devised a few tricks of his own which he was ready to unleash.

His final warm-up before the Championships was a trade union team event in Berlin. He played on the top board of four for the Berlin Steel Workers team. He had no connection with the steel industry but Udo Grosz had asked him to join the team as a favour some months previously, and he felt bound to honour his commitment.

In the fifth round, he was paired against one of the more promising German students, Ernst Reisen, a fair-haired, serious fellow with glasses. Lothar expected to win without trouble. Reisen, however, defended his position tenaciously, finding a series of best moves. After a tense struggle, Lothar resigned on the forty-fifth move.

'You played well,' he said after the game. 'I didn't realise you had that in you.'

'Working with Hans has made a big difference.'

'Hans?'

Reisen looked down at the floor. 'Sorry, I thought you knew. Hans Adler is my coach now. I didn't mean to reveal it that way. I know you two go back a long way.'

Lothar knew he shouldn't have been surprised that Hans had a new pupil, but he still felt like a jilted lover. He had lost the game too. It was a bitter pill to take. But he had no one to blame other than himself. After gathering his thoughts alone on a park bench, staring at the swans, regretting so much that had happened over recent months, he made a decision. It was time to make up. Walking up the hill, he knocked on Hans' front door, for what must have been – oh – the five hundredth time in his life, but the first since they had split. Lothar carried the most expensive bottle of white wine he had been able to find as a conciliatory gesture. His former coach opened the door with his habitual cigarette in hand. His shirt and trousers were even more creased than usual and his stoop more pronounced.

'Lothar, it's been a long time. How are you?'

Lothar held out the wine. 'I need to apologise, Hans.'

Hans put his arms around him in a bear hug. In all those meetings, Lothar couldn't remember them ever hugging before. 'It's good to see you, Lothar. I'm sorry about today's game. Even if Reisen is my new student.'

'You've taught him well.'

'Thank you, that's generous. Now take your jacket off and join me for a drink.'

Lothar followed Hans into his cramped kitchen area. Dirty plates were strewn across the worktop and a half-eaten lump of cheese lay next to a stale loaf of bread. 'Freya away, is she?'

'She's taken the children to her mother's for a week. Which is good timing, because I just took delivery of a very early birthday present.' With a flourish, Hans opened the cupboard to reveal a bottle of Oban Single Malt.

'A bottle of Oban? That must be worth a small fortune'. Picking up the bottle, he inspected it carefully before handing it back to Hans. Even the gold embossed label looked expensive. 'How on earth did you manage to get something so specialised?'

'Let's just say I've got a few connections in the West.'

'Is that wise?'

'Says the man who goes drinking with Tony Marlowe.' Hans had unscrewed the top of the bottle as they were talking. He took a sniff of the Oban. 'Ahh, that smells good,' he said.

'You know about my friendship with Marlowe?'

'Lothar, you spent an evening drinking with the man in front of fifty other Masters. You know how chess players gossip. You can't have expected that to stay secret.'

'Who are your friends in the West, Hans?'

Hans bit his lip and handed him a glass of whisky. 'You can't say a word of this to anyone.'

Lothar looked out of the window. A group of kids were playing football in the courtyard below. It reminded him of when he had been that age. Life had been simpler then, that was for sure. 'You can trust me,' he said.

'Gavrilov wants me to coach him. It would mean emigrating to Switzerland.'

'Viktor Gavrilov? The runner-up in last year's World Championship?'

'Yes, that's the one. How many other players called Gavrilov do you know?'

'When you say emigrate, you mean defect? That's how the government would see it, in any event.'

'It's no government of mine. I don't care what they think.'

Lothar thought about the reaction from the government, from the police, if they knew what Hans was plotting. 'How would you get across the border?'

'There are ways. If it was just me, I would do it like a shot. I'm not sure how Freya and the children would cope in Switzerland, and that's what's holding me back. They don't know anything other than East Germany. The adjustment wouldn't be easy. If I have to stay, then I will. There's nothing here I can't handle.'

He remembered his conversations with Udo Grosz. He knew that Hans had had problems with Grosz in the past. 'I wouldn't be so sure about your own safety, Hans. There are people who bear grudges against you. They'd make trouble for you in the blink of an eye.'

'I'm yesterday's man, Lothar. Nobody cares about me now. I'm not a threat to anyone. Not like you, a promising young Grandmaster. You still have prospects. You need to be careful.'

He nodded. 'I intend to look after myself. You should do the same.'

Hans raised his glass. 'A toast, my friend, to us both. Whatever happens, may good luck follow us.'

Lothar raised his own glass and clinked it against Hans'. 'To the future.'

As he walked home, he reflected on his friendship with Hans. Through thick and thin, they had found a way to stick together. The argument over Hungary behind them now, he did not intend to lose touch with his friend again. Since his own father had died, Hans had been the closest thing he had to a father figure in his life. Aside from his mother and Anna, there was nobody else in the world who meant as much to him as Hans.

Little did he realise that it would be a long time, and in very different circumstances, before he would see Hans Adler again.

Chapter Thirteen

Betrayal

He had read about it, of course. He had seen the television programmes too. The bombings, the destruction, the loss of half a million lives. At university, he had even met a professor who was born in Dresden, who had seen the rebuilding at first hand. Nothing, though, could prepare you for the reality.

The strangest thing was the contrast between old and new. In the centre of the city stood the magnificent Town Hall, home to this year's national championships. The spire of the hundred-metre-high clock tower, at the top of which stood Hercules, guardian of the people of Dresden, dominated the town. Lothar had spotted the spire, two hundred and fifty years old and a survivor of the war, from the window of his boarding house over half a mile away. Now that he stood outside the Town Hall, he marvelled at both the tower and the famous Golden Arches — four gold-plated doors, in front of which stood two bronze lions. The front of the Town Hall had been entirely reconstructed after the war. The transition was seamless. The architect had made an impressive job of it.

Walking through the gates, he came to a courtyard. In the corner was a set of steps. Lothar followed these up until he reached a platform which gave him a view of the historic city centre. Old and new: it was the feature of the town.

After he had surveyed the city, he walked out of the Town Hall — he would be spending enough time here once the tournament began — and headed back down the hill. To the right, he found shops, taverns and a market square. To the left, a row of grey prefabricated flats, just like home. On the front of the nearest block of flats was the largest mural he had ever seen, ten metres wide at least. A woman wearing a peasant's headscarf held a flame aloft in her right hand. Behind her, workers swept the streets, mothers held their children, and old men played folk music. Amongst them stood Vladimir Lenin, smiling benevolently at his people.

The town was beautiful and the main square crowded. But he saw few people smile and nobody laugh. The people of Dresden had been through quite a trauma, that was for sure.

That evening, Lothar dined at his boarding house, a simple meal of soup and bread, before returning to the Town Hall for the opening ceremony. Around fifty people had gathered in the courtyard. Some of them were competitors. Others were friends, families or local people. Just when the crowd was beginning to grow restless, the front door of the Town Hall opened and an elderly man dressed in ceremonial robes and with a huge chain around his neck stumbled hesitantly into the courtyard.

'That's the Mayor of Dresden,' whispered a man to Lothar's left. The man rested his arm on Lothar's and leaned across. 'He's a good speaker, is the Mayor. This should be worth listening to.'

Lothar thanked the man and turned back round. Contrary to his neighbour's expectations, it appeared the Mayor's speech was going to be a short one, and he had already missed the first half of it.

'In conclusion, I must praise the game of chess, which represents all that is good in our society: intellect, a passion for the truth, courage in adversity and the will to win. Ladies and gentlemen, a toast to chess players everywhere.'

Lothar heard a chuckle, and turning around, saw the scruffy, unshaven figure of Johan Martins just behind him. '*Passion for the truth*, that's a new one,' said Martins, stubbing out his cigarette on the ground and shaking Lothar's hand. 'If you're talking about chess players, then I'd say *passion for alcohol* is more realistic.'

Lothar smiled and turned back towards the speaker.

'Now,' said the Mayor, 'time for the draw.' Holding up twelve numbered balls to the audience, he placed each of the balls in turn in a gold-emblazoned leather bag. There was a pause while a man to the left of the Mayor – Lothar recognised him as the Chief Arbiter – whispered in the Mayor's ear. The Mayor nodded and continued. 'May I call to the front the greatest ever East German player, Herr Thomas Jensen.'

Jensen was a popular local hero and a huge roar went up when his name was called. Waving to the crowd and acknowledging their cheers, the grey-haired Jensen walked up to the front, shook the Mayor by the hand, and pulled out the Number Eleven ball, which he passed to the Chief Arbiter. The arbiter wrote a large 'Eleven' against Jensen's name, and the veteran returned to the crowd to further applause. Next up was Konrad Welde, followed by Ernst Reisen, the player who had beaten Lothar just recently. Lothar had not yet seen Sebastian Bahl, but when the Mayor called out Bahl's name, a spectacularly dressed figure emerged from the crowd. No wonder he had not recognised him. Bahl had cut short and washed his hair and, discarding his normal grey suit, the six-foot-tall Grandmaster was dressed in an outrageous yellow and red striped blazer, which barely covered his portly frame. To complete the effect, he had on a matching yellow and red bow tie. When the ridiculously clad Bahl drew, of all things, the Number One ball, he held a single finger in the air before beating his chest with his hand. 'Champion!' he shouted, to the Mayor's bemusement.

'Follow that,' Lothar said to Johan Martins.

'Don't worry, I will,' said Martins.

Sure enough, when Martins strode up to the front, his worn grey trousers and beaten-up shoes a contrast with the expensively attired Bahl, he took a glass of beer from the table in front of the Mayor, turned to the crowd, and downed the drink in one. Slamming the glass back down on the table, Martins shouted the lyrics of a popular beer festival song: '*a toast, a toast, a cheer and good times.*' Lothar smiled. The people of Dresden must have wondered, he thought to himself, who these oddballs were, and what they were doing in their town.

When everyone else had had their turn, the Mayor called Lothar to the front. Selecting the only ball remaining, Number Twelve, his fate was cast. In the first round, he would meet the highest-rated player in the field, Thomas Jensen. In the last round, he would face, of all people, the newly blazered Sebastian Bahl. In both games he would have the black pieces, and neither of these were pairings he was looking forward to. If he was to win the tournament, though, it was an undeniable fact that he would have to beat the best.

By the time he sat down on the stage for the opening round the next day, Lothar felt oddly calm. With over five hundred spectators seated below, plus numerous press and photographers, it was the largest audience he had ever played in front of. He had wondered if he would feel nervous, but actually he felt concentrated and determined, so focused that he hardly noticed the excited chatter of the audience.

As the clock struck two, the Chief Arbiter called the start of play, and Lothar and Jensen shook hands, his opponent smiling warmly. Lothar pressed down his opponent's clock and Jensen replied by pushing forward his Queen's pawn two squares. Pausing for effect, Lothar pondered before bringing out his King's Knight. When Jensen pushed his Queen's Bishop pawn,

Lothar paused again, before bringing out his King's pawn two squares. Jensen drew a sharp breath. Lothar had ventured the Budapest Gambit, a brave, some might even say foolish opening, where black sacrifices his King's pawn as early as the second move. Jensen had not anticipated such a bold choice, and he deliberated carefully before hesitatingly taking the offered pawn. Over the following turns, Lothar brought his pieces into attacking positions, while Jensen defended against his threats.

By the twentieth move, Lothar had brought his Queen, both Rooks and his King's Bishop into the game. He was now two pawns down, and objectively Jensen had much the better position, but the great man was not used to being attacked in such a direct manner. Having already unhooked his tie, Jensen now undid his top button, and began mopping his brow with his handkerchief as he sought to find the refutation of Lothar's aggressive plan.

After further thought, Jensen advanced his Queen's Rook pawn to the fifth rank. Given time, the pawn could one day make a new Queen, but time was one thing Jensen did not have. After stopping to check and re-check his calculations, excitedly Lothar picked up his Rook and snapped off the pawn in front of Jensen's King.

'Check.'

'Lothar Hartmann's gone mad. He's sacrificed a Rook,' he heard a spectator say.

Jensen turned pale. He had not seen the sacrifice coming. Unlike the spectators, however, he was able to work out what was about to unfold. His response was forced: King takes Rook.

Doing his best to keep his hand steady, Lothar picked up the black Queen and slid it across the board, landing it next to the King, on a square where his opponent could capture it. 'Check.'

As he played the sacrifice of his Queen, his hand shook. There was further rumbling from the hall and the arbiter had to ask the spectators to be quiet. Realising something special was about to happen, the other competitors began to crowd around the board. Only Sebastian Bahl remained seated, grimly hunched over his board, staring at his own position and ignoring the surrounding excitement.

Sportingly, Jensen smiled and, picking up his King, captured Lothar's Queen.

Now came the *coup de grâce*. Lothar moved his Knight forwards towards Black's King. Check and mate!

The crowd broke into thunderous applause. Ernst Reisen slapped him on the back – 'a work of genius, Lothar' – and Johan Martins suggested that they head immediately to the bar for a beer. An extremely dignified man, Jensen shook him warmly by the hand. 'A fine game, young man. Immortal, even.'

Lothar found out afterwards that this was the first match Jensen had lost as White in the East German championship for over ten years. That night, he celebrated by drinking two glasses of beer with Johan Martins. Evenings with Martins had a habit of getting out of control, but this occasion was different. By ten o'clock he had said his goodbyes to Martins and was back in his room and early to bed. Having made such a good start, he was determined not to squander it.

In round two, Lothar continued his good start by defeating the experienced player Andreas Tarrant. With each of them using their allotted two hours for the first forty moves, and then another hour each for the next twenty, the game took no less than six hours. By the end, Lothar was in a state of near exhaustion, arms dangling from his chair, vision blurred. Seeing his nervous state, Ernst Reisen and Johan Martins dragged him out for some food. He was so tired, he could hardly finish the meal.

The following day, he drew quickly with his old friend and roommate in Amsterdam, Rainer Müller. The action in the third round happened on the neighbouring board, where Sebastian Bahl beat Christoph Roth sacrificing not just his Queen, but both Rooks to boot. When Roth offered his hand in resignation, Bahl punched the air, and shouted out 'Yes!' like a World Cup footballer. Bahl joined Lothar in the lead, on two and a half points from three games.

That evening, Lothar spent the evening with Roth, Martins, Müller and Reisen at a tavern in the centre of town drinking beer and eating black bread. Contrary to popular reputation, chess players are capable of being sociable, and the banter was good, drink-fuelled as it was. The night was a warm one and they had selected an outside table, overlooking the market square. When the time came to pay the bill, there was no doubt that Martins, as was his habit, had drunk by far the most alcohol. He had not eaten any of the bread, however, and the other four resignedly agreed to split the bill evenly among themselves, given Martins' usual financial circumstances. They all put their cash on the table, and Ernst Reisen counted the notes and coins carefully. Roth put the money in a heap in the centre of the table and they debated whether to order another drink or move on to a new bar.

As they deliberated, a youth with short hair sauntered past their table. Relaxed by the beer and the company, the friends noticed too late that the young man had grabbed hold of the money they had left on the table and was now running down the street. First to react, Roth rose to give chase, with Lothar just behind. On a good day they might have had a chance, but the beer slowed them, and with a head start the thief was soon out of sight.

They returned to the table despondently. 'What a day,' said Roth. 'I lost my game, now my money too. It's alright for the rest of you. At least you got results today.'

'It's not alright for me,' said Martins. 'I can't afford to pay another bill.'

'But you didn't pay the first time, Johan,' said Lothar.

'The principle is still the same.'

'If you say so.'

Counting their remaining money between them, they had nowhere near enough to pay. With unfortunate timing, a waiter appeared at their table.

'Gentlemen, perhaps you would like to pay the bill now?'

There was an embarrassed silence. Reisen spoke first. 'There is a slight problem.'

The waiter looked at Reisen and raised his eyebrows. 'A problem?'

Reisen held out the small amount of money they had gathered between them. The man looked at it dismissively, before nodding his head in the direction of the kitchen. Within seconds, a second waiter appeared. He was carrying a meat cleaver. The first man was blocking their exit.

At this point, Lothar made possibly his boldest move of the tournament so far. 'We were wondering,' he said, standing up straight, having recovered his breath, and projecting a confidence that he didn't feel, 'how many plates and pans we would need to wash, to pay our bill?'

The two waiters looked at each other. The first man frowned. The second raised his meat cleaver. Lothar's position as the tournament leader, so promising, suddenly seemed at risk, and in the most bizarre of ways. Then the first man laughed, a loud, hearty laugh. 'You want to wash our dishes? Hahaha. The thought of it. Famous chess players, scrubbing our dishes. This is too funny.'

The second man began laughing as well. Dropping the meat cleaver on the table – for which Lothar breathed a silent word of thanks – he leaned down and rubbed his sides in mirth. 'Wash the dishes. Ha! Yes, we can let you wash our dishes. You can sweep the floors too.'

Five hours later, when a group of East Germany's top chess players had washed and dried several hundred dishes, swept the floor, thrown out the rubbish and remnants of uneaten food, and reset the tables for the following day, the waiters finally let them go. The only experience in his life of manual work, it was not something Lothar wished to repeat any time soon.

The following day Lothar was paired against Konrad Welde, like Sebastian Bahl a rival from his junior days. Unlike Bahl, Welde was someone with whom he got on reasonably well. His gapped teeth and pebble-thick glasses gave him a comical air, but he was not unpleasant. Lothar had the white pieces and began the game by moving his Queen's pawn. Welde replied with the King's Indian Defence, one of the most aggressive choices available, and a sign that he had come to fight.

For some reason, Lothar felt ill-prepared, and no matter how hard he stared at the board the good moves would not come. While he advanced his forces on the Queenside, Welde was building a fearsome attack, advancing his army towards Lothar's King.

Lothar managed to defend against the checkmate threats, but only by making great concessions to his position, expending considerable time in the process. After a scramble where they each played twenty moves in less than five minutes, they emerged in an endgame in which he had a lost position, a Rook for a Knight down.

Believing that he was about to win, Welde went off contentedly to buy himself a coffee while Lothar sat at the board with his head in his hands. Martins looked on sympathetically, while Sebastian Bahl, who had already won his game, stood by the board in his striped blazer, a sardonic smile on his lips.

Needing to take desperate measures, it was here that Lothar saw a trap. Waiting for his opponent to return to the board, he played an innocuous-looking move, delicately sliding his Knight towards the edge of the board on the Queenside. Giving his best film star impression, he sighed wearily as he did so, acting as if on the point of resignation. Welde thought for a few seconds and then quickly took a pawn with his Rook, a smile flashing across his face. In response, not even pausing for thought, Lothar picked up his Knight and captured a harmless-looking black pawn, slamming down the clock as he played his move. Only now did Welde realise that his Rook was misplaced. There was no way for it to get back in time to stop Lothar's humble pawn advancing to the end of the board and becoming a new Queen.

In one move, a lost game had become a win. It was Welde's turn now to hold his head in his hands, before eventually looking up sadly, holding out his hand and resigning. As a result, Lothar joined Bahl in the lead on three and a half points from four rounds. Welde took the defeat with grace. The look of frustration on Bahl's face when he realised that Lothar had won was a picture.

As he walked back to his boarding house that evening with Johan Martins, Lothar reflected on the day's events. With a defeat, he would have been almost out of contention for the tournament. By winning, he had kept himself firmly in the hunt for the championship. He would need to raise his game though, otherwise he was surely due his comeuppance.

Two games remained before the rest day on Sunday. On Friday, he beat the former champion Heinz Malkinson with Black in his most straightforward contest of the week. Saturday was entirely another matter, however. Paired against his recently acquired friend, Ernst Reisen, the player who had vanquished him only a week before the tournament, and the new protégé of Hans Adler, he contemplated offering a draw before the start of the game. He was not sure what he was going to do until the point when they sat down at the board, but as the arbiter announced play he shook Reisen's hand and firmly pushed forward his King's pawn two squares.

With his very first move, he had already varied from his previous game against Reisen, and he expected his opponent to give his response at least a little thought. Nothing doing. With barely a flicker, the younger man brought out his Queen's Bishop pawn two squares, the Sicilian Defence. Soon, they were into a variation favoured by the legendary Bobby Fischer. They were following a series of moves that Lothar and Hans had analysed, and which – if Reisen continued with his current strategy – would lead to his certain defeat.

On the twelfth move came the critical point. Reisen's best option, he knew from his home analysis, was to develop his King's Bishop one square. If instead he played the natural move, developing his Queen, then Lothar would bring out his Bishop, giving check. The idea looked ridiculous – Black could take the Bishop in three different ways – but each way would lead to his ruin.

For the first time, Reisen stopped to think, leaning forward, stroking his chin and staring at the board intently. Lothar did his best to stay motionless, not giving anything away. Had Reisen seen his trap? He was particularly proud of the idea when he found it. Hans said it was one of the best *novelties* he had ever seen on the chessboard, and he had been waiting for over a year to play the move in a real game.

Eventually, when Lothar felt he could calm his breathing no longer, Reisen moved. To Lothar's joy, his opponent had brought out his Queen. In response, he snapped out his Bishop. 'Check!'

Reisen looked up at him, surprised, and shook his head. Then, without thinking, he calmly moved his King one square to his left and shook his head again. Lothar felt a sudden tightness in his chest. What was this? His opponent had three ways to capture his Bishop, and yet he had ignored all of them. The move Reisen had played, a King move, had not featured in his reckoning at all. He did not understand it. Staring at the position, he began to realise the horror of the situation. Reisen's King was out of the firing line, and Lothar's Bishop would have to retreat again. Then, his opponent would have a *tempo* to start building his own attack. Far from winning, he was actually in trouble.

As he considered the position further, sweat now clinging to his armpits as he failed to find any decent plan, a dreadful thought came to his mind. How had Reisen found the refutation of his attack so quickly? There was no way he could have discovered it over the board, unaided; such a thing was impossible. He surely knew about his intended Bishop sacrifice. He must have known about it, studied it, and worked out the solution. The truth dawned on Lothar. Hans had showed Reisen his idea.

Redoubling his efforts, Lothar put his hands over his ears and hunched over the board. Eventually, in desperation, he found a plan. It looked crazy, but by swapping off his Queen and both Rooks, he could emerge into an endgame a pawn down. Technically, he was much worse, but he knew that Reisen had been aiming to land an immediate checkmate, and he may not be ready psychologically for such a shift in the position. Besides which, he did have one ace up his sleeve, which was his Queen's Rook's pawn. There was no black pawn standing against it. Could that lone pawn, just as it had against Konrad Welde, become a new Queen?

The game played out in a most unexpected way. As they entered into the endgame, Reisen sank into deep thought. He fixed his eyes firmly on the dangerous pawn. Clearly he had seen what had happened to Welde, and he was not going to make the same mistake. Indeed, he brought his entire remaining army across to the Queenside to surround and destroy the lone pawn. In the meantime, Lothar had brought his pieces over to the Kingside, and he launched an attack on the black King. From nowhere, he was threatening checkmate. As he stared at the board, he realised that Reisen had no decent response. He was about to win the game, from a position which had seemed hopeless only a few moves previously.

As a bemused audience looked on – they were no more able to fathom what had happened than he was – Reisen stretched out his hand to resign. Crestfallen, his opponent muttered the briefest of words before running off the stage. As for Lothar, at the end of the first week he was the clear leader with five wins and a draw from six rounds, just ahead of Sebastian Bahl. The spectators were already speculating that his last round match-up with Bahl would decide the title. He knew full well, though, that he had four difficult rounds to get through before then, and there was no room for complacency. More than anything, his overriding emotion, despite his success, was anger. He could not stop himself fuming at Hans' treachery. In showing Reisen his novelty, he had nearly cost him not just a game but also the Championship itself. It would take some time to get over this.

Sunday was a rest day. Some of the younger players took part in a rapid tournament. Lothar needed a break from chess, and he did not want to bump into Reisen, a man he no longer considered a friend, so he stayed in his room most of the day, taking only a short walk to the Town Square to unwind. In the evening, the Mayor arranged a reception for the Championship competitors. Chess players have a unique ability to hunt down free food and drink, and over sixty people turned up at the event claiming to be Masters. As one of the few who was legitimately entitled to attend, Lothar made the most of the feast, gorging himself on bratwurst, salami and cake, and downing four glasses of beer. There was no sign of Reisen, and he was pleased about that. With each drink, he was feeling ever more annoyed about yesterday's betrayal. Had Reisen or Hans been here now, he would have been ready to tell them what he thought of their behaviour, in no uncertain terms.

Once they had had their fill of cake, Udo Grosz, who was making a brief visit to Dresden in between political appointments, gave a short speech wishing all the competitors luck, before handing around his trademark Bison cigars as gifts. Towards the end of the evening, when Lothar had already drunk far too much, Grosz cornered him in the bar, putting his huge arm around his shoulder. To Lothar's relief, Grosz had already given his last cigar away, so he wasn't subjected to the noxious fumes.

'Congratulations, Comrade, on a fine performance in the first week. I'm only sorry that I won't be able to stay to see you win the Championship.'

'Thanks Udo, I'll try my best.'

'I know you will, Lothar. I'm very excited by the opportunities that we are going to find for you. As an aside, your performance shows how little you needed Hans Adler. A great player will come through, coach or no coach.'

'I agree, Udo. I don't need Hans. I'm better off on my own.' He downed his beer as he said this and picked up the fresh glass that was already waiting at its side.

Grosz tilted his head and peered at him. 'That's a change of heart, isn't it, Lothar? Previously, you've always defended Adler to the hilt.' Lothar thought he saw the flash of a smile across Grosz' face, but when he looked again, he was deadly serious. 'What's made you see the light, Comrade?' Grosz asked.

'Let's just say Hans let me down, Udo.'

Grosz folded his big, bearlike arms and looked at him pensively. 'I'm guessing he gave away one of your opening secrets?'

Credit to the man, thought Lothar. He was sharp. 'Spot on. How did you know?'

'Oh, it wouldn't be the first time. A bitter coach, realising that his better days are past, and his best student has moved on, seeks to gain revenge. It's the classic story.'

'You guessed right, Udo. Nearly cost me the game today against Reisen. Took all my ingenuity to get out of it.'

Grosz shook his head. 'Disgraceful. Do you want me to take any action? We may be able to get his licence suspended for that.'

Even in his drunken and angry state, Lothar realised that seeking punishment would be going too far. 'No, Udo, that won't be necessary.'

'Fair enough, Comrade. I'll place an even-money wager with you that Adler won't be here long anyway. No doubt he's already plotting some sort of escape, following that renegade Gavrilov to Switzerland.' As he said the word *renegade*, Grosz curled his lip and rolled the 'r' for emphasis.

Lothar's hand slipped and the top of his beer frothed and spilled over his glass. 'You know about Hans and Gavrilov?'

Grosz paused and his face suddenly grew animated. 'No. I don't know about Hans and Gavrilov. Tell me, Lothar.'

Lothar stumbled. His head was throbbing. 'Nothing, Udo. I'm not sure what I meant.'

Grosz raised himself to his full height, so that he towered over Lothar. 'Not sure what you meant?' His voice was incredulous. 'Come on, man. You just gave the game away. You told me in so many words that Adler is planning to defect, that he's going to work with Gavrilov. Are you now denying it?'

'Udo, the truth is... the truth is I don't know.'

Grosz jabbed a finger into Lothar's chest. His face had gone red and he was glaring at Lothar as if he was the devil himself. 'You, Hartmann, just told me that Adler is planning to defect. Deny it and I'll throw you in jail.' Raising his voice so that he was almost shouting, he poked Lothar in the ribs again, this time viciously hard. 'Tell me, Lothar. Tell me. Tell me!'

Lothar began to sweat. He could see people turning around to look at him. Why had he drunk so much? If he had been sober, he would never have put Hans in the position he had just done, no matter what secrets his former coach had given away. 'Udo, I'm sorry, I don't know what I'm saying. Maybe Hans was thinking of going to Switzerland at one stage. But he won't do so now. I'm sure of that. He's loyal, Udo. Hans is loyal.'

Grosz paused and, just as quickly as it had appeared, his anger dissipated again. Putting his arm around Lothar's shoulder, the President smiled, the callous smile of a jackal.

'Comrade, I was only teasing you. If the Swiss want Adler, then they are welcome to him. Hah! Enough of that lapdog of the West. Let's have another drink. A nice spirit to finish the evening.' Grosz turned to the barman. 'Two vodkas, please.

Make them doubles. Next week, this young man will be crowned champion of East Germany. A toast to his success!'

Grosz' car arrived shortly before midnight to take him back to Berlin. Lothar left at the same time, taking the short stroll back to his boarding house. With all the emotion, and the drink, he was unsteady on his feet and unsure of his vision. Sitting outside on the steps of the boarding house, smoking a cigarette, wasn't that Ernst Reisen?

After the difficult, confusing conversation with Udo Grosz, the anger he had felt earlier in the evening had subsided and he was determined to be polite to Reisen. His former friend beat him to it. 'Lothar, I'm sorry about yesterday. I shouldn't have rushed off like that after our game. It was rude.' Reisen offered his hand, which Lothar shook.

'You should have beaten me, Ernst. With all that preparation, and the position you got against me.'

'I know, Lothar. I was so surprised when you went down that line. Didn't you read the latest edition of *64*?'

Lothar felt a compression in his chest and his head began to spin. 'What do you mean, the latest edition?' In his mind, he pictured the copy of the Russian journal *64*, the most famous chess publication in the world, that had arrived shortly before he packed for Dresden. It was still sitting, unread, in the bottom of his suitcase.

'The article on the Soviet Championships? Voronin played your Bishop sacrifice. He'd been preparing it for three years, apparently. Vasily Smirov thought for half an hour then refuted it over the board. They're calling it one of the great defences of all time. I could hardly believe it when you followed exactly the same line as Voronin.'

'So it wasn't Hans who prepared you for our game?'

'Hans? Heavens, no. Hans would never help me prepare against you. It was the first rule when we signed up together. He wouldn't do that to you, Lothar.'

Everything had become clear. He had made a terrible mistake. 'Of course not, Ernst. Hey, it's late. I must go to bed. Let's grab a beer during the week.'

'Look forward to it, Lothar. Well played again. Good luck in tomorrow's game.'

His heart had sunk to its lowest point. He needed to escape, to get some sleep, to get away from this nightmare, at least temporarily. 'Thanks, Ernst. Good luck to you too, and goodnight.'

'Oh, don't forget to read *64*,' called out Reisen as he headed through the front door of the boarding house. 'You don't want to miss any other *novelties*!'

CHAPTER FOURTEEN

No Country for Old Men

Lothar woke up with a throbbing head, a queasy stomach and a desperate craving for coffee and cigarettes. Stumbling out of bed, he thought about the night before. Switzerland! What on earth had he been thinking? How foolish had he been to betray his friend, his mentor? Even if Hans had helped Reisen with his preparation, he would have had no business giving him away. To allow Grosz to trick him like that, it was awful. This was East Germany, where the authorities did not tolerate dissent. The merest hint of disloyalty was liable to lead to punishment. To talk to a traitor, as the government regarded Viktor Gavrilov, was akin to treason. In his drunkenness, his anger, he had given away Hans' biggest secret. The stupidity.

For the rest of the morning he sat at his desk with his head in his hands, wondering what to do next. He could warn Hans, but in doing so he would have to admit the enormity of his mistake. He wasn't sure he had the strength. Besides which, knowing what was about to befall him was hardly likely to help his former coach. He could try phoning Grosz, to explain that he had been wrong about Switzerland. He knew though that the President wouldn't believe him. There was even a chance that Grosz had known about the plan to defect already. Conceivably, Hans' flat was bugged, and Lothar was being set up as a fall guy. Whatever the circumstances, the die was cast. His only hope was that the incident would blow over. Grosz had had a number of drinks as well. Perhaps he would have forgotten about the whole thing?

That afternoon, battle resumed. He would be facing his friend Johan Martins. He was hardly in a mood to play, and they agreed a pre-arranged short draw. Returning to the boarding house, he spent the evening in his room, waiting for a message from either Udo Grosz or Hans Adler. When there was no news, good or bad, he took that as a promising sign.

In the following two rounds, Lothar remained distracted, unable to think of much other than Switzerland and Hans' potential arrest. Somehow, he managed to beat the talented student Christoph Roth, before drawing with Eduard Berger. With two rounds to go, he continued to lead with seven and a half points from nine games, half a point ahead of Sebastian Bahl.

By Thursday morning, when there had still been no news from either Hans or Grosz, he began to relax. It seemed his worst fears would not be realised. If Grosz was going to make a case against Hans, he would surely have done so by now. The police had not come to question him. Perhaps there was no reason to worry? For the first time in several days, he felt able to concentrate on the chess again.

Thursday afternoon brought the tenth and penultimate round. If he won today, and Bahl lost to Konrad Welde, he would win the tournament outright. Standing in his way was former champion Lazlo Vogel, a strong Grandmaster whom he had first met all those years ago at the local rapid chess contest, and a player he had still never beaten. He appreciated Vogel's strength. He was on good form himself, though, and his head was now back in one piece.

Sitting down at the board shortly before the start of play, shaking hands with the sharply dressed Vogel, his pristine suit and tie contrasting with Lothar's leather jacket and jeans – souvenirs from his trip to Amsterdam – he began to feel a tightening of his stomach. Not since the final round of the school championship, his first foray into the chess world, had so much rested on a single game. A record number of people had bought tickets that day, and the arbiters had brought in an extra ten rows of chairs.

As he tried to compose himself before the start of play, taking deep breaths and willing his mind to go blank, Lothar could feel the eyes of the crowd burning into the board. A murmur ran around the room and he shifted uncomfortably, feeling the sweat underneath his armpits and the pressure in his chest. Make the wrong move and six hundred pairs of eyes would see it. He set his jaw. He was determined that today would not be a day when he let people down.

At two o'clock sharp, the arbiter announced, 'Let play commence,' and pressed down Lothar's clock. Lothar pushed forward his Queen's pawn two squares, and Vogel responded by bringing out his King's Knight, leading them into a Grünfeld Defence.

On move nine, Lothar played a new idea that Martins, Reisen and he had found in the bar, an unexpected thrust with his King's Rook pawn. The idea was brutal. He intended to push his pawn up the board, before sacrificing it and making space for his Queen to give checkmate. It was a simple plan, but surprisingly hard to counter.

As Lothar picked up his Rook's pawn, Vogel's face twitched. Blinking rapidly, his opponent clutched his hands to his face. Clearly he had never before contemplated such a strange pawn thrust. After painstaking thought, he hesitatingly moved forward his own pawn to barricade Lothar's advance. This was only a temporary respite, and by the twentieth move Lothar had a strong attack, with his pieces bearing down on black's King. Meanwhile, Sebastian Bahl was struggling against Welde, and the Championship was almost within his grasp.

On the twenty-fifth move, as Lothar deliberated, he was disturbed by a commotion behind him. Bahl and Welde had finished. To his surprise, Bahl had won. Lothar asked Johan Martins what had happened. 'Welde threw the game,' replied Martins, in a whisper. 'Bahl is desperate to win the tournament, and he and Welde go way back.'

Lothar returned to his board, reflecting sadly. To win the national championship, it was not enough to be the best player. It wasn't even enough to beat your main rivals. The only way to win was to be so far ahead of the competition that they could not catch you even when they cheated.

Turning his attention back to his board, he looked again at the options: move the Knight or the Rook. Suddenly, he saw a third possibility. Of course, it had been obvious. Picking up his Queen, he removed Vogel's Bishop from the board and pressed down the clock. In one fell swoop, he had captured an enemy piece and kept his attack going.

The moment he released his hand from the clock, he heard a buzz of noise from the hall. Looking up, he saw Vogel staring at him incredulously. Bemused, he looked back down at the board, still with no idea as to what was wrong.

Shaking his head, Vogel picked up his Knight and captured the white Queen. A backward capture, supposedly the hardest move to spot, it was a turn Lothar had completely overlooked. He was now simply a Queen down. The game was lost.

Lothar's heart leapt seven beats. What had he done! As the chatter in the hall seemed to rise to a crescendo, his cheeks went red and his head began to throb. Memories came back of the blunder he had made against Sebastian Bahl in Tallinn a couple of years earlier. This mistake was worse, though. Terrible, awful and humiliating. He felt simultaneously panicked, embarrassed and in despair. The stupidity, the carelessness, the grim consequences. Tipping over his King in resignation, Lothar offered his hand to Vogel. His opponent was deeply apologetic. 'I'm sorry, Lothar, I didn't want to win that way.'

Barely able to speak, Lothar mumbled something incoherent to Vogel, rose unsteadily to his feet and staggered off the stage and out of the playing hall. Johan Martins tried to speak to him as he left, and all he could do in reply was shake his head. Returning to the boarding house still in a haze, Lothar sat alone in his room for the rest of the afternoon thinking about what he had done. He had blown it. All that hard work over the last ten days thrown away because of a moment of impetuosity. Gradually the sadness and despair were overtaken by anger, and he began to curse: at himself, at his foolishness and at this torturous game called chess which could bring so much joy, but also on occasion make him so unhappy.

The evening came, and he staggered out of his room and trudged slowly down the stairs to the phone box outside the boarding house. His former coach would know what to say, he felt sure. When he couldn't get through after the third attempt, he rang home instead. There was a click on the line and Anna answered.

'Bad news,' he said. 'I've done something really stupid.'

'What do you mean? What's happened?' Anna's voice was concerned yet sympathetic at the same time. He had missed her.

'I've handed the tournament to Sebastian Bahl,' he said. 'I lost today. A shocking blunder. I need to beat Bahl tomorrow, or else.'

Anna paused. 'Lothar, you need to forget about what happened today. Go out and enjoy yourself this evening. Tomorrow is another day. You can beat Bahl, which means you're still in it. Remember that.'

This was, Lothar realised, good advice. He took a deep breath and tried to compose himself. No point in worrying Anna

further. 'Enjoying myself may be pushing it, but I'll try my best.'
He paused, wondering whether to raise the question, fearing he
would not like the answer. 'Have you spoken to Freya recently,
by the way? I've been trying to get hold of Hans for a couple of
days but no one is answering.'

He heard a crackle on the end of the line. It was a question
he had to ask himself on every phone call. How many people
were listening on the other end?

'Funnily enough, I rang earlier and couldn't get through
either,' said Anna. 'Maybe they've taken the children away for a
break. I'll try again and leave a message if I get through.'

'Thanks, my love. Speak to you tomorrow.'

'Good luck, Lothar. Remember, try and have some fun this
evening too.'

Putting the phone down, he reflected on what Anna had said.
She was right. He had to forget about today's game. He needed
company too. Luckily, in Johan Martins he had a friend who was
available for a drink day or night. After downing a stein of beer
each, Martins and Lothar met with Rainer Müller and Ernst
Reisen, playing pool in a smoke-filled local bar. Martins and
Müller began a drinking contest, downing horrid concoctions
of vodka and beer in one. Meanwhile, Reisen tried to impress
the locals with card tricks. They did anything other than talk
about chess. It didn't make Lothar feel any better, but at least
he was distracted.

The next day he would be facing Sebastian Bahl with the
black pieces. He was now half a point behind his foe. If he won,
he would be champion. Any other result and the title was Bahl's.
It was win or bust.

Rising late the next morning, he found two telegrams slipped
under his bedroom door. The first read: '*Lothar. The right result*

today and you will be Champion. Be brave and success will come your way! From your biggest supporter, Udo Grosz.'

The second consisted of two words only. *'Best, Hans.'*

So Hans was OK? Feeling as if he had emerged from the other end of a dark tunnel, he left early for the venue, arriving fifteen minutes before play. As he made his way to the front of the hall, he saw two familiar faces in the second row.

'We told the nice man at the box office who we were, and he gave us these great seats,' said Anna, hugging him.

Lothar turned to his mother and put his arms around her. 'I told the man,' she said, waving her stick in the air, 'I'm Lothar's mother. I didn't take a three-hour train journey to come and stare at my son through a pair of binoculars.'

'I'm so glad you've both made it,' he said. 'It means a lot to me.'

'Yes, well, you need to make sure you win now. Make the effort worthwhile,' said his mother. She had become noticeably more irascible and blunt since the death of his father. He loved her for it.

Anna squeezed his hand. 'Good luck, my love. You can beat Bahl. I know you can do it.'

Lothar hugged them both again and climbed up the steps to take his seat on the stage. By the time Sebastian Bahl arrived, two minutes before the start, he was focused purely on the game. He hardly noticed the sneer Bahl gave as he sat down at the board. He had the black pieces, he was half a point behind Bahl, he had lost his last round, and he did not care. Today, he had come to win.

After a short speech, the Tournament Director announced play, and the game commenced. Lothar had met Bahl four times in his career, and honours were even at two wins apiece. Unsurprisingly, given their dislike of each other, the two of them always fought to the bitter end. He didn't see that changing today.

Sitting behind the white pieces, Bahl grimaced and shook Lothar's hand weakly before opening with his favourite King's pawn, forward two squares. Pausing, Lothar unleashed his prepared surprise: pushing his Queen's pawn a single square, he played the Pirc Defence. The Pirc may look to the uninitiated as though it is a passive opening. In fact, it gives Black great chances to create complications and to play for a win.

If he was taken aback by the unusual opening choice, Bahl did not show it. Confidently, his opponent pushed forward his Queen's pawn two squares, before developing both Knights and a Bishop, using an approach adopted recently by Vasily Smirov, no less.

On the tenth move, Lothar had another shock in store for his opponent. With all his pieces developed, and feeling content with life, Bahl rose from the board, stretched and stood behind his chair surveying his position, his hand fiddling with his bow tie. While it is not specifically forbidden in chess law, most players regard standing rather than sitting at the board as a discourtesy at best and gamesmanship at worst. Lothar had no time for that type of behaviour, and it was with extra force that he pushed forward his Queen's Knight pawn two squares, offering a sacrifice.

As Lothar's hand left the piece, Bahl jumped in surprise. Returning to his seat, he stared at the offending pawn for some time, shaking his head. Eventually, puffing up his chest, Bahl snapped the pawn off the board with his Bishop. As he did so, he looked up and glared at Lothar. Lothar held his gaze for a second before turning back to the board. Picking up his Bishop, he captured the Knight in front of Bahl's King. A key defender removed, he had placed Bahl's King in grave danger.

Realising the difficult position he was in, Bahl plunged into thought again. He hunched his vast body over the board and his breathing became heavy. Eventually, Bahl shook his head and, placing his stubby fingers over the white King, began a race to find safety. Over three successive moves Bahl slid his monarch across the board from right-hand side to left. The defence was desperate but it was also ingenious, and not something Lothar had foreseen. Suddenly a position that had seemed so promising for him had turned again, and when Bahl captured a second and then a third pawn, it was Lothar's turn to be placed under pressure. As Bahl looked on, the hint of a smile on his lips, Lothar stared at the board, realising that now it was he who needed to rescue his game.

Suddenly, his concentration was disturbed. What was that under the table? Had Bahl really just kicked him? He felt it again. Yes, it was a kick, a second one. Unbelievable. Looking up, he saw Bahl meet his eye. Quietly, so that no one else could hear, Bahl whispered softly, 'You're going to lose.'

Lothar looked at his opponent in astonishment. 'What did you say?'

Bahl stared back. 'Nothing. I didn't say a word.'

'Kick me again and there will be trouble.'

Bahl glared back. The arbiter rushed across to their table. 'What's going on here? Gentlemen, behave yourselves, please, both of you.'

Shaking his head, Lothar looked back at the board. From the corner of his eye, he could see the arbiter standing watching over them. At least that should stop Bahl kicking him again. But what to do about his position? He was three pawns down in a match for the national championship, and his opponent had just abused him. He had to find a way to regain the momentum, and quickly, before one of his opponent's pawns made a new

Queen. Closing his eyes, he sat back and allowed the pieces to dance in front of him. Clearing his mind of all other distractions, only the board and pieces remained. As though in a dream, the pieces floated before him, a perfect vision. There! It came to him. The pawns his opponent had captured had opened up lines for him to attack. Salvation lay in offence. With a new sense of vigour, he opened his eyes again. He was ready to resume battle. Reaching out his left hand, he picked up his Rook and brought it across the board to attack Bahl's King. Now he felt the game was perfectly balanced again. His attack against Bahl's extra pawns.

On the thirty-eighth move, with both players desperately short of time, Bahl pulled his King back to the first rank. As he made the move, he put down his pen on the table and crossed his arms confidently. Perhaps it was an act, or maybe he really was counting on this as his saving move, but Lothar already had a response planned. Taking a moment for a deep breath, feeling like he was about to lift the weight of the world off his shoulders, he picked up his Rook and played the sacrifice Rook takes pawn. It was check, and if Bahl captured the Rook, Lothar's Queen would leap into action, giving mate the following move.

As Bahl stared at the wreckage in front of his King, the flag on his clock fell. He had run out of time. The arbiter reached over to stop both clocks. The game was over. Lothar had won. Refusing to shake his hand, Bahl rose and walked out of the hall without acknowledging either Lothar or the arbiter. Lothar was champion of East Germany, and he had won the tournament with a tremendous attack against his biggest rival.

The spectators burst into applause. For the first time, he looked up at the audience. People were standing and cheering. His mother and Anna were both crying. He acknowledged the acclaim shyly, with the briefest gesture of his hand. He had done it. He felt almost overwhelmed, as though he wanted to burst into tears of happiness there and then. Turning back to the table, he signed his score sheet, handing it to the arbiter. He picked up Bahl's score sheet as well, left behind by his opponent, and handed that across too. Underneath Bahl's score sheet, he saw a telegram. '*Sebastian. The right result today and you will be Champion. Be brave and success will come your way! From your biggest supporter, Udo Grosz.*'

So Grosz had sent them both the same message. Even for a politician, the man was shameless. Acknowledging the cheers of the audience for a final time, and waving to his family, he sprung off the stage and through to the annexe at the back. Ernst Reisen, whose game had finished several hours previously, rose to shake his hand. Reisen's face was worn and his voice was frail. 'Congratulations, Lothar.'

He knew immediately that something was very wrong. 'What's up, Ernst?'

'It's Hans. They've arrested him. He's in jail.'

'Arrested?' He felt the blood rush to his cheeks. A moment ago he'd been so happy, and now his world was turned on its head. 'What's happened?'

'I've been on the phone to Freya all afternoon,' said Reisen. 'That's been difficult, I tell you, since the Stasi are no doubt listening to every word we say. Poor Freya is beside herself.'

'What's the charge?' Lothar asked. In his heart, he knew what the answer would be before Reisen replied.

'Udo Grosz found evidence that Hans was plotting against the state. Apparently, he was planning to defect to Switzerland. You've known Hans for years, Lothar. Did he say anything to you?'

His heart raced twelve dozen to the minute and his throat felt as dry as sawdust. What had he done? How had he put his friend in this position? He tried to compose himself. 'Hans didn't say a word, Ernst. But then I've not seen much of him lately.'

'I'm going to set up a petition for his release,' continued Reisen. 'Will you sign it, Lothar?'

'Of course,' he said, knowing already that such a petition would be doomed to failure. Why on earth had he spoken about Hans to Grosz? A few loose words and he had condemned his friend. On the day of his greatest triumph, the enormity of his mistake, his stupidity, was now apparent.

Chapter Fifteen

Enemies of the People

In September, Lothar's mother, increasingly frail and absent-minded since the death of his father, suffered a fall and broke her hip. In hospital, complications set in. She caught an infection and passed away three days later. At the age of twenty-four, he was now without both his parents. He felt distraught, numb, angry, in denial: all those things, and more. Above all, he felt an emptiness in the pit of his stomach. With the passing of his mother, the last link with his childhood was gone.

Anna helped him sort through his mother's possessions. They cleared the flat, handed the keys back at the municipal offices, and within three days a new tenant had moved in to his parents' old apartment. Lothar spent several days sitting at home, staring into space, before Anna dragged him away for a week's break. He couldn't escape the aching in his soul, but in the countryside, the fresh air, open spaces, he did at least try to think of the happy memories, the good times his family had enjoyed together. He suspected it would be a long time before he could get himself back into any kind of balance.

Over the summer, Anna had graduated with distinction in literature. On their return from holiday, she took a temporary job in the local post office. The work was undemanding, but it allowed her time to focus on her writing, which had recently become a passion. She had already had several short stories published and was now working on a novel. She politely rebuffed his attempts to find out what the novel was about.

'When can I have a read?' he asked.

'I'll let you see it soon enough,' Anna said teasingly, walking out of the kitchen. He followed her into their bedroom.

'Is it autobiographical?'

'All novels are about their writer. Everybody knows that.' She turned her back on him and began folding away linen in the closet.

'Am I in it?'

'Of course not. I'm hoping to sell some copies.'

Lothar grabbed his girlfriend from behind and tickled her.

'Ouch!'

'That will teach you to be cheeky.'

Anna turned back round and kissed him on the cheek. 'I'm your girlfriend. I'm allowed to tease you. And it doesn't matter what you say, you're not seeing the novel yet.'

While Anna wrote, he shut himself in the spare room and spent hours working on his chess. The practice was not as productive as he had hoped, and he found himself frequently losing all grip on what he was doing, daydreaming idly, when he should have been focusing on the board. What a strange year this had been. The Championship, yes. But the loss of his mother was causing him more agony than he could say.

On top of that, he was also desperately guilty over what had happened to Hans. His dreams were haunted by nightmare flashbacks of the meeting with Grosz where he had given Hans' secret away. He had let his friend down, and he needed to find a way to recover the situation, to help Hans escape the iron clutch of the Stasi. The trouble was that, so used to fighting his battles on the chessboard, he had no idea how to take on the might of the state. Grandmaster he might be, but the Stasi were playing a game of chess at a whole different level.

Eventually, when he could not stand the continuous empty feeling any longer, Lothar made up his mind. It was time to meet with Udo Grosz. He had to throw himself on the President's mercy and ask him to forgive Hans. As he reached into the bureau for his address book, the phone rang. It was Grosz' secretary, Petra, calling to arrange a meeting. The timing was uncanny.

Never more at home than at the Central Chess Club – as President, this was where he held court – Grosz greeted Lothar in his usual extravagant manner, grabbing him in a bear hug as he welcomed him into his office. 'Comrade! It's been too long. I'm sorry I'm so busy with politics these days. I don't get to spend the time I would like on chess.'

Motioning to Lothar to take a chair, Grosz offered him one of his foul Bison cigars. Why a man of his means chose to buy such low-quality tobacco, he couldn't imagine. Politely declining the offer, he took a seat at Grosz' cluttered desk, covered in old committee papers, newspapers and unwashed coffee cups.

'So, Lothar.' Grosz leaned back and blew a large circle of smoke out of his cigar, 'How is life treating you as East German champion?'

'I'll be blunt, Udo. I'm missing Hans. I'm doing my best to improve my game, but without a coach beside me, I lack direction. I won't make it to the top without him.'

'But Lothar, you won the national championships on your own. Why do you need Hans' help now?'

'I managed to survive for a while on my own, Udo. Right now, though, I feel like a sports car. Without a good engineer, I'm never going to win the biggest race. I may not even make it out of the garage.'

Grosz pursed his lips. 'Interesting analogy, Lothar. You do know that the state doesn't approve of motor racing? Honecker himself has said that fast cars are tools of the West, playthings for the capitalists. Leaving that aside, there are others who could help you.'

'I'm not working with Manfrit Nester again.'

Grosz waved his hand in the air. 'Nester doesn't coach any more. Just tell me who you want.'

'I want to work with Hans again, Udo. I need you to arrange his release. You know the truth as well as I do. Whatever offers Hans may have had, he was never going to go to Switzerland.'

'If only it was that simple, Lothar. I'm afraid I don't have that type of power. In fact, the reason I asked you here today is because of Hans Adler. There are people in Honecker's cabinet who are out for blood. The party needs something to keep the masses in order, and politicians love a show trial.'

'A show trial?' His heart began to pound like a drum.

'I'm afraid so. Adler is in a lot of trouble, Lothar.'

He started to protest, but Grosz gestured for him to be quiet. 'Lothar, I have little time for Adler. He let you down, and he's let down the whole of East Germany. There is never any excuse for plotting with enemies of the state.' Grosz picked up a pencil from his desk and began to doodle on a piece of notepaper. 'Nevertheless, I can see that a trial would not be good for chess. The publicity would be terrible. It could put our work here back years. As for you, Lothar, well, it could be the end of your career.'

This was going from bad to worse. 'Why would I need to be involved in a trial? What has this got to do with me?'

'Because, Comrade, the primary witness would be you, our new national champion. Lothar, we don't want you appearing in court. Think what the West would make of it. Besides which, Hans Adler is unaccountably popular. Jensen has already said he would refuse to play in the same team as you, if you gave evidence.'

'You've spoken to Jensen about this?'

'Of course. He's our top-rated player. Jensen agrees with me. We mustn't have a trial. We have to punish Adler, though. We are treading a very delicate line, Lothar. I will need your help.'

Lothar looked at Grosz silently. The President paused and inhaled deeply from his disgusting cigar before blowing the smoke over him.

'What do you want me to do, Udo?'

'I want you to give written evidence against Adler. Nobody will ever know it was you, but it will be enough to keep him behind bars for a few more weeks, and to end any thoughts he has of returning to the chess world. We will let him out before Christmas. Then we can say to Honecker that we've dealt with the problem, without letting the bloodsuckers have their way.'

'You want me to destroy Hans' life? What if I say no?'

'Now don't exaggerate, Lothar.' Grosz picked up an empty coffee cup from his desk, inspected it with a frown, and scraped at the mould inside. 'A few weeks in jail never did anybody any harm. When Adler returns, we'll find him a job delivering post, or sweeping the streets. Of course, we won't let him teach chess anymore. But after the trouble he's got himself into, surely even he will see that's a good thing.' Grosz leaned back, and stretching his arms behind him, stifled a gentle yawn.

'If I refuse to help?'

'Then, Comrade, there will be no escaping it. The hawks in the Cabinet will get what they want, we'll have a show trial for Hans Adler, and we will call you to give evidence, to confirm that Adler was considering escaping to Switzerland. Lie in court, and we'll try you for perjury. Tell the truth, and everyone will know that you gave evidence against your own friend. Oh, and we'll bring that little girlfriend of yours into this as well.'

'What has this got to do with Anna?' Underneath the table, he felt his fists clenching. It was all he could do to restrain himself from jumping across the table and punching Grosz.

'Our spies tell us she is very friendly with Adler's wife. I would be amazed if she didn't know all about his plans. But we'll see how she gets on when we interrogate her.'

'You're planning to arrest Anna?'

'Not arrest, Lothar, interrogate. There is a difference.'

'Udo, I can't believe you're doing this. After all the time we've spent together.'

'I'm giving you a choice. Don't you see that?'

'A choice of the devil and the deep blue sea.'

Grosz sighed deeply. Not a man who was used to being said no to, he hadn't reckoned on Lothar's stubbornness.

'Lothar, I'm going out to buy some cigars. While I'm out, I'd like you to read this.' Grosz reached into his worn brown leather briefcase and pulled out an envelope inside of which were three sheets of pristine typed yellow notepaper. 'When I get back, you can tell me whether you're going to sign. I'll have the car lined up to go and collect your girlfriend, in case you give the wrong answer.'

As he waited for Grosz to return, Lothar reflected on what would happen to Hans if he signed. Hans was not just a mentor and coach; he was his oldest friend. His concern for Hans paled into insignificance, though, alongside Anna. He tried to imagine his girlfriend being interrogated. A thirty-six-hour session, with no sleep, no food, the endless barrage of questions, hostile, intimidating, designed to break her. There was no way that she would be able to survive that.

When, twenty minutes later, Udo Grosz returned with three new packets of Bison cigars, he found Lothar seated where he had left him. 'So what is the answer, Lothar?'

'Give me your pen, please, Udo.'

'Splendid, Comrade. I am glad you've seen sense.'

Lothar signed the document with betrayal in his heart. The statement would damn Hans Adler. His sympathies with the West, his friendship with Daniel Lorenz, his dislike of authority and the Party, his consistent subversive views and behaviour. They had put everything bad about Hans that they could in there. Where some of the information had come from, he had no idea. He understood now, though, if he had not done before, that the Stasi had eyes and ears everywhere.

'What happens to me now, Udo?'

'You've helped the state, Lothar. We are grateful. We'll look after you, support you financially. Most importantly, that dog Adler won't know that you signed the statement. As long as you continue to work for us, we will keep your secret safe.'

'Who am I working for, Udo?'

Grosz smiled wryly, a viper surveying its prey. 'You're an informer now, Comrade. You do know what they say. Once a member of the Stasi, always a member of the Stasi. May Lenin be with you.'

That evening, Lothar did not return home. He spent hours walking the streets of East Berlin, passing bar after bar, too ashamed even to go in for a drink, fearful that another customer would engage him in conversation and uncover his awful secret. Eventually, passing a beaten-up supermarket, he bought a bottle of vodka and a newspaper. Finding the nearest park, he placed the newspaper on a damp bench, and sat in the rain drinking the vodka. By the early hours, when he had drunk nearly a quarter litre of spirits, and his clothes were soaked through, he could no longer remember what he had done, or why he was so disgusted with himself. A passing police officer arrested him and, taking pity, drove him home. Anna was already asleep and was unamused by his drunken attempts to waken her. By the time he woke up the following morning, she had left for the library. It was a relief not to have to explain what had happened the day before or why he had returned so late. There was no way, he reflected, that Anna could ever understand what he had done. Nor would she be able to forgive him. No, he must bear the awful guilt for his sin alone, his cross to carry, perhaps for the rest of his days.

In early December, Anna's father fell ill and she went to stay at her parents' house for a few days. When he looked at the clothes strewn on the backs of chairs, the empty bottles of beer on the floor and the four days of unwashed plates that had accumulated in the sink, Lothar was embarrassed at the squalor he had created. On Sunday, Anna sent him a telegram to tell him that she would be returning that afternoon, and like a teenager who has held a party while his parents are away, he hurried to tidy the flat before she got back.

Taking a couple of black plastic sacks from the kitchen cupboard, he threw the bottles of beer and food waste into one sack, and the old newspapers and magazines into the second. He put the waste in the bin outside their flat and stored the papers in the hallway cupboard, in case there was anything in them which Anna still wanted. Then he washed and dried the plates and, turning to their bedroom, put the clothes back in the wardrobe. He felt almost domesticated. Shutting the wardrobe, he breathed a sigh of relief. For once, he had earned himself a coffee.

As he turned, he saw something odd. Anna's dark blue diary lay on top of her chest of drawers. Sandwiched within it were what looked like typewritten sheets, at least fifty pages of them, in small print. Intrigued, he reached down and opened the cover. Normally so careful to keep her writing hidden – he did not even know the hiding place – in her hurry to see her parents, Anna had left the unfinished manuscript on top of her desk.

Enemies of the People, said the title page.

He turned to the second page. '*A novel by Irina Karlova.*'

Anna was using a pseudonym. A Russian one at that. Intrigued, he turned to the first chapter and began scanning quickly down the page. '*The people of Arcadia ... a happy people ... government elected with one hundred and one per cent ... the great leader, Erich.*' Hmmm.

He put the story back down on the desk, carefully placing the papers back inside the diary so that Anna wouldn't know he had looked at them. So his girlfriend was writing a political allegory? He picked the manuscript back up again and turned to the second page.

'*Erich had brought stability. Crime eliminated ... Dissent ... Executions ...*'

Lothar put the story back down again uneasily. This was East Germany. You simply didn't write things like that. Not if you wanted to avoid arrest. He picked the manuscript up for a third time and then put it back down without reading any more. The fewer details he knew about the contents, the less he could give away if he was questioned.

By the time Anna returned home, he had recovered his poise. Unpacking her suitcase, and making them both a coffee, she came through to the living room. 'How have you amused yourself while I've been away?' she asked.

'Oh, watching television mainly. You've missed some very good programmes on agriculture. Apparently annual production is at record levels again.'

She smiled. 'What did you think of the writing?'

'What writing?'

'My novel. I know you've read it.'

'How do you know?'

'Because you left the front page on your bureau. You'd never make a spy, Lothar.'

Goodness, he had been careless. He cursed at himself. 'I only looked at a few pages. What I did see, I thought it was an interesting read.'

'But?'

'I understand why you've written it, but I'm worried. Supposing you get found out. The Stasi have put people in jail for far less.'

Anna scrunched up her face. 'Stop being melodramatic, Lothar.'

'Anna, listen to me for a moment. This isn't a country that tolerates dissent.'

'What are you suggesting? That we do nothing?' She had raised her voice and her fists were clenched. 'Lothar, we live in a totalitarian state. Would you want to bring children into this world, where people are afraid to speak, to say what they think? Where ordinary members of the public, including, might I add, your friend, are arrested for their thoughts? I want my life to be useful. To help effect change. I can't live in this society. That's what the book is about.'

Lothar lowered his own voice, trying to sound sympathetic. 'I understand, but this isn't the way, Anna.'

'I wasn't proposing to use my own name.'

'How long do you think a pseudonym will protect you?'

Brow furrowed, Anna tidied the plates from the table and, ignoring his question, turned her back on him, carrying them into the kitchen. He followed behind her.

'I'm not saying I disagree with your views, Anna. I worry though that you'll get yourself into trouble.'

'Get you into trouble more like.' Anna dropped the plates into the sink with a crash and turned the hot tap on full blast.

'That's not fair, Anna. I love you and I'm worried about you. I admit I'm terrified of being arrested. I'm concerned for both of us, and that's the truth.'

'Typical chess player. The only one of you with guts is Hans Adler.'

'Hans is like a father to me. But he spoke his mind and look what happened to him.'

It was the wrong thing to say. Before the words had left his mouth, he realised how stupid he had been. The curse of the chess player. A mind attuned to maths, to puzzles, and to winning and losing, he was unable to find the right words when it really mattered.

Leaving the plates in the sink, the hot water still running, Anna stormed out of the kitchen and, grabbing her coat, headed out of the flat, slamming the door behind her with a force that shook the apartment. These arguments were becoming all too frequent, Lothar reflected desolately as he tidied up the kitchen. If only it was as easy to sort out the mess in his life.

CHAPTER SIXTEEN

The Traveller

'Konrad,' he said, buckling up his seat belt and trying to ignore the spluttering of the engine as they prepared for take-off, 'can I ask you a question?'

'As long as it's not about air travel,' replied Welde, adjusting his new black metallic glasses. 'I'm regretting travelling with Interflug already. That engine does not sound healthy. Next time we go to Czechoslovakia, Lothar, we should get the train.'

The plane had come to a halt, and they watched as the captain, who had left his cockpit, stood talking with the stewardesses. The captain kept motioning to the control tower. Lothar wondered if they were about to disembark.

'Konrad,' he said, 'I'm pleased the Federation asked you to be my second for this tournament. You're a strong player and I can learn a lot from you. There's one thing that worries me, though.'

Welde looked across at him. 'The only thing I'm concerned about right now is this rickety old plane.'

'It's Bahl,' Lothar said. 'You know that he and I dislike each other.'

Welde had both fists clenched and he had turned his eyes back to the captain. 'Yes, everybody knows that,' he said. 'The two of you don't exactly keep it secret.'

'He's your friend, Konrad. Can I trust you to work with me?'

Welde swivelled around in his seat. He looked ghostly white. 'Lothar, I get on well with Sebastian, that's true. I know he can be difficult sometimes. I see another side to him though. He's a bright guy.'

'He's a bad sort. He's got nothing good to offer the world.'

Welde rubbed his nose. 'You do know about his childhood, don't you? About what he went through? With his parents?'

Lothar looked at Welde blankly. 'I don't know anything about Bahl's childhood.'

'He suffered,' said Welde.

They both went quiet momentarily, before Welde broke the spell. 'As long as I'm working with you, Lothar, I'll give you my full commitment. I guarantee it.'

While they had been talking, the captain had returned to the cockpit and the engine had miraculously started first time. A man sitting in the row behind them gave a small cheer, and Konrad mouthed the words *thank God*. For the first time since he had arrived at the airport, Lothar began to relax. Bahl would be nearly three hundred kilometres away from them in Berlin. Surely not even he could cause trouble from such a distance?

Rising from the board, feeling exhausted, exhilarated and almost delirious all at the same time, Lothar staggered up, handed his score sheet to the arbiter and hauled his body across to the other side of the playing hall, where he collapsed into the arms of the waiting Konrad Welde.

'You did it, Lothar. You beat Vasily Smirov. A world champion. Magnificent play!'

'Thanks, Konrad. A six-hour game. I'm going to need a drink to recover, that's for sure.'

'Of course, Lothar. See you in the hotel bar in half an hour?'

Regaining his balance, Lothar shook his head. 'It's not every day you beat a former World Champion, Konrad.' he said. 'Something special is called for, I feel.'

'What do you have in mind, Lothar?' Welde's voice was croaky and Loather sensed his unease.

'All will be revealed, Konrad.'

Welde stared at his brown shoes. 'As long as we're not going to the red light district.'

'You can trust me, Konnie. I'm a respectable chess player. I just beat a World Champion.' Welde looked reassured. 'Oh, and put your finest outfit on. We're not doing things by halves tonight.'

Welde hesitated again and gritted his teeth. 'OK, Lothar, I'll see what I can do.'

Thirty minutes later, he met Welde at the hotel reception. Welde was in an aqua blue velvet jacket and matching trousers. The jacket looked several sizes too large and the trousers fell well below his ankles.

'Goodness, where did you get that outfit?'

Welde looked at him defensively. 'You said wear something smart.'

'It's certainly striking, I'll grant you. I've never seen you wear it before, though.'

'I borrowed it from reception.' Welde pointed towards a porter standing behind the concierge desk. The man waved back and held his thumbs up.

'What was wrong with your grey suit?'

'I always wear my grey suit. I wanted to dress up. Don't you like it?'

'It's fine, Konrad. The blue goes well with your purple shirt as well.'

'Thanks, Lothar. Where are we headed?'

'Follow me,' he said, leading Konrad out of the hotel and towards the old town. 'I found a little bar in my travels earlier today. It looked interesting.'

The bar he chose may not, in retrospect, have been quite what Konrad was expecting. Leading his compatriot through the cobbled streets of the old town, they arrived at the top of the hill, where they turned down a side road, passing bookshops, bootmakers and a tobacconist. On the other side of the road were terraced cottages, with curtains drawn, winter fires flickering inside. At the end of the street, they reached their destination. The Traveller was the self-proclaimed oldest bar in Prague, dating back to the 1400s, so the buxom barmaid who spoke to him earlier had claimed. 'Ivan the Great once dined here,' she said, 'when he was travelling through Eastern Europe. Would sir like to see the very table where he ate?'

Lothar had not had time to stop earlier but had promised himself he would return. Opening the heavy oak front door, and ushering Konrad in ahead of him, he took a deep breath, savouring the history. Through the door was a single room, no more than seven feet high and ten feet deep, with sloping grey walls and dark beams on the ceilings. At the end of the room two locals sat at a long bar, with steins of beer in front of them.

Welde looked doubtful, lingering at the door, but Lothar pulled him towards the bar where a brunette in a low-cut top – not the cheery girl he had seen earlier – stood idly drying beer glasses with a grey towel. 'What will it be, gentlemen?' said the brunette.

'What do you have?' Lothar asked in broken Russian.

The barmaid looked behind her. 'This is a Czechoslovakian bar. We have beer and we have vodka. What else could one want?'

It was a fair question. He pulled a five-koruna note out of his wallet. 'We'll have a lager each,' he said, 'and a vodka too. We are celebrating.'

The brunette smiled, pulled the cash from his hand, and poured them two glasses of lager, along with a large measure of vodka. '*Na Zdorovie,*' she said.

'*Prost!*' they replied, downing their vodkas in one.

Hearing the German salutation, the nearest of the locals, at a guess sixty years old, with a red beard and wearing a Russian fur hat, gave a shout of appreciation. 'Visitors!' he said, walking over to them, putting his arms around their shoulders. 'What brings you here, my friends?'

'We are Grandmasters,' Lothar explained, 'here for the chess tournament.'

'Ah, Grandmasters! We love chess in Prague.' The man shook their hands enthusiastically. 'I am Alexander,' he said, before turning to the friend at his side. 'Rudi, these are chess players, all the way from East Germany. Come and meet them.'

Rudi seemed even more impressed than his friend. As they sat talking, the two local men took it in turns to buy the Grandmasters vodka, and more vodka, while asking them about their lives as professionals. Of course, Konrad and Lothar couldn't allow these hospitable old men to buy all the drinks, and so for every round of vodka that the locals bought, they matched it with a glass of lager. The East German visitors both enjoyed the attention and, drunk as they were, they were happy to carry on ordering round after round.

Awaking with a start, Lothar looked at his watch through bleary eyes. One in the morning. The temperature had dropped by several degrees and his fingers felt stiff and cold. What was that solid oak feel behind his back? Turning around, he saw the front door of The Traveller. Rubbing his eyes, the truth was apparent.

He had fallen asleep outside the bar. Feeling in his pockets, he found his wallet. He checked inside. There was a solitary five-koruna note left.

To his right, he heard a groan, and then a snore. Welde lay asleep in the middle of the road, his arms stretched out behind him. An empty glass of lager lay at his side.

Rising hesitantly, he stumbled up and grabbed Welde by the shoulder. 'Konrad, wake up!'

Welde spluttered. 'Eh? Where are we?'

'Konrad, we have to go. Now.'

'What's happened?'

'Follow me, Konnie. Come on, let's go.'

A semi-conscious Welde rose and followed him back down to the Old Town. At the main road, Welde came to a halt, rested against a lamp post and, fumbling, took out his wallet. 'How much money do you have left, Lothar?' he asked.

'Five koruna.'

'That's five more than me.'

'We've spent a lot of money this evening.'

'We have. I'm also feeling rather cold.'

He looked at Welde. His compatriot was shivering. 'One question, Konrad.'

'What's that?'

'Where's your blue jacket?'

'Oh, God.' Welde cursed and kicked the side of the kerb.

'You left it inside? We can go back.'

'No way am I going back in that place. Those locals might have looked harmless, but they could drink Rasputin himself under the table.'

Welde looked like he was about to burst into tears. Lothar put his arm around him. 'Come on, Konrad. It will be OK. It's only twenty minutes' walk back from here.'

'We've got no money left, Lothar. How are we going to survive for the rest of the trip?'

'I'll wire the Federation tomorrow for more funds. We can say we were mugged. It's better than saying that we lost a drinking contest with two old men.'

Welde scrunched up his face. 'Tell me, Lothar, one thing. Why do we go on these crazy drinking sessions? You, me, practically every chess master we know. What are we doing to ourselves, to our bodies, never mind to our game?'

Lothar thought of Mikhail Voronin. 'We're not athletes, Konrad, we're artists. Take Fyodor Dostoevsky. Did he worry about how drink affected his writing?'

'*I drink so that I may suffer twice as much!*' said Welde, throwing his hands in the air like an actor.

'What's that?'

'Dostoevsky, *Crime and Punishment*. I read it at school. Always loved that quote.'

Lothar nodded, secretly ashamed that, unlike Welde, he had never read any Dostoevsky. Reflecting on what his friend had said, however, he recognised that he might be on to something.

'Why do we want to suffer, Konrad? What are we trying to escape? The communist system?'

'More than that, I think,' said Welde. 'Probably life itself.'

Lothar wanted to ask more, but his compatriot turned to one side, made an awful gasping noise, and threw up on the side of the road. Welde was right. What on earth were they doing to themselves?

On their return, the East German Federation was due to announce the names of the team for the biennial Olympiad, held in Greece. The squad was limited to five places and competition was fierce. Team members would receive a bonus of five hundred Marks. It was also an opportunity to travel outside Eastern Europe, a rarity even for the strongest players in the country.

As national champion, Lothar assumed that his selection would be automatic. He was also desperate to play. Outside of the World Championship, competing in the Olympiad was just about the greatest honour in chess. He had reckoned, however, without East German politics. He had also underestimated the cunning of Sebastian Bahl. Heading down the steps of the Central Chess Club one evening, after having taken part in a coaching session for promising juniors, he met Udo Grosz coming the other way.

'Comrade, what a surprise! I'm so glad to have met you this evening.' Grosz threw his burly arms around him and hugged him.

'Good evening, Udo. How are you?'

'I'm in need of a stiff drink, my dear friend. Will you join me?'

Lothar wondered how he felt now about Grosz. In so many ways he was a monster: a bully, an intriguer, a cheat, so devious and determined in getting his own way, so careless about those who he had stamped on to get there. The man had a strange charm, though, a boundless enthusiasm for chess, a larger-than-life energy that had helped him and others to achieve successes they could never have dreamed of.

Conflicted, he followed Grosz into the nearest bar, where the President ordered the most expensive bottle of red wine he could find. They took a seat in the corner and Grosz looked at him with a sombre expression. Lothar suspected he had been practising in the mirror. 'You will not like what I'm about to tell you,' said Grosz.

'What's happened?'

'It's that four-eyed scoundrel, Konrad Welde.'

'Welde? He's not that bad, is he?'

'I've never had any time for Welde, Lothar. He criticised me once at an after-dinner party, called me a crooked and incompetent bureaucrat.'

Lothar thought about what Grosz had just said. He imagined that nobody called him a bureaucrat and got away with it.

'What has Welde done this time?' he asked.

'He's made a complaint about your behaviour in Prague. He requested a personal appearance at the committee of the Central Chess Club this morning. He described you as arrogant and patronising and said that he was deeply offended when you asked him to act as your second in future tournaments.'

'Why was he offended?'

'He said that he is a Grandmaster in his own right and shouldn't have to play second fiddle to you. He criticised me, too. Said that I should never have asked him to go to Prague with you.'

Lothar shook his head in bewilderment. 'I thought Welde enjoyed himself in Prague. We had an evening out on the town together. Why did he accept the engagement in the first place if he didn't want to act as a second?'

Udo Grosz gave a deep sigh. 'Welde mentioned the night out in Prague. He said you were a bad influence. He claims you led him astray. He lost a velvet jacket as a result.'

'Ah, yes, the jacket.' He pictured the vivid aqua blue jacket in his mind. 'I think I did Konrad a favour there.'

Grosz had finished his first glass of wine already. He poured himself another and topped up Lothar's. 'This isn't really about Welde. If you'll forgive the analogy, he is just a pawn in a bigger game.'

'What do you mean, Udo?'

'Sebastian Bahl is behind this. He doesn't want to get his own hands dirty, so he set Welde up to do the dirty work for him. A public denunciation, criticise you in front of senior officials when you're not present to defend yourself. It's the classic tactic of the bully. Welde is naïve enough to go along with it.'

Lothar reflected on Grosz' last statement. *The classic tactic of the bully.* He supposed it took one to know one. 'What are Bahl and Welde trying to achieve?' he asked.

'Bahl wants you excluded from the Olympiad. He's set up a petition to have you dropped from the team, and for Welde to take your place.'

'A petition? Who's signed it?'

'Several people, Grandmasters included.'

Lothar drew a deep breath. The duplicity of Bahl and Welde was something else. 'What did the committee decide? Are they going to leave me out of the team?'

Grosz lit a Bison cigar. 'The committee hasn't made up its mind yet, Lothar. There are some who want your blood, and others who support you. The next meeting is on Friday week. I would say the decision is on a knife edge.'

'Udo, I have to play in the Olympiad. I've had my heart set on this since I learned the game. What can I do to persuade the committee?'

Grosz paused. 'As you ask, there is one thing you can do. It would help me too.'

CHAPTER SEVENTEEN

Crime and Punishment

Three days later, Lothar met with Konrad Welde in a bar off the Market Square. Small, thin, frail at the best of times, the bespectacled Welde shook his hand hesitantly, checking his seat carefully as if for a booby trap before sitting down opposite him. 'Good to see you again, Lothar. We had a lot of fun in Prague, didn't we?'

'How could you do it, Konrad?'

Welde jumped back in his seat. 'I'm sorry, Lothar, but I don't know what you're talking about.'

'Don't play the innocent with me, Konrad. I know that you spoke to the committee about me. I know you called me arrogant and you criticised my drinking.'

'Lothar, I can explain.' Welde hesitated and stared at his shoes. 'It wasn't what it seems. It wasn't... personal.'

'What was it then?' Behind him, an elderly man reading a newspaper looked up. Lothar realised he had raised his voice.

'I was doing what was right for the team.'

'For the team? How?'

'I don't believe you're a team player, Lothar.' Welde look embarrassed as he said this, and his face went red.

'What the hell do you mean?'

Welde broke down more quickly than expected.

'I'm... I'm not sure.'

'You're not sure? Come on, Konrad, pull yourself together.'

'Lothar, I'm sorry. I had to tell the committee the truth. What I believe to be the truth.'

'Why didn't you tell me your concerns directly?'

'I... I didn't want to upset you.'

'So how do you think I feel now?' He had raised his voice again. He couldn't help himself, he felt that angry.

'Lothar, I didn't want to say anything. But Bahl had me in a vice.' Welde was shaking now. Lothar suspected he was close to cracking under pressure.

'Bahl? How does Sebastian come into this?'

'He knows about my student days, my time working for an underground group.'

'You were a member of the underground? Seriously?' He tried to picture the bespectacled Welde leading a revolution, dressed in his nondescript grey jacket. He failed and gave up.

'I used to be a radical, Lothar. When I was growing up, I hated the Stasi, the totalitarian regime. I used to dream that one day people would be able to choose the government they wanted.'

Any one of those statements would have been enough to convict Welde. All three together and they would throw the keys away.

'What happened? Why did you change?'

'It's easy to be a dreamer when you're young, Lothar. I read my Dostoevsky, thought that I could be a radical, an idealist, like him. But then real life takes over. Compromises, deals, acceptance of the system. It's the only way to get ahead. I'm sorry again, Lothar, for what happened. You do understand I had no choice?'

Lothar was interested in Konrad Welde's philosophy on the world. Compromises and deals. It was almost an exact match for how he was living his own life. Was that what the system was forcing them into? He thought again about what Udo Grosz had made him do to Hans. He also thought about Anna, and what she would want. His parents too, God rest their souls. He reflected further. Konrad wasn't a bad man. If anything, he was a victim.

Coming to a decision, Lothar offered his hand. 'OK, Konrad, I understand. I appreciate you had no choice. I'm sure we can sort things out.'

For the first time since they had sat down, Welde smiled. 'Thank you, Lothar. You're a good friend. I'm sorry again about what happened.'

Standing up, Lothar picked up his jacket from the chair. 'Stay well, Konrad. Don't give up on the dreams either.'

On the way home, remembering the conversation he had with Welde on that drunken night in Prague, he stopped at a bookshop and bought a second-hand copy of *Crime and Punishment*. Gambling addict and drunkard. Dostoevsky sounded like his kind of author.

The next day he met with Udo Grosz in his office. Grosz looked at him expectantly. 'Well, how did you get on with our friend?'

'I'm sorry, Udo. It didn't happen.'

Grosz turned a shade of red. 'What do you mean, it didn't happen? You told me yourself that you were meeting Welde for a drink. Did he cancel the meeting?'

'No, the meeting went ahead. But he didn't say anything.'

'He didn't say *anything*? Not a single thing we can use against him?'

'Sorry, Udo. Nothing. He was full of praise for you. For the government too. He's very loyal.'

Grosz put out his cigar and stared at him. 'Really?'

'Really, Udo. I'm sorry. What happens now?'

Grosz screwed up a piece of paper and threw it at the bin behind his desk, missing by a foot. 'I guess we will have to see what the others say, won't we?'

'The others?'

'Sorry to disappoint you, Lothar, but you're not the only person I asked to help on this one. Just as well, given that you've drawn a complete blank. Now, on your way, I've got phone calls to make.'

When the East German Federation announced the Olympiad team, to Sebastian Bahl's disappointment, Lothar's was the fourth name on the list, behind Jensen, Müller and Vogel. Bahl himself took the final place. What Bahl didn't realise was how much ill-will he had created in Lothar. Bahl had tried to sabotage his place in the national team and Lothar was determined to get his revenge on him, even if he didn't yet know how.

As for Konrad Welde, called to a special meeting of the East German Federation, he was suspended from all chess indefinitely. The Federation did not say in public what the charges were or why he had been banned. But a promising career had been curtailed because he had upset the wrong person at the wrong time.

Sometimes a disunited and disharmonious team can play well. The East German Olympiad team which travelled to Greece did not enjoy such good fortune.

Things went badly almost from the off. Lazlo Vogel was delayed at the airport when he was unable to produce the correct papers. His teammates expected him to follow them to Greece on the next flight, but after a further delay, Vogel telegrammed three days later to tell them that he would have to withdraw. Lothar found out afterwards that Vogel had a cousin who lived in Greece, and the authorities feared he would defect while over there.

Down to a squad of four players before the first round, they experienced further bad luck when Jensen, the grand old man of East German chess and their first board, suffered a severe allergic reaction to the rich local food. While he was confined to his room for most of the first week, emerging only to play his games, the rest of the team had to battle with their leader only on half power.

An opening round victory against Chile – its right-wing regime hated in their country – gave some hope that they might be able to function as a team. They even managed a celebratory dinner together that evening, animosities temporarily forgotten. In the second round, the Hungarians soundly beat them, and in the third round they lost to the Netherlands. None of them played well, but Sebastian Bahl had the best result so far, with a win and two draws. Lothar had lost two games from three, over-pressing both times when he realised the team was in trouble. That evening at dinner, Bahl took his opportunity to taunt him.

'What was that nonsense you played today, Lothar?' he asked, a sly smile on his lips.

'Excuse me, Sebastian?'

'That opening? Sacrificing a pawn for no compensation. What were you doing?'

'He defended well. Otherwise my attack would have crashed through.'

'Do you seriously think that?' Bahl shook his head dismissively and pushed his soup to one side. 'I don't know what's worse: your game today, or this broth.'

Lothar could feel the anger rising inside him. 'You don't know what you're talking about, Sebastian.'

'Says the man who just lost horribly, again.'

This was too much for Lothar. He rarely lost his temper, but when he did, he knew himself that he tended to lose all control. 'You'd better start showing some respect, Bahl.'

'Or what?'

'There will be trouble.' Lothar raised his fist threateningly.

Bahl looked over plaintively to their team manager, Neuer. The same Wolfgang Neuer whom Rainer Müller and he had bumped into in a nightclub in Amsterdam. 'Wolfgang, did you hear that? Lothar is threatening me.'

Neuer raised his finger in admonishment, but before he could say a word, Lothar stood up and shoved his plate to one side. 'I've had it with you guys. I might keep playing, but I'm not part of this team any more.' Stunned into silence, Neuer still had his finger in the air. 'Oh, one other thing. If you think, Wolfgang, that you're going to take any action against me, then I have two words for you. *Bar Red.*'

Rainer Müller followed Lothar as he stormed out of the hotel. A mellow man, Müller did his best to calm him, but it was to no avail. Lothar spent the rest of the evening fuming in the taverna opposite the hotel.

The next day, Udo Grosz phoned him. Under strict instructions, Lothar apologised to Bahl and Neuer, they shook hands and, on the surface, resumed normal relations. Inside, however, he was still seething. Ironically, in his anger Lothar found his form, winning game after game. After nine rounds, he was the team's top scorer with six wins. Meanwhile, his teammates had all struggled, every single one of them having lost more games than they won. By the time Jensen was back to full fitness, they were already out of contention for the medals.

With one round to go, heading for their worst result for over twenty years, they were paired against, of all teams, their neighbours, and long-standing enemies, West Germany. As Neuer explained to them in a heated meeting before the start, this was their shot at redemption. Win and all would be forgiven. Lose, and there would be little point in going home.

Never before had he played in such a tense match. Evenly balanced on paper, the West Germans were desperate for victory as much as they were, and they fought every game to the bitter end. When, several hours in, most other teams had already finished and found a spot at the bar, all four of their games were still in full flow. To his left, Jensen sat with head in hands, his shirt bathed in sweat as he tried to extract the most from a small advantage. To his right, Müller fidgeted, tapped his toes, strummed his fingers on the table, did anything he could to get his thought process flowing. Even Sebastian Bahl, normally so disinterested in the fortunes of his teammates, kept jumping up from his seat to look in turn at the three other boards.

In the final hour, Jensen launched a mating attack and they scored their first victory. Their joy was short-lived, however, when Müller blundered and lost. When Bahl was forced to agree a draw by perpetual check, the match was tied at one win each, leaving the fate entirely on Lothar's shoulders. Playing with the black pieces against the up-and-coming student Eric Laufman, he struggled on until the ninetieth move, trying to make something of a minuscule edge. When only the two Kings were left on the board, the two players finally shook hands and agreed a draw before adjourning to the bar. Whatever the quarrels between their nations, Lothar's argument was not with Laufman, and he had no reason to be hostile to him.

The next morning, he awoke late. One drink with Laufman had turned into six. His head was throbbing, his throat dry. Pushed under the door, he found a telegram from Udo Grosz, summoning him to his office on his return home. In light of his arguments with Bahl and Neuer, he assumed there was real trouble to come. In genuine fear as to what might happen to him on his return to East Germany, he wondered if he could ask for political exile where he was in Greece. The climate was too warm for his liking, though, and more importantly he could not leave Anna stuck in Berlin. There was no choice but to return home. On the flight back, pleasantries no longer required, Sebastian Bahl ignored him completely. Surprisingly, Neuer made an effort to be friendly, perhaps fearing that he would tell the tale of his Amsterdam exploits.

On landing at the airport, Grosz had a car waiting, and a chauffeur took him straight to the Central Chess Club, where the President sat in his office, stony-faced. It was not what he had expected.

'I'm afraid I have bad news, Comrade.'

'Bad news? What about?'

'It's Hans Adler.'

A shock jolted through his body. 'What about Hans?'

'He's defected to the West.'

Lothar could breathe again. 'I thought he was still in prison?'

'We released him on bail last week. Adler has an uncle who lives in West Germany. The uncle smuggled him out through the border, in the boot of his car.'

'What about Freya and the kids?'

'They escaped too.'

'How?'

Grosz turned away from him. 'We have no idea,' he whispered so softly that Lothar could hardly hear him.

'So what happens now? Do we write Adler out of history, forget he existed?'

'I'm afraid not,' replied Grosz. 'In fact, one might say it's the opposite strategy.'

Grosz handed him a copy of that morning's newspaper. 'Top Grandmaster slams former coach' ran the headline. Lothar read the article with increasing unease. 'Current East German champion Lothar Hartmann has denounced his former coach, the defector Hans Adler. Twenty-four-year-old Hartmann said last night that: *"Adler is a drunkard, a capitalist, and an enemy of the state. He has made a living by exploiting other people's talents. With no discernible ability of his own, he is a parasite and a curse to our society. We are better off without him."*

'But I didn't say any of this. I would never speak about Hans in that way. I'm going to issue a refutation immediately.'

'I think you've forgotten something, Lothar.'

'Forgotten what?'

Grosz pulled a yellow envelope out of his briefcase. 'Remember this? Your denunciation of Hans Adler. I'm sorry, Lothar, I hate doing this to you. But you'll back up the story in the newspaper.'

'Or?'

'Or we release your signed statement against Adler. Do what we say, or you're finished in East German chess.'

Something in Grosz' expression – smug, self-satisfied, so sure of his own superiority – made Lothar feel ill. The betrayer of his coach and friend, he had himself now been betrayed.

'Udo, this isn't on. I thought I was going to be in trouble for the Olympiad. For arguing with Neuer and Bahl, for not beating the West Germans, for going to the bar afterwards with Eric Laufman. I would have understood you disciplining me for that. But I can't see any justification for the way you're behaving now.'

Grosz put down his cigar. 'Lothar, believe me, there are plenty of people who want you disciplined after Greece. You need to realise you are getting away lightly. Do you know why I'm not going to take any action for what happened at the Olympiad?'

Lothar shook his head.

'Because you were our top scorer in Greece. While you keep winning, nobody can touch you. Better make sure you don't lose though. When that happens, my friend, I won't be able to protect you any longer. You'll be left out for the wolves.'

That evening Lothar returned home to find Anna packing. The offending newspaper article lay on the dining room table.

'Anna, please, I can explain.'

'Don't come near me, Lothar. I don't want to hear it. How could you speak about Hans like that, after all he's done for you?'

'Anna... it's not what it seems.'

Anna raised her head and looked directly at him. Her eyes were red and she had been crying. A single wisp of hair had fallen across her forehead and he wanted to brush it away, just like the troubles in their relationship.

'Lothar, nothing in this country is ever what it seems. We both know that. I'm sorry, I can't live any more with someone who is complicit in the lies.'

'Anna, I can explain.' He followed her into their bedroom, where his girlfriend had grabbed her case and begun to shove clothes, books and toiletries into it. 'It wasn't me. Those weren't my words.'

Ignoring him, Anna carried on packing, throwing her things into her case before heaving her bag into the hall. At the door, she turned round. 'I'm sorry, but it's always someone else's fault, isn't it? It's over, Lothar. We're finished.'

Desolate, he stood at the window and watched as Anna strode down the road, case in hand. He thought that she might look back, at least acknowledge him, but there was nothing, not even a glance. He remained at the window until she was just a speck in the distance, and he could see her no more. Returning to the kitchen he sat for the rest of the evening with his head in his hands. What had he done? Why had he been so foolish?

So began life on his own.

PART THREE – THE ENDGAME

CHAPTER EIGHTEEN

Notes from the Underground

*Chess, like love, like music,
has the power to make men happy.*
Siegbert Tarrasch

The weeks passed. Since moving out, Anna had been staying with a friend in a district two kilometres out of Berlin. Every couple of days, Lothar sent her a letter, sometimes even including a small poem, but she did not respond. Breaking up was a new experience for him, and he had good days and bad. At his best, he was able to acknowledge what had happened, ready to move on. On other days he felt depressed and low, uncertain of how he had reached this position or what he was going to do next. The black moods were difficult to take and there were several days when he didn't leave the house.

One autumn morning, on his way to the Central Chess Club, he spotted a familiar figure coming the other way. There she was, dressed in jeans and a short-sleeved white blouse. She had cut her hair and was carrying a handful of books, as well as a rucksack.

Anna smiled and there was an explosion in his heart. 'Lothar, what a surprise. How are you?'

'I'm fine thanks, Anna. I didn't expect to run into you.'

'I'm on my way to the university. Did you know I've started a PhD?' Anna shifted her glasses and peered at him. 'You look well.'

'Thanks. I heard about the Doctorate. Max told me that you're studying Russian literature.'

'Yes, Bulgakov. *Heart of a Dog, Master and Margarita.* I've always loved gloomy, angst-ridden writers.'

'Bulgakov? Do they allow you to study him? I thought he was on a banned list.'

'It's OK to study Bulgakov as long as I don't admit to liking him. You should read some. How is the chess?'

'I qualified for the last eight of the World Championships.' How proud he felt when he said that. He wondered how she would react.

'Yes, I heard. That's amazing.' Anna ran her left index finger along her lip. 'I always knew you'd be great. You can do anything when you put your mind to it.'

'Thanks, Anna. That means a lot to me.' He paused and composed himself. 'I'm sorry about what happened. I'd like to try again. What do you say?'

Anna looked at him sadly, her doe eyes mirrors into his soul. 'Lothar... What we had together was special. I won't ever forget you. But our time has come and gone.'

'Anna...'

Too late. Picking up her rucksack, she had already begun to walk away. 'I have to meet someone at twelve. It's been lovely to see you. Take care.'

With that, she was gone. Anna, the beat his heart missed.

The World Chess Championship is a unique test in that it can take up to three years from the first qualifying contest through to the final itself. It is a marathon which rewards not just great talent and ability, but energy and perseverance too. When Misha Voronin won the title in the early 1960s, he had to play no fewer than seventy-two competitive games to do so. Lothar was now through to the knockout stage, which gave him a fighting chance. But if he was honest with himself, he knew that the hard work was only just beginning.

When the organisers made the draw for the quarter-finals, he avoided both Boris Korneev, the Soviet Union's new star, and Viktor Gavrilov, the runner-up in the last two championships. His opponent in the last eight, the Dutchman Loek De Jong, was a strong competitor nevertheless, arguably the best player to come from the West since the war, the great Bobby Fischer excepted. De Jong had also of course been the only man to beat Lothar back in Budapest, when he had gained his Grandmaster title in such dubious circumstances.

Now forty-eight years old, De Jong said that this would be his last attempt at the World Championship. Lothar wasn't sure whether to believe such talk. De Jong was nothing if not unorthodox, in his approach both to chess and to life. An educated, articulate man, he was well read, a quality that is unusual amongst master-level players, and he had active political leanings. Determined and aggressive, he gave few early draws, and had won many high-quality tournaments.

The two of them were due to play their ten-game match in the autumn. Several countries put in bids to host the contest, including Russia, Hungary and Holland. De Jong was adamant that he would not travel to the Eastern bloc, and Lothar did not want to play on De Jong's home turf. That left Mallorca in Spain as the only choice. The prize fund was ten thousand dollars, with sixty per cent going to the winner. In practice, he did not expect to see much of the prize money – win or lose, the East German authorities would take a generous slice before anything reached him – but he was focused on a bigger objective than cash. This was his opportunity to achieve greatness. Grandmasters come and go, but World Champions are permanent. In the back of his mind, it was also a chance to impress Anna. If she saw him at the top of the chess world, then surely she would understand him better, maybe even get back with him.

In early November, he flew out from Berlin to Palma, Mallorca. Ernst Reisen, a trusted ally, had agreed to act as his second. They were joined by no fewer than four other officials. Neuer was there, to keep a watchful eye over him, as were three bodyguards. He was mystified by the level of security, until Reisen told him the authorities were fearful he would use the trip to Palma as an opportunity to defect to the West.

The match began badly, De Jong winning the first game. In the second game, the Dutchman again had him on the ropes, ready to deliver a knockout punch, but he somehow survived to hold on to a draw. The third was little better. He was lucky not to lose that too, and the press said that he was dead and buried.

Depressed with his poor form, Lothar took a time out before the fourth game. Walking down to the harbour with Reisen, they stood and gazed at the yachts and fishing boats. The largest of the yachts were twice the size of his flat. He imagined what it might be like to live on the water, a seafarer. Reisen must have been thinking the same thing. 'Get on board one of those and we need never go back,' said his friend.

Lothar looked over his shoulder. Two of the bodyguards were some twenty metres behind them. In their shades and summer shorts, they looked for all the world like holiday tourists. How different the truth was. 'Those guards would think nothing of jumping in to stop us,' he said. 'Besides which, even if we did get away, the Stasi would have us shot.'

'Seriously? They've not shot Gavrilov.'

'We're not as famous as he is. Celebrity gives you protection.'

'You really think they'd shoot us?' asked Reisen.

Lothar paused and reflected. A large yacht was sailing out to sea, and the passengers aboard were waving back to land. They looked happy. 'No, you're right,' he replied. 'They wouldn't shoot us. They'd most probably poison us in the back with an umbrella. The question is this. How does one get to be as famous as Gavrilov?'

'You need to start by beating De Jong,' said Reisen. 'You want to hear my ideas?'

The following day, on the advice of Reisen, Lothar changed style, adopting a more cautious approach. With his new safety-first strategy, he drew both the fourth and fifth games quickly. De Jong seemed bemused by his rope-a-dope tactics, and in the sixth it was the Dutchman's turn to over-press. Refuting the sacrifice of a piece, Lothar levelled the scores.

When Lothar won the seventh game, the press declared him the certain winner. Once more, they were premature in their forecasts. He blundered badly in the ninth, and with one to play De Jong made it two wins each. It was now anyone's match. In a nervous session the evening before the final round, Lothar and Reisen considered a number of different tactics, eventually deciding to make the game as complex as possible from the off. Reisen felt that, as the younger man, Lothar would cope with the tension better than De Jong.

The following day, over four hundred spectators crowded into the auditorium to watch the final game, a place in the World Championship semi-finals at stake. Arriving at the board early, in his best suit and tie, with his shoes newly polished, he tried his hardest to look calm and collected. His hands were shaking though, and as he went to play his first move, he fumbled and knocked over two of his own pieces. De Jong smiled benevolently and paused while he reset the board. Someone of the Dutchman's experience wasn't going to be put off either by the occasion or by his nerves.

On the tenth move, Lothar played an unusual thrust of his King's Knight pawn. He had prepared this move at home with Reisen before the game, but it was a new idea to De Jong. The Dutchman looked at him suspiciously, before staring at the bold black pawn. After a little thought, he rubbed his hands together purposefully, and took the pawn. An audible chatter broke out amongst the audience, and Lothar felt his heart pound. He had already stumbled once in the game, on the first move. Now was the time to stay calm, and to begin his own advance on the other side of the board.

The battle was now set, with each player thinking only of checkmate. On the thirtieth move, Lothar played a clever Rook retreat, which appeared to parry all De Jong's threats. In the audience, he saw Reisen clench his fist. Surely victory was now in his grasp?

In a match full of twists and turns, the surprises had not yet ended. Just two moves later, Lothar overlooked a tactic, giving De Jong a chance to relaunch his attack with a Knight sacrifice. The Dutchman played the move quickly and confidently, and it was now anybody's game again. On the fortieth move, they adjourned for dinner with the position, and the fate of the match, completely unclear.

Lothar left the board feeling despondent. Victory had been in his grasp and he had blown it. Reisen saw things differently, though. The game was still there for the taking, as long as Lothar kept his composure. He also had youth on his side, which was surely an advantage in such an energy-sapping contest.

When they resumed, Lothar noticed that De Jong's palms were sweaty. For the first time in the match, the veteran seemed to have lost his confident air. When, on the forty-fifth move, he attacked one of De Jong's pawns, the Dutchman surprised him by leaving it undefended. As he captured the pawn with his Knight, his opponent shook his head. He had missed the obvious riposte, and now Lothar was firmly in the ascendancy. Just three moves later, he won another pawn and his opponent had to resign. Lothar had won the match and was now through to the last four of the World Championships. The audience applauded thunderously, and the two players stood and bowed, actors on the stage at the end of an epic performance, taking their acclaim.

A dignified man, De Jong accepted his defeat with grace, joining Lothar and Reisen for dinner the following evening, and never once showing the crushing disappointment he must have felt. It was only when Lothar received a telegram from Erich Honecker that he realised the magnitude of what he had achieved. He was now just one match away from a contest against the world's best player, Boris Korneev.

During the match, Lothar had focused only on the chess, and had forgotten about his troubles at home. Returning to an empty flat, bereft of Anna's books, her paintings, her flowers, most importantly of Anna herself, he felt again the pain of being on his own. Only the yucca plant, which still stood proudly on the bookcase, remained. Its solitary presence made him feel Anna's absence more. Over the following days, amongst the many telegrams and cards which arrived to congratulate him, he hoped each time for word from his ex-girlfriend, but nothing came. Sitting alone in the empty living room, starting bleakly at the wall, he thought about visiting her, but had no idea what he would say. In reaching the last four of the World Championships, he had achieved something that no other East German had ever managed. Success had brought him fame, and some money, but it had not brought him happiness.

At Christmas, Lothar planned to play in the annual Hastings Congress in England, a prestigious event that dated back to 1895. Unfortunately, the East German authorities rejected his exit visa application, and he was unable to travel. Bumping into Thomas Jensen at the Berlin Chess Club, his teammate told him that Hans Adler, after a nomadic few months, had settled on a life in England, where he had become the coach to the English junior team. The Federation must have feared that his application to play in Hastings was a plot to follow Hans and defect to England.

Had he made an effort, he could easily have found an alternative tournament in East Germany, or even Hungary or Czechoslovakia. He was listless though, and spent Christmas on his own, drinking beer and reading *Crime and Punishment*. When he finished that, he turned to *Notes from The Underground* and *The Gambler*. He knew that he should be spending more time preparing for the next round of the World Championships, but with his crash course in great literature, he began to realise what he had been missing.

On New Year's Eve, Max and his new girlfriend Katrin invited Lothar to a party at their flat. He made an effort to look smart, shaving for the first time in a week, getting his hair cut and putting on a new shirt. It was five years ago to the day that he had first met Anna. A lot had happened in that time, some good, but much that he wanted to forget. Time to start mixing again.

Clutching a bottle of wine in his hand, he rang the doorbell shortly before seven. Taking his coat and leading him through to the lounge, Max took the bottle from him, while Katrin kissed him on the cheek and handed him a glass of white wine from the table in the corner.

'Lothar, how are you? So good to see you again!' Katrin introduced him to a group of other guests. 'Have you met Phillip before? This is Alicia and her husband Walter. Oh, and of course you know Anna.'

Lothar smiled. Inside his heart was pounding and it felt like an electric shock had just gone through his body. Anna looked a little pale, but otherwise she was unchanged. She had on the blue dress that she had worn to Hans' birthday party, all that time ago. He kissed her on the cheek, the other guests already forgotten.

'How are you?' he asked.

She bit her lip. 'I'm doing well, thanks, Lothar. I'm still making progress with the dissertation. I saw you won your match as well. That's fantastic!' As she spoke, a serious looking man with round-rimmed glasses and long black hair walked across to them and took her hand. 'Ah, here he is,' continued Anna. 'Lothar, I'd like you to meet Dominik Habeck. Dominik, this is Lothar Hartmann, the chess champion.'

Lothar shook Habeck's hand warmly but inside his chest was about to explode. The blood rushed to his head and his vision became blurred. He had no idea what he said next. Perhaps it made sense, perhaps it didn't. All he knew was that his world felt like it was about to collapse. Anna had met someone else. There was no turning back now. Their relationship was over, and that was final.

Shortly afterwards Anna and Habeck left the party to meet other friends, and he found himself standing alone in the corner of the living room, staring into an empty glass of wine. Periodically someone would refill his glass. Sometimes people even tried to talk to him, but they got no response.

Towards the end of the evening, Max pulled him into the kitchen, ushering him to take a seat and pouring them each a glass of vodka.

'I'm sorry, Lothar. I didn't want it to happen this way. Anna had told me she couldn't come tonight. She only changed her mind at the last minute.'

Lothar tried his best to look stoic. 'I guess I had to find out sometime, Max. Who is he, anyway, this Habeck? What do you know about him?'

Max drew a sharp breath. 'He's a political radical, a critic of the government.'

'Oh.' He had had too many drinks to make much sense of anything, but that didn't sound good. 'Not exactly a steady profession,' was all he could manage.

Max gave a bitter smile. 'Precisely. It's probably only a matter of time before Habeck gets himself arrested,' he said. 'Which means danger for Anna too. I would ask for your help, but there's no talking to my sister right now. You know how stubborn she can be.'

Lothar walked home in a haze. In pursuit of his ambitions at chess, goals that had driven his every action, his every move, he had lost his friendship with Hans, and now he had lost Anna too. What's more, he had put his former girlfriend in danger. No matter how much alcohol he had downed, he went to bed feeling as sober as he ever had on New Year's Eve.

CHAPTER NINETEEN

Carpe Diem

In the draw for the semi-finals of the World Championships, Lothar was paired with the grand old man of chess, and famous political émigré, Viktor Gavrilov. Having competed at the top level for over thirty years, Gavrilov had the look of someone who had lived a full and exhausting life. Yellow smoker's teeth, wrinkled and pockmarked skin, thinning hair, red of complexion, he appeared closer to seventy than his actual fifty-five years. He was not to be underestimated, though. He had contested the last two Championship finals and was still a considerable force to be reckoned with, even now.

While privately Lothar admired his opponent, respecting both his magnificent chess and his fighting character, he was conscious that the authorities in Eastern Europe hated Gavrilov. Born in Leningrad, Gavrilov had always been a maverick, resistant to authority, unwilling and unable to take orders. After a series of scrapes and arguments with the Soviet Chess Federation, while taking part in a tournament in Amsterdam Gavrilov sought political asylum. He became one of the most famous defectors from the Soviet Union of the 1970s, taking up residency eventually in Switzerland. It was Gavrilov of course who had tried to persuade Hans Adler to become his coach.

The match was fixed for May. Finding somewhere to play had been problematic. Gavrilov would not travel to the Eastern bloc, fearful for his life, and the authorities would not allow Lothar to accept many venues in the West. Eventually, after prolonged discussion, they settled on Madrid. Gavrilov requested to play under the Swiss flag, but Neuer, who was leading the negotiations on the East German side, refused. At Lothar's suggestion, the two players resolved the issue by agreeing to play with no national flags. Neuer was unhappy with this, but there was little he could do about it, at least for the moment.

Gavrilov was a legend, and Lothar appreciated that the match would be tough. He was, however, nearly thirty years his opponent's junior. With fourteen games to play, he resolved on a strategy to wear him down through attrition. Landing in Madrid a week early, his party, which included Reisen, Martins and a rotating crew of security guards, settled into their villa on the outskirts of Madrid and began their preparations. Given his plan for the match, Lothar spent more time than usual on physical fitness, including swimming, tennis and weight training, as well as acclimatising to the intense Spanish heat. Three days before the match started, Neuer joined them. The security guards had not allowed Lothar to leave the villa, but after much pleading Neuer did at least relent on that, provided that the guards accompanied him at all times.

Arriving for the first game at the Royal Theatre, a venue more accustomed to opera than sporting events, Lothar felt a sense of history. The setting was the grandest he had ever seen, with marble archways, gold-leafed pillars and no fewer than twelve hundred seats for spectators, most of which had already been sold. His team had their own box, way above the stage, and followed the contest through opera glasses. As he sat down at the board, he thought of the great artists who bestrode the stage before him: Maria Callas, Placido Domingo, Luciano Pavarotti. Now he would be facing a great artist of the board, Viktor Gavrilov. His personal problems put to one side, he felt inspired and ready to play his best-ever chess.

The strategy to wear his older opponent down did not immediately work as planned. In the very first game, Gavrilov turned down an early draw offer, fighting until move ninety, when they only had their two Kings left. At the end of the game, it was Lothar who could barely move, exhausted by the energy-sapping contest. Gavrilov meanwhile bounded through the audience, signing autographs and smiling as fans took photos with him. In the second game, it was Gavrilov who did the pressing again. Once more, Lothar was lucky to survive. After two further draws, Gavrilov outplayed him, beating him soundly in the fifth game. When he replayed the moves afterwards with Reisen and Martins, they concluded that he had played well. It was simply that his opponent had proved stronger. Never mind. There were nine games still to go, and tireless as Gavrilov had been so far, he could not believe that the older man could continue at this pace. He needed to be ready to take his chance when the time came.

In game eight, Lothar tried a new opening, the Sicilian Dragon, where Black creates a fight from the earliest possible stage. It was almost impossible, but again the veteran showed far more energy than him. Missing one chance, he fell into a worse position and lost again. That evening he was inconsolable, sitting in his room on his own, staring into space, drained of energy, unwilling or unable to say a word to his friends. He was playing well, but Gavrilov was simply too good.

In game nine, for the first time in the match, Lothar gained the advantage in the opening. He had Gavrilov sweating, but at a critical point he missed a spectacular sacrifice of his Queen, which would have won the game instantly. Worse, the move he played allowed Gavrilov to launch an attack, which he conducted in exemplary fashion. At three games down, the match appeared to be over.

In the final week, the most extraordinary thing happened. Mentally, Lothar had given up on the match. To defeat Gavrilov, whom he had never beaten a single time in his life, three times in one week was nigh-on impossible. Reconciling himself to his fate, he began to relax, and suddenly found some form. He won the eleventh game, when Gavrilov blundered while under pressure, and very nearly won the twelfth as well. Gavrilov was renowned as a superstitious player, and for the thirteenth game he arrived looking distinctly uncomfortable, refusing for the first time to allow the crowd to take photos with him before the game. Lothar won with a crushing attack and suddenly he was only one game behind.

Pleading a summer cold, Gavrilov claimed a medical time out, and Lothar, Reisen and Martins enjoyed a break of two days while they plotted for the final game. He had the white pieces and needed to win to take the match into a tiebreak. After much discussion, they settled on that most romantic of openings, favourite of the great players of the nineteenth century, the King's Gambit. In a daring strategy, White offers a pawn on the second move of the game. In return, he is able to develop rapidly and to threaten Black's King. He needed a decisive result and the King's Gambit appeared to be just the opening.

After twenty moves, it seemed that their plan was working to perfection. Gavrilov took the first pawn, and then, gritting his teeth, grabbed a second pawn as well. When Lothar offered a Bishop sacrifice, Gavrilov took that too, but Lothar now had a huge attack on the black King. As he pondered how to continue the attack, Lothar could see Gavrilov shaking. Was it his imagination, or had his opponent aged five years over the past week? If the two of them had been in a boxing ring, then connecting with one more punch would surely finish the older man off.

Somehow Gavrilov managed to avoid mate, but he was forced to sacrifice a Rook, and Lothar was now ahead one again. On the thirtieth move, Gavrilov sacrificed a Knight as well, shrugging despondently as he did so. Assuming that this was a desperate measure, and that he was about to resign, Lothar took the piece quickly. Almost jumping off his chair, Gavrilov brought his Queen crashing down towards Lothar's King. Check! Only now did he realise. He could not capture Gavrilov's Queen, nor could he evade the checks. So close to a victory, he had allowed his opponent to give a perpetual check, and the game was drawn. Lothar was out, defeated by three wins to two by one of the titans of chess.

After such a heart-breaking defeat, Lothar would have liked to head straight back to East Berlin if he could. In the past two weeks, he must have spent sixty hours sitting opposite Gavrilov at the board. In addition to that, he had clocked up countless hours of analysis back at the villa with Reisen and Martins. He was tired and upset at the opportunities he had missed. They had not booked their flights until the following day, though, and they still needed to attend the closing ceremony. Thinking of the sponsors, and the many people who had worked tirelessly to arrange the match, he put on his best suit and geared himself up for one further public showing before returning home.

As Lothar, Martins and Reisen drew up outside the Royal Theatre in their hired grey Volkswagen, a Stasi man in the driver's seat, they saw a limo pull in just ahead of them. A security guard jumped out of the front, followed by a broad-shouldered Asian man with grey hair and a designer suit, another two security guards, and a tall, angular man carrying a leather briefcase. Stepping out of the Volkswagen, Lothar saw that the grey-haired gentleman was Felix Kim, President of the World Chess Federation. He didn't recognise the tall man with the briefcase.

'They look like the Mafia,' said Martins. 'Be careful if they try to offer you a deal, Lothar.'

They followed Kim and his entourage into the building. Their own bodyguards trailed at a respectful twenty metres behind them, alongside Neuer and a couple of the Stasi men. Ahead, he saw Gavrilov, supported by his wife, ambling towards the main hall. In contrast to their party, he couldn't see that Gavrilov had either security or an entourage anywhere in sight.

At the closing ceremony, Lothar sat next to Gavrilov's second, and one of his old adversaries, the British Grandmaster Jon Forester. A dry man with a wry sense of humour, Forester told him he suspected that Kim was in the pay of the Soviet government. 'The poor fellow will be feeling bad about this match,' said Forester.

Lothar looked at the Englishman blankly.

'He's desperate to please the Soviets, his paymasters. If the old boy could have found a way to disadvantage Gavrilov, the defector, he would have done so.'

As a Grandmaster, Lothar was used to cunning ploys and intrigues, but even he was surprised by this. Such machinations at the top of world chess hadn't occurred to him.

Forester leaned closer towards him and whispered. 'I hope you don't think I'm talking out of turn. I was wondering how you feel about Gavrilov?'

'I think he's a great player.'

Forester stroked his chin. 'We both know that. What I mean is this. Is he a hero or a villain? Given what he's done, defecting from the East, we expected you to hate the man. But we watched you talk at the end of the match. You seem to get on well.'

Lothar looked around nervously to see where Neuer was sitting. He saw his bald pate three rows behind, out of earshot.

'I have respect for Gavrilov, the player and the man,' he said to Forester.

Forester patted him on the forearm. 'I understand, old chap. Perhaps we can talk about it more later. Look, Kim's about to start his speech.'

They turned towards the stage, and Lothar puzzled over what Forester had just said, as well as what he might have to say later.

After the prize giving, the two teams, their entourages and the organising committee dined in a banqueting hall at the back of the theatre. Surrounded by Neuer and the Stasi men, the conversation on their table was restrained. Even Martins seemed subdued. By ten, coffee had been served, Neuer had checked his watch several times, and Lothar suspected he would give the instruction to leave shortly. Just when he feared there would be no opportunity to talk to Forester again, the Englishman appeared at their table, accompanied by Felix Kim. 'Mr President, sir, allow me to introduce you to Lothar Hartmann.'

The President shook his hand warmly. 'My commiserations, Lothar. You played a very fine match. Keep working, and your time will come.'

Lothar thanked the President. Before he could say more, Forester had already guided Kim around the table to Neuer, where the two men hugged, old friends.

'Wolfgang,' said the President. 'It's been too long! How are you?'

While Neuer and Kim talked, Forester returned to his side of the table. 'Lothar, there's someone I'd like you to meet. Come this way.'

Lothar stood up from the table, leaving Martins and Reisen with the Stasi men. 'I won't be long,' he said, following Forester to the other end of the banqueting hall.

Squeezing past the table where Kim had been sitting, Forester guided him through a side passage at the back of the hall, at the end of which was a door which led them out onto the street. Emerging into the open air, he saw the tall, angular man he had spotted earlier with Kim, leaning on a railing, smoking a cigarette.

The man extended a hand. 'David Laws, President of the British Chess Federation. Delighted to meet you.'

He shook David Laws' hand. 'I saw you with Kim earlier.'

Laws clenched his teeth. 'An accusation I can't deny, I'm afraid. The man is as unscrupulous as they come. But he's President of the World Chess Federation, so we can hardly ignore him.'

Laws stamped out his cigarette on the ground and tutted. 'Disgusting habit. I'm sorry. Do you smoke?' Lothar nodded. 'I guess we are OK then,' said Laws, pulling a packet out of his top pocket, lighting cigarettes for them both. Another chain smoker, Lothar thought to himself. The chess world was full of them. A few yards behind, Forester appeared to be standing guard at the door.

'We don't have much time, so I'll come to the point,' said Laws. 'Our people tell us you may not be entirely happy in the East. We wondered if you might be interested in, shall we say, a change of scenery?'

Lothar's heart missed a beat. Did this mean what he thought it did? He tried to remain calm. 'What do you have in mind, Mr Laws?'

Laws turned his head and looked behind him. The street was empty. A solitary car stood on the other side of the road. 'We offer a new life, Lothar. A fresh start. We'll set you up in England, find you a house, a place in the national team.' Another car came slowly past and Laws turned around again and took a deep breath. The car continued on. 'We'll provide you with security too, at least until the Cold War is over.'

'What about my friends?'

'You mean your second, Reisen, and that other fellow with holes in his shoes?'

'Reisen and Martins, yes. Can you get them out too?'

Laws pulled a long face. 'Not straight away, Lothar. Maybe in the future.'

Lothar nodded. 'I'd need to talk to them first. I can't just leave.'

Laws shook his head. 'I'm afraid, Lothar, we don't have that sort of time.' He gestured to the other side of the road and pointed to the silver Mercedes with a chauffeur sitting in the front. 'That's our car. Come with us now, and we can be at the airport in half an hour. We have a private flight ready to go at midnight. No passport or visa needed. You'll be travelling with the British Secret Service. Political asylum.'

'You'd do that for me, Mr Laws?'

'As I said, Lothar, this is war. *Carpe diem.*'

'*Carpe diem?*'

'Seize the day, Lothar. Will you join us?'

Lothar took a final drag of the cigarette and ground it out under his feet. So here it was, the biggest decision of his life. Bigger than any puzzle he had ever faced at the chessboard. The chance for a new life. It was an opportunity to start again, perhaps the only one he would ever get. He looked at the Mercedes parked opposite. A few small steps and he would be a free man. He would be escaping from the tyranny, the oppression, the overbearing state which watched his every move. His heart leapt at the thought. But at the same time, it was impossible to ignore everything, and everybody, that he would be leaving behind. His breath was constricted and the blood rushed to his head, overwhelmed at the magnitude of it all.

He needed more time. He turned away from Laws, continuing to grind at the cigarette under his feet until it was dust. He had to think it through, like a puzzle on the board. Quick decisions. He was good at those. It was how he made his living. First of all, the practicalities. What did he need? He felt inside his pockets. Aside from his wallet and cigarettes, what else? Technically, nothing. Secondly, how would he fare aboard? Continue to play chess at his current level and he knew he could make a comfortable living, even in the West. Tony Marlowe was in the UK, Hans too of course. He had friends and allies who would support him.

Those were the plusses. Undoubtedly major things. But there were downsides. Of course there were. What about his flat, his neighbours? What about Reisen and Martins? What pressure might they come under if he fled the country? Friends of a defector, they would have been with him the day he escaped. He would be putting them in an invidious position. He needed to think. Come on, think! He had to press Laws again on the help he could offer.

'Mr Laws,' he said. 'One other question.'

Before he could continue, there was a screeching of brakes and a grey Volkswagen pulled up in front of them. Neuer jumped out of the passenger seat. 'There you are, Lothar. Thank goodness. We thought we'd lost you. It's been a long day. We need to get back to the villa.'

One of the security guards had opened the back door of the car, and Neuer pushed him towards the back seat, shutting the door firmly as he clambered in. Neuer heaved himself back into the passenger seat and the car pulled away, leaving David Laws and Jon Forester watching them as they drove off into the distance.

'I thought we'd lost you there, Lothar,' repeated Neuer.

'You nearly did, Wolfgang,' he replied. 'You nearly did.'

CHAPTER TWENTY

A Beautiful Sadness

The thing about Paul Kask, Lothar thought to himself, as he gazed at the bust of Estonia's greatest ever chess player, was that he always kept his dignity. Arguably the strongest man never to compete in a match for the World Championship, it was said that the Soviet authorities conspired to stop the Estonian taking the crown from their favourite, the pure-bred Russian Mikhail Dasaev. When asked, shortly before his death at the tragically early age of fifty-nine, why he never became champion, Kask, bitter about the annexation of Estonia by the Soviet Union in 1944, replied: 'I was unlucky, like my country.'

Now, ten years after Kask's untimely death, Lothar found himself for the second time in his life in the beautiful city of Tallinn, taking part in an anniversary event to celebrate the life of the great Estonian.

Lothar had always admired Kask. Bold, calculating, not afraid of risks, the Estonian stood out for openly speaking his mind to the Soviet authorities. Lothar had hoped that playing in the land of one of his heroes would inspire him. It seemed though that the heart-breaking defeat to Gavrilov had left a scar from which he had not yet recovered. He performed indifferently, feeling unwell throughout the event and finishing in mid-table. The low point came when, after a late night with Johan Martins and Ernst Reisen, he overslept and missed the start of the final round. Hurrying from his hotel through the turrets that mark the entry point to the old town, down the winding streets towards the Town Hall at the foot of the hill, he arrived at the venue, out of breath and sweating, five minutes late. Fighting his way through the spectators, he found a crowd standing around his board. It transpired that the games had started early that day. He was now over an hour late, and having overstepped the one-hour limit, had lost by default. What a humiliation!

Feeling despondent about his chess, seeking to find something good to take away from the trip, at the conclusion of the tournament he took Martins and Reisen to the bar where he had stayed up drinking all night on his last visit to Tallinn. The owner was still there, and what's more, he remembered him. Martins was so impressed with the bar that he repeated Lothar's trick, staying there all night.

Continuing their tour of the Baltic states, Lothar, Martins and Reisen took part in a tournament in freezing cold Riga, home to the genius Mikhail Voronin. Lothar again played badly, struggling with the temperature, drinking more than he should, and losing too many games. Walking down the ancient cobbled streets back to his hotel one evening, he stumbled, fell and badly sprained his ankle, walking with a limp for the rest of the week.

Voronin's health had been poor for some time, and he was unable to attend the tournament, as he was in hospital with a kidney infection. When the President of the Latvian Chess Federation presented a special merit award at the closing ceremony, Lothar was distressed to realise that the sallow, frail man who made his way slowly to the stage, supported by a walking stick, was none other than Voronin himself.

At the reception, Lothar sat next to the great champion. The light in Voronin's eyes still shone deeply when they talked about chess. The body might be ailing, but his passion for the game would never die. As the evening came towards an end, the great champion rested his arm on Lothar's shoulder. 'My friend,' he said, in his thick Slavic accent, 'I believe that I must apologise.'

Bemused, Lothar asked him what for.

Voronin shook his head mournfully. 'For the advice that I gave, those years ago, in East Berlin.'

'You told me that the chess player is an artist, Misha. Your advice helped me to become a Grandmaster, and East German champion.'

Voronin ran his hand through his thinning hair. 'Lothar, I realise now I was wrong. The chess player, he needs to be artist, this I accept. I would not have achieved success without imagination or wits. I would never have become champion if I had played ...' Voronin stumbled for the expression, '*by the book*. That much is true. However, the Grandmaster, he also needs to be sportsman. Look at Smirov. Do you see him drinking, partying, up all hours?'

'Smirov has a very dull style. I'm not sure I want to emulate him, Misha.'

'Smirov, he was Champion of World for five years Lothar. I manage one year. What does that tell you?' Voronin lit another cigarette. 'It is too late for me now. I am hooked. I love the drink, cigarettes, late nights. You, Lothar, are still young man, not yet thirty. You can change.'

Lothar shook Voronin's hand. Genius of the chessboard, and a gentleman too. If he could achieve half of what the Latvian had done in his career, he would be a proud man. He needed to reflect on what Voronin had said about drinking, too.

He knew before she replied that something was wrong. Grosz' secretary Petra's eyes were red, and half-used tissues were scattered over her desk. She nodded towards the two workers who were removing Grosz' nameplate from the door. 'Didn't you hear? Udo was beaten into second place in the elections.'

'Beaten by whom?' Lothar struggled to hide his surprise. He had not even realised the President of the Federation was elected. He'd thought the job was Grosz' for life.

'By Georg Schneider,' Petra said haltingly, her face downcast.

Lothar cast his mind back to those days in junior competitions, when the five-foot-tall Georg Schneider, a Stasi member himself, had been master of all he surveyed. He wondered what Grosz had done to lose his job to such a character. Nothing happened by chance in their country. Had Grosz upset senior Party officials, maybe even Honecker himself, with his constant bravado and self-promotion?

Lothar found out later that Grosz had left the headquarters of the Federation in tears. For all Grosz' undoubted flaws, it surprised him that he felt a small element of pity, even after what he had done to Hans. Grosz had been a huge part of his life, and the times had not been all bad. He wondered where Grosz would go, what he would do next. This was a strange country, where very few people were in charge of their own fates. Grosz, more than most, must have felt he had control of his life. It turned out that he was wrong.

Whether it was the conversation with Voronin, or the departure of Udo Grosz, he did not know. Whatever the cause, Lothar began to reflect seriously on his life. Firstly, his friends. He seemed to be drawn to these odd, unconventional characters. Joker, Martins, Tony Marlowe, even Rolf Lehmann, going back to his school days. He admired their bravery, their willingness to be their own people. Was it the influence of his uncle, so much his own man that he risked his life and liberty to leave the country? How much of his rebellious streak dated back to those formative years?

Secondly, alcohol. He had let things slide, drinking too much and allowing himself to wallow in pity. The split with Anna was a part of it. Finding his life hard without her, he was using vodka and beer to alleviate the pain. There was more to it than that though. He thought back to that conversation with Hans, when he won his first junior title. What was it Hans had said? *People drink to forget.* Finally, Lothar understood what his coach had meant. In this oppressive society, where your every move was watched, every phone call potentially eavesdropped, your future dependent upon the patronage of a small number of corrupt officials, how could you function normally? Yes, drink was an escape, not just from his love life, but from his whole world.

Whatever the causes, Voronin was right. The alcohol had become a problem. It was taking its toll physically as well as on his chess. He had put on over two stone since he left college, and a long walk would now leave him out of breath. When he found that he couldn't even climb the steps to his flat without taking five minutes to recover, he realised that he had to make a change, and to do so fast. He began going to the gym, as well as making a concerted effort to cut back on his drinking. He also started studying the game seriously for the first time since the match with Gavrilov. Time would tell if he had the strength of character to deliver on his good intentions.

During the summer, Lothar took up running. He wasn't able to go far at first, but it was a good way of getting out of the flat, and with each successive run he felt stronger and fitter. Out of breath at first after even the shortest distance, it was also the final spur, if he needed one, to give up cigarettes. He came to know the contours of Friedrich Park well, its large green expanse providing a perfect escape from the city. He found the exercise peaceful and relaxing, and as he felt his physical health begin to improve, so too did his mood gradually lift. Looking back on his relationship with Anna, it still hurt to know that it was over, that he would never have those happy times with her again. But the memories were special, not ones he would swap for anything in the world. It was a beautiful sadness, knowing that the pain he felt now was only possible because of the happiness he had once had. It made him feel alive and human, like standing in the pouring rain, getting drenched to his skin. The rain in time would pass, as would his pain.

One afternoon, as he came back through the main entrance to his flat after a run, Lothar bumped into a gaunt, red-haired woman, late twenties, carrying boxes up the stairs. Dressed all in black, she had a stud in her nose, ripped jeans, and the look of a goth or a punk about her, he wasn't sure which.

'Can I help you with those?'

'Thank you, no, I'm fine,' the woman said curtly. She carried on walking up the stairs, and he followed behind her.

'Are you moving in?' he asked.

'Yes, flat number ten, on the fourth floor.'

'I live just opposite you, flat number eight. I'm Lothar Hartmann.'

'Pleased to meet you, Lothar. I'm Monika Kohler.' The red-haired woman stretched out her hand for the briefest moment, nodded at him unsmilingly, and then continued up the stairs.

Lothar frequently bumped into Monika Kohler as he was coming into or out of their block of flats. Like him, she seemed to keep strange, late hours. She often had friends with her, all of whom dressed in black and had piercings or tattoos and messy punk hair. He very rarely saw Monika smile, but for some reason she fascinated him. Living as a punk in East Germany, without an apparent job, or source of income, or any role in society, simply wasn't the done thing. He marvelled at how she managed it.

Towards the end of the summer, returning late one night from an evening training with Ernst Reisen, he saw a blue van parked outside their block of flats. Monika stood by the van, her arms crossed, looking morose.

'Hello, how are you?' he said.

Monika nodded. 'Fine.'

'Are you sure? Can I help you?'

Monika looked him up and down. He knew exactly what she was thinking. Could she trust him? She paused and drew a deep breath. 'I need to unload the van. A guy was supposed to help me, but he's let me down. There's too much for me to handle.' She said this through gritted teeth, hating admitting a weakness, he imagined.

The door of the van was open, and he could see at least six large cardboard boxes in the back. 'What's in the boxes?' he asked.

Monika glared. 'What are you, Stasi?'

'No. I just want to know what I'm helping move into your flat.'

'Heroin,' said Monika blankly.

Lothar looked startled. For the first time, she laughed. 'Come on, I'm joking. This is East Germany. You think I want to get arrested?' Monika leaned over and opened one of the boxes. He looked inside. Musical instruments.

Lothar smiled. 'I'll help you,' he said.

Monika nodded, handed him a box, took a second box for herself, and shut the van door behind her. 'You take the heavy ones. I'll take the light. Should take three trips,' she said.

He held the door at the foot of the stairs open for Monika and then followed her up, leaving the boxes outside her front door before returning to complete two more trips. After the third journey, they stopped outside Monika's door. He wondered if she might invite him in, but with the merest nod of her head she thanked him for his help and wished him good night.

'Sleep well,' he said, as Monika shut her front door. The enigma that was Monika Kohler remained, but at least he had now established some sort of contact.

What was it about Prague, Lothar wondered, as he sat with Reisen in the police station. First there had been the incident with Konrad Welde. The lost velvet jacket, and the threat to his place in the Olympiad team. Now this business with Johan Martins, which threatened to cause even more problems.

The tournament in Pardubice had been nothing but a success. The three friends – Lothar, Martins and Reisen – had dominated the event, winning the top three prizes. In the evenings, they had sat in one of the bars overlooking the market square, sampling fine beer, relaxing, without ever allowing things to get out of control. Even Martins had been restrained. It was on their return to Prague that their troubles started.

Lothar and Reisen had reserved hotel rooms just off Wenceslas Square, in the centre of the city. They had booked Martins, who was neither well off nor organised, a room in a student hostel. Reisen had brought the booking form with him, which he gave to Martins as they got off the train at Central Station.

By the time they arrived at Wenceslas Square, Martins had lost the form and none of them could remember which hostel he was booked into. There began a fruitless hunt for the elusive hostel which took them, high roads and low, through the entire centre of Prague. None of the many hostels they found had heard of Martins. The one hostel which did have spare rooms took one look at Martins, bedraggled, torn jacket, soles coming off the shoes of his feet, and turned them away.

By the early evening, dispirited, they needed food. Leaving Martins in a local bar, Lothar and Reisen walked the short distance to their hotel, and after a wait at reception, deposited their bags and met downstairs half an hour later. Of course, leaving Martins alone had been a mistake. By the time they made their way back to the bar where they had left him, not an hour previously, he was gone.

Seeing their bemused expressions, the barman, an elderly man with a thick beard, guessed what had happened. 'Are you looking for your friend, the other German, the dishevelled one?'

'Yes, that's right. Have you seen him?'

'Bad news, I'm afraid.' The barman shook his head sadly.

'Bad news?'

'He's been arrested.'

Lothar gulped. 'What for?'

'He was talking to an Englishman. Goodness knows what the English fellow was doing here. An off-duty policeman was in here as well. He didn't like the look of the Englishman, and he thought your friend might be a spy. So he called his colleagues. Five policemen turned up and arrested them both.'

It was bizarre, but the Czechoslovakians really had accused Martins of spying. Politically clueless, a man less likely to engage in espionage he couldn't imagine. Lothar and Reisen waited two days in Prague for the police to free Martins, knowing full well that they would be in trouble when they got back to East Berlin.

On their return, events panned out as badly as Lothar had feared. Say what you like about Udo Grosz, but he would have found a way to protect them. Georg Schneider owed them no such loyalty. A Special Committee of the East German Federation, convened by Schneider, and chaired by Wolfgang Neuer, suspended Lothar from all chess activity for six months, the second ban of his career and his first since student days. His crimes included disrespect for his country, consorting with an unknown enemy – totally unjustified, as he never even met the Englishman, who was, it turned out, a writer – and leading the younger Martins astray. The Committee also suspended his stipend and banned him for a further year of international travel. An immediate result of this was that he lost his place in the Olympiad team which would be travelling to Hungary shortly afterwards. He suspected that Neuer was also taking revenge for his perceived misbehaviour in Madrid – fraternising too closely with Gavrilov, and the Englishmen David Laws and Jon Forester – although he didn't say as much.

Reisen received a similar punishment. Only Martins came through unscathed. The Committee gave him a formal warning but no suspension. He heard afterwards that they were worried about Martins' ability to survive without the meagre income which his play brought in. It was a rare moment of empathy from a faceless bureaucracy.

Back home, while colleagues departed for Hungary and the Olympiad, he found himself stranded alone in cold, snowy East Berlin. With little planned for the month of December, banned from playing, he occupied his time revisiting old haunts, including the university campus, the library, the lakes and the woodland where Anna and he had hiked on weekends. Those had been happier and more innocent times.

While browsing in a bookshop near the campus, Lothar found a copy of *The Master and Margarita*. On a whim, he bought it and spent the following two days reading it solidly from cover to cover. So this was what Anna's dissertation was about? He must have read the passage where Margarita chose to live in poverty-stricken love with the Master at least four times. It was a beautiful piece of writing. The following week, he returned to the bookshop, buying the complete works of Bulgakov, plus Tolstoy too.

The week before Christmas, Lothar's elderly neighbour Elsa fell on an ice patch and broke her wrist. The break aside, there was no lasting damage, but she was shaken by the fall. The doctors told Elsa she needed to rest, and Monika and Lothar took it in turns to help her husband Benjamin with household chores. Monika was still guarded with him, rarely exchanging anything more than the merest pleasantry. When Benjamin caught flu, though, with no immediate family to help them, Monika and Lothar had no option but to work together. At the end of the week, he still knew almost nothing about Monika. He had no idea where she was born or brought up, where her money came from, whether she was in a relationship or who her friends were. They had, however, established a degree of trust, and when he caught a mild dose of flu himself, Monika collected his shopping and medication.

Returning to his flat at the same time as Monika on New Year's Eve, impulsively he asked her to join him for drinks with Benjamin and Elsa, and she accepted. It was the quietest New Year's Eve he had ever known. Benjamin and Elsa said goodnight at midnight, and Monika wasn't much later. It was an enjoyable night nevertheless.

Before she left that evening, Lothar was finally able to ask his neighbour about her life. 'What do you do for a living, Monika?'

Monika gritted her teeth and turned to look out of the window. 'I'm a musician in a punk band.'

'Don't be embarrassed. That's fantastic. What do you play?'

Monika laughed. He noticed that when she laughed, she opened her eyes wide and her blue pupils dilated. 'It's a punk band. I don't play anything. I look mean and sing badly. Same as the rest of the band. What do you do?'

'I'm a chess player.'

Monika pulled another face. She could be wonderfully expressive. 'Get away? Isn't that kind of geeky?'

'Yes, I guess so. That's what I like about it. What did you think I did?'

'I thought you were an accountant.'

'No! That really would be geeky. Didn't you wonder why I'm about so often late at night?'

'That's why I thought you were an accountant. Those people don't like to be seen in daylight. How did you get into chess anyway?'

'My uncle taught me. He escaped the country when he was young. My parents encouraged me, God bless their souls. I wouldn't have made it without their support. How about your parents? Are they still alive?'

'They both died when I was young,' said Monika. 'It's going to sound odd, but I'm relieved in a way that they didn't see me grow up. I would have been a disappointment to them. They wanted a daughter who had a great career, who made something of herself. They would have expected me to be married by now as well.'

'Are you seeing anyone?'

Monika stubbed out her cigarette. 'It's complicated.'

'Complicated how?'

'I'll tell you when I know you better.'

'I'll hold you to that.'

'How about you, Lothar? Any women on your horizons?'

Lothar stood up and looked out of the window. A solitary man stood on the street corner smoking a cigarette. He wondered if he was Stasi. 'I was seeing someone.'

'What happened?'

'It's complicated.'

'You'll tell me more when you know me better?'

'I will.'

Monika laughed and stood up to leave. 'Goodnight, Lothar. You know, I wasn't sure about you. But you're OK.'

Lothar switched off the telly and turned out the lights. He thought about pouring a final vodka, but instead sat quietly in the dark and reflected. What society was this that he lived in? Equally, what role had he played in supporting it: the tyranny, the collusion, the cheating? The questions were complex, but he had to find an answer. As important as that, he had to find a better way of living, a means of acting on his convictions. He had treated the big decisions in his life – his relationship with Anna, his allegiance to Grosz and the state – as though they were moves on a chessboard. But surely there was more to the world than that? Heart and soul, what had happened to them? Putting the half-empty bottle of vodka back in the cupboard, he locked the front door and went to bed. Perhaps in the morning, things would seem clearer.

CHAPTER TWENTY-ONE

The Manifesto

It took some weeks before Monika told him the full story, but her boyfriend Gregor, it transpired, was an underground political radical, a historian by training, who was agitating for the downfall of the government. The Stasi had caught him and he was in prison awaiting trial.

'How did they catch Gregor?'

'The usual. The Stasi bugged our flat, intercepted our mail and questioned our friends. Then when they couldn't find any concrete evidence, they made baseless allegations that they hope will stick.'

'They didn't find his writing? Anna used to hide hers under a floorboard.'

Monika sighed. 'Writers, they have a habit of doing that. I made sure Gregor never brought his political stuff anywhere near our flat. The Stasi turned the place upside down but they couldn't find anything. Unfortunately, one of our friends — we don't know which — was working undercover and gave Gregor away.'

'Maybe they bugged you?' he said. 'Are you worried they might be listening to us now?'

'You know what,' said Monika. 'They may well be bugging me. But I honestly don't care.' She raised her voice to a shout. 'You effing losers. You can't arrest us all, can you?'

Over the following weeks Lothar met a number of Monika's friends. Punks, goths, heavy metal freaks, they were an odd assortment of nonconformists, idealists and dreamers. He hadn't realised that such people could survive in East Germany.

Monika was a member of a punk band called The Disciples of Doom. The membership of this anarchic group seemed to be ever-changing, with no fixed composition. The band played in bars and clubs in the rougher part of East Berlin, where it had attracted a cult following. It was hardly his type of music, but he went to one show. Monika was a mainstay of the band, shaking a tambourine and sometimes shrieking into a microphone through blood-red lipstick.

After a particularly violent gig, where Monika told him the band had led a hundred-strong audience in chants of 'Honecker out', and members of the crowd had fought afterwards with local skinheads, he asked her why the government, intolerant, authoritarian and brutal as it was, allowed the band to continue.

'Two reasons, Lothar. Firstly, arrogance. The government are afraid of writers, poets and intellectuals, because they know those guys can beat them in an argument. It's a contrast with musicians, who they see as a bunch of thoughtless kids. Our opinions are worth nothing to them.'

'The second reason?'

'Gorbachev, Lothar. That man is going to change the world, mark my words. Honecker sees it happening too. He doesn't know how to react, but he's worried.'

When Georg Schneider summoned Lothar to a meeting at the Central Chess Club, it felt just like the old days. Schneider, like Grosz a Stasi member, had even taken over Grosz' office, which looked unchanged from when he had visited last. He wondered if the disgusting Bison cigars were still in the top drawer of the desk.

'Hartmann,' began Schneider, peering up at him through newly acquired spectacles, in his familiar high-pitched voice, 'we are hosting a large international event next month. Smirov is playing, as are De Jong, Marlowe and Jensen.'

'I'm banned, Georg. I'm not allowed to play until June.'

Schneider looked at him benevolently, fiddling with the button on his waistcoat. 'Hartmann, you've served your time. Hopefully you've learnt your lesson too. You were always a good Party member, a faithful servant. We've not forgotten the way you helped us with Hans Adler. We are willing to forgive and forget. Time to return to the fold, eh?'

'What about my international ban? Does that end too?'

'One step at a time, Hartmann. Let's see how you get on at the Berlin tournament, and then we can discuss your longer-term future.'

Schneider held out his hand and Lothar shook it. He didn't trust the man any further than he could throw him – and even with his small frame, that wasn't far – but now wasn't the time for heroics.

The Bogoljubov Memorial Tournament in Berlin was the strongest event held in Europe that year. In a major coup, just a week before the start of the event Schneider secured an acceptance from Boris Korneev. The new World Champion had been almost unplayable over the past year, and Lothar was intrigued by the opportunity to take on the Azerbaijani for the first time.

Having not played for nearly six months, he was not feeling match sharp, and began the tournament cautiously, drawing with Jensen and Smirov. In round three, he faced Dutch number one Loek De Jong. Never one to agree an early draw, De Jong was also out for revenge after his defeat against Lothar in the World Championships. Forced to fight, Lothar defended with all his might, surviving an attack before winning a piece and the game. Strange to say, it was the first game he had won that year.

The round after, Lothar won again, and he was now in second place behind Korneev. The television and press built the game up as a clash of the champion and the pretender, Lothar's return to the tournament scene the greatest comeback since Muhammad Ali. The evening news even devoted twenty minutes to the game.

Lothar knew full well that the media had exaggerated. This was certainly the best he had played for a long time, but based on his form over the past year he wasn't yet ready to challenge Korneev. He enjoyed the contest with the World Champion, and at times he even had the Champion under pressure, Korneev grimacing theatrically as he held his head in his hands. By move forty, though, normal service was resumed. Korneev had survived the attack and launched a lethal counterattack of his own. Lothar resigned on the forty-fifth move, the players receiving a standing ovation for a spectacular game. He appreciated the acclaim, but Korneev had outclassed him. It was not for nothing that one of his opponents described Korneev as 'a monster with a thousand eyes, who sees all'.

Lothar finished the tournament in third place, behind Smirov and the peerless Korneev. Two days later he received a phone call. There was a familiar click on the line which told him that an operator was listening, followed by the high-pitched voice of Georg Schneider. 'Hartmann, it's your President here. Congratulations on a wonderful performance.'

'Thank you, Georg. I'm grateful for the opportunity.'

'Hartmann, I need to discuss a delicate matter with you. Will you come to the Central Chess Club this afternoon?'

He arrived at the club shortly before three. He noticed that Schneider had a new black leather chair. The seat was much higher than the old one, and it gave the pocket-sized President the appearance of being taller than he really was.

'Thank you for coming in, Hartmann. I'd like to talk to you about the World Championship. We have two places available for the qualifier in London this September. Jensen picks himself. We are still considering the second spot. You and Bahl are the obvious candidates.'

'I'm flattered, Georg. Does that mean my travel ban is ended?'

'Yes, Hartmann, we will end your ban. With one condition.'

'What's that?'

'The state needs your help. Are you willing to assist your government?'

Lothar felt the familiar tightness in the pit of his stomach. Did these people never give up? 'Georg, you know that I'll do anything I can, as long as it's lawful.'

'By virtue of the state asking you to help, it goes without saying that what I'm about to request is lawful.'

Lothar looked at Schneider impassively. There was a knock on the door and Schneider's secretary, a round woman with wavy brown hair, brought in two coffees. He thought about Udo Grosz. He would never have been seen in the afternoon with a coffee, except perhaps an Irish one.

The secretary left the room, closing the door softly behind her. Schneider played with a pad of paper on his desk, his eyes not meeting Lothar's. 'Hartmann, for a Grandmaster, a pillar of our society, you have mixed with some interesting people. There was Hans Adler, the defector. Also, Anna Schuster, the writer.'

Lothar tasted his drink. It was lukewarm and the milk smelt sour. 'Anna has never harmed anybody.'

'I'm not here today to talk about Miss Schuster,' said Schneider. 'We are worried, Hartmann, about the young woman who lives opposite you, Miss Kohler. We have had a number of tip-offs about her. There are accusations that she is a radical, a revolutionary, an anarchist even.'

'I wouldn't know about that, Georg. She's my neighbour, but that doesn't mean I socialise with her.'

'I'll be blunt with you, Hartmann. We think that you do know Miss Kohler. We have evidence that you've spent time with her, and the delinquent group of associates that she calls a band. We even have some photos' — Schneider pulled a cardboard wallet out of his top drawer — 'which show you with Kohler. Here's one, for example, where you're in the crowd at one of her gigs. The front row, no less.'

'I've only been to one gig, Georg. How can you possibly have a picture of that?'

'We are the Stasi, Hartmann. We have eyes and ears everywhere. Look, here's another photo where you are unloading musical instruments from a van. Not that the so-called Disciples of Doom have much use for instruments, from what I hear.'

'I'm Monika's neighbour, Georg. She asked me to help unload the instruments. What do you expect me to do in that situation?'

'I expect you to put the state first, Hartmann, and not some anarchist punk rock band.' Schneider spat the words *punk* and *rock* like chewing gum out of his lips.

Lothar took a deep breath. So the Stasi had been following him all this time. He should have guessed.

'What do you want me to do, Georg?'

'We have reason to believe, Hartmann, that at some point in the next few weeks, Miss Kohler will be taking possession of a package.'

'What package?'

'Have you heard of *The Manifesto for a Free Society*?'

'No, I can't say I have.' He would have said this to Schneider whatever the circumstance, but *The Manifesto* really did mean nothing to him.

'*The Manifesto* is a pamphlet written by one of these self-important fellows who claims to be an intellectual and thinker. An underground type who is trying to bring down the government, to destroy our society. Rumour is that *The Manifesto* contains damning allegations about Honecker and the government, of fraud, corruption, bribery. There is no substance to the stories, but the mere release of them could do incalculable damage.'

'Who is the writer?'

'Gregor Kramer, the boyfriend of Monika Kohler.'

'Isn't he in jail?'

'Yes, but no matter how hard we search – his flat, his office, his parents' home – we've never been able to find *The Manifesto*. We've heard now, though, through our sources, that the original copy is due to be delivered to Miss Kohler. She'll get one of her band members to smuggle it out of the country. If they succeed, this could be the makings of a revolution.'

Lothar thought about what Schneider had just said. Outside the window, he heard shouting, followed by the sound of police sirens and a gunshot.

'Is the system so fragile that one book could bring it down?'

Schneider glared at him. 'I'm not debating with you, Hartmann. The offer is this. We believe *The Manifesto for a Free Society* will be delivered to Monika Kohler in the next month. We know you're close to Kohler. Find out when the delivery is due, and phone us when it arrives. We will arrest Kohler and secure *The Manifesto*. In return, we will end your travel ban. Nobody will ever know that you've helped us, but you will have safeguarded East German society from revolution.'

'Can't you watch the flat yourself?'

'We would risk tipping Miss Kohler off, if we did that. Not even the Stasi can make ourselves invisible, Hartmann. Besides which, the package could be delivered tomorrow, or in three weeks' time.' Schneider looked wistful. 'Our resources are not what they were.'

Lothar took a sip from his drink and reflected long and hard. There were several different moves open to him, but only one of them appeared playable.

'If I help you, will you guarantee me the place in the World Championship qualifier, ahead of Bahl?'

For the first time since he had sat down, Schneider smiled. 'We will be happy to pick you for the London event, yes, once you have done your bit.'

Lothar downed the remnants of the foul coffee and shook Schneider's hand. He had decided on his next move. Time to resume the game.

CHAPTER TWENTY-TWO

The Accidental Anarchist

The day after Lothar met Schneider, Monika Kohler invited him to lunch. His neighbour had spent the previous week decorating. Stripping the paper off the walls, she had painted the hallway and bedroom a striking combination of mauve, red and black, a colour scheme that struck him as extreme even for a punk. The bedroom still had that newly decorated aroma, pungent and heavy. In the living room, she had pinned rugs to the walls, and hung a blanket across the window. A joss stick burned unhealthily in the middle of the room. Monika prepared a simple meal of bratwurst and brown bread, and afterwards they sat talking over coffee.

'I see from the papers that you did well in the chess, Lothar. You never tell me these things.'

'It's best not to take too much notice of journalists, Monika. They write what they want to. Today a hero, tomorrow a nobody.'

'They say that you're going to challenge again for the World Championship.'

'*They* say a lot of things.'

Monika punched him lightly in the ribs, her red hair matching the colour of the wall behind her. 'You should be proud of your achievements.'

'Thank you. There is one player who is better than me right now. You should see Korneev in action. It's like sitting down at a chessboard with God. An aggressive, violent God.'

'If there is a God, then that's exactly how I imagine him,' said Monika.

'Like Boris Korneev?'

'No, silly. Aggressive and violent, a God which bends the world to his whim. Allowing corruption and intolerance to flourish, mediocrity to prosper, talent and good intention to go to waste.'

'A God like that would appreciate your music, Monika.'

Monika punched him again, harder this time. 'The Grandmaster thinks he's funny.'

'I try. By the way, I keep meaning to ask you, what's happening with Gregor? Isn't his case due to come to trial soon?'

'The court has set a date for the end of September.'

'Monika, that's great. Gregor will be cleared and released, and you can return to a normal life.'

Monika sighed. 'I wish it were that simple, Lothar.'

'What do you mean?'

'Gregor's lawyer has already told him, there's no chance of release. He's seen the evidence. Most of it they've fabricated. They've accused Gregor of fraud, theft, of attacking other prisoners in jail. If you saw Gregor – he's got a build like you, like a chess player – the thought of him attacking anyone is ludicrous.'

'So what do we do?'

Putting her hand to her lips, Monika reached across to the table where she switched on the radio. Music now blaring, she turned back to him and whispered, 'I can't say any more here. It's not safe.'

He nodded. Speaking in a normal tone again, Monika continued. 'I don't think there's anything we can do, Lothar. Let's hope things work out. Hey, it's a lovely day today, far too hot to be stuck indoors. Let's walk across to Friedrich Park and stretch our legs.'

They put on their shoes and took the short stroll down to the park. As they walked, Monika told him that while she was decorating, she had discovered wires under the wallpaper. 'I'm glad I decided to paint the walls. If I hadn't stripped that awful wallpaper off, I would never have found out.'

'Why don't you rip the wires out?'

'I don't want to alert them that I know. Better to play innocent. Especially right now.'

'Right now?'

Monika was about to say something but went quiet as a man passed the other way, carrying a newspaper and umbrella. Office worker or spy: who could be sure? They carried on walking, past a thicket of trees and bushes, until they found a secluded spot on the other side of the undergrowth.

'Follow me,' said Monika. 'I know this place. We can sit on that log.'

'Do you have all your private discussions here?'

'You'd be surprised,' said Monika. 'Now sit down. I need your help, Lothar. But I also need to know if I can trust you.'

He looked at Monika and bit his lip. 'If you'd asked me that question a year ago, I'm not sure I could have answered. A lot has happened, though. I don't see the world in the same way now.'

'If I tell you my secret, then I'm putting my life in your hands, Lothar. Other people's too.'

'My establishment days are over, Monika.'

Goodness, he thought to himself, Monika was certainly putting her faith in him. A loose word, if they were somehow overheard, and she was finished. What had he done to earn such confidence, and would he show the same faith in her position?

Monika ran her hands through her hair and blew a deep breath out of her cheeks. 'OK, Lothar. Here goes.'

He returned home that afternoon knowing exactly what Monika Kohler's plan was. He also had a fully formed plan of his own, not that he was telling anyone what it was yet.

One week later, Monika Kohler took possession of a large brown cardboard box. Monika helped the van driver carry the box up the stairs, proclaiming loudly as she did how she was looking forward to unwrapping a new set of musical instruments. Lothar watched from the spyhole in his front door as she loaded the box inside her flat, shutting the door carefully behind her.

At three o'clock on Thursday 24 July 1986, two police vans pulled up outside their block of flats, sirens wailing. Eight police officers got out of the vans and ran up the stairs. A fair-haired man at the front of the group banged loudly on the wooden door of flat number ten. 'Police, open up now! Open the door or we break it down.'

From his vantage point opposite, Lothar watched as Monika opened the door. She was dressed in her jeans and a red top that matched her hair. He couldn't see anyone behind her.

'Ms Kohler, I am Inspector Maier of the East Berlin police force. These men are my colleagues. We have reason to believe that you are hiding anti-government material in this flat. We have a warrant to search your property.'

Monika examined the warrant and sighed. 'Gentlemen, I've no idea why you're here, but you are welcome to come inside. I've nothing to hide.'

Maier waved his men inside while he stood waiting at the entrance. Lothar heard shouting, banging and what sounded like furniture being moved. After five minutes, the men emerged. Two at the front were holding a large cardboard box which they brought out to the hallway. Monika had remained motionless at the front door while they did this.

Inspector Maier looked at Monika. 'Can I ask you please, *Madame*, what is in this box?'

'The box that's not been opened yet? You want me to tell you what's inside that?'

'Yes, the box that's not been opened yet.'

Monika crossed her arms and stared at the Inspector. 'Why don't you open it yourself and find out?'

Maier pulled a penknife out of his jacket. 'Thank you, *Madame*. It's certainly a heavy package. Let's see what's inside.'

The box was tightly secured with tape. Maier cut the tape then ran the knife roughly across the top of the box, ripping the lid open. Looking inside, he exclaimed loudly. 'It can't be!'

Monika looked at Maier calmly. 'What have you found, Inspector?'

Maier glared at Monika. Reaching into the box, he pulled out an electric guitar and three tambourines.

'Ah, my tambourines. A guitar too. What a lovely surprise,' said Monika.

'This box is all you found?' Maier asked his men.

'Yes, we searched everywhere, sir,' replied a young officer with a crew cut.

'There is nothing else in the flat?'

'Nothing of value, sir.'

Maier screwed up his face momentarily, before regaining his composure. In that flicker, all was clear. It was game over, and he had lost. 'I'm sorry, Ms Kohler, for any trouble that we have caused you. Please do put in a claim in the unlikely event that the men have caused any damage.'

Monika uncrossed her arms. 'Goodbye, Inspector,' she said coldly. 'I'm sure everything will be in order.'

Maier rose, turned, and led his men back down the stairs. As he passed Lothar's front door, the Inspector stopped for a second and stared. Lothar thought he was going to knock on the door, but after another moment Maier shook his head and moved on.

The following week Lothar met Schneider again in his office. The President of the Federation glared as he peered at him over his black-rimmed glasses.

'I'm sorry, Georg. I guess Monika Kohler must have changed her plans. She's not said anything to me.'

Schneider cursed. 'We were certain that the *Manifesto* would be smuggled in when Kohler took delivery of her new instruments.'

'Perhaps your information was incorrect?'

Schneider almost spat at him. 'Stasi information is never incorrect. No, the double-crossing Kohler has been devious this time. Rest assured though, Hartmann, we will get her. We always do.'

'Georg, you know I've done everything I can to help you. I tipped you off about that box being delivered, didn't I?'

'Yes, Hartmann, you did.'

'The qualifier in London starts in a month and a half. Have I earned my place?'

Schneider sighed and put out his cigarette. 'You'll fly out with the others. Neuer will be leading the delegation. Report to his office tomorrow to sort out your visa.'

'Thank you, Georg, I won't let you down.'

Schneider glared at him again. 'You'd better not, Hartmann. You'll be representing the nation. No drinking, no fraternising with Westerners, and no going anywhere without Neuer's permission. Not if you want to be allowed out of the country again. Oh, and when you return from London, we can discuss how you're going to help us get Miss Kohler. Mark my words, Lothar, that woman isn't going to enjoy her liberty for long.'

Standing up to leave, he shook Schneider's hand, turned around, and as he walked through the door he closed it behind him without looking back. He understood clearly now, if he had not before, that the Stasi would never leave him alone. Before he had left the building, he had already made his decision. The time for compromises was over.

Pulling on a sweater – it was unseasonably chilly for early September – Lothar packed a case full of clothes and a second full of chess books. At the airport, he and Jensen were joined by no fewer than six officials. Jensen whispered to him during a bathroom break that the government was obsessed by the possibility of a defection.

'By you or me?'

'No, by their own agents. They've got them spying on each other, so that if any one of them tries to break loose, the others will get hold of him. See the burly one at the front, the one who looks like a boxer, that's Stein. He's Head of Security. Don't get on the wrong side of him, whatever you do. He'll break your arm first and ask questions later.'

'It's madness, isn't it?

'It's a new level of paranoia, that's for sure,' said Jensen.

Walking back to the departure hall, he saw a familiar figure had joined their group. The newcomer was wearing a yellow and red striped blazer and waving his hands theatrically as he talked to Neuer.

'Who let Bahl into the tournament?' he asked.

'Didn't you hear?' replied Jensen. 'Schneider negotiated us a third spot. He found some money to pay the organisers, and now Bahl is in.'

Lothar pursed his lips. Bahl was an unwelcome addition to the team, and he wasn't looking forward to his rival's presence at breakfast, dinner, or any of the other innumerable team meetings that Neuer was no doubt planning. He had bigger fish to fry in London though, and he had to do his best to put his foe to the back of his mind. He had tried until now to avoid thinking too much about the next two weeks, but the critical point, the moment which would determine his future, was growing ever closer. He needed to be focused, to be vigilant, to seize the opportunity when it came.

London was grey, damp and foggy. It rained on the first two days, which Lothar had heard was common in England, whatever the time of year. Only on the third day did the sun come out. So concerned was he about their security, Neuer had rented their party a townhouse three miles out of the capital. A guard stood outside the front door day and night. Lothar's room was spartan, with space only for a narrow single bed, a closet, a small desk and a washbasin, but the house did at least have a generously stocked bar and a library of old Hollywood films. He spent several happy evenings acquainting himself with the work of Alfred Hitchcock and Martin Scorsese, film directors previously unknown to him. On the one excursion that Neuer allowed, they walked past Big Ben, the Houses of Parliament and Buckingham Palace. Lothar asked Neuer if they could go shopping, and the older man told him that he would consider a trip at the end of the tournament, if they performed well.

Taking his seat on the stage at Westminster Central Hall for the first round of the World Championship qualifier, Lothar looked across at his rivals. To his left was Thomas Jensen, immaculate as ever in a brown suit and tie. Straight ahead sat Sebastian Bahl, in his yellow and red blazer. To his right was Lev Ivanov, and next to him the Soviet Vasily Smirov. The tournament was going to be a tough test. The biggest challenge, however, would not be the chess.

The competition developed into a tussle for first place between Lothar, Smirov and Bahl. Lothar won a number of close games, holding draws with Smirov and Bahl. Meanwhile Smirov and Bahl were both playing spectacular attacking chess, winning round after round. He had never seen Bahl play so well, and only his own success made his compatriot's bragging each evening bearable.

At the end of the eighth round, when he had won again, Lothar shook his opponent's hand, set up the pieces and headed back to reception to find his bodyguard. Security was so tight that they wouldn't even allow him to catch the tube back to the house on his own. As he left the tournament hall, he saw a grey-haired man with hunched shoulders and a moustache coming the other way. The man intercepted him and put his hand on his shoulder.

'Hello, Lothar. You played a fine game today.'

Lothar smiled. Of all people. His old partner in crime. He had wondered if he would see him during the tournament, but until now he had kept a low profile.

'Hans! How have you been?'

His former coach looked at him warmly. 'I'm good, thank you, Lothar. England is treating me well.'

From a distance, he spotted Neuer approaching. Hans caught his expression. 'Good luck, Lothar,' he said, clutching his hand. 'I hope that this trip ends successfully for you.'

With that, Hans was gone. Neuer had already accosted him. 'What are you doing, Lothar, consorting with the enemy like that? We could have you arrested just for talking to that defector.'

'I'm sorry, Wolfgang,' he said. 'Adler came up to me to say hello. It was awkward. I thought Stein or the other bodyguards were supposed to stop that happening. Where are they?'

'Yes, well, I'll have a word with Stein. It will not happen again. Well played today, by the way. Now, let's get you back to the house.'

Lothar followed Neuer back to reception where they found one of the bodyguards. Clasped tightly in his fist he was still holding the crumpled piece of paper that Hans had given him during the fleeting moment in which his former coach had gripped his hand.

Friday 26 September 1986. The final round. He had spent the morning in his room, trying to calm his racing heart. Now the moment had arrived. Taking his seat at the board, he reached out and warmly shook the hand of his compatriot, Thomas Jensen. On the board next to him, Sebastian Bahl was facing Lev Ivanov. Four players would qualify for the quarter-finals of the World Championships, and such had been their form that Lothar, Smirov and Bahl had all already secured their places. The discussion in the press room was over which one of them would win the tournament, gaining the prestige that came with first place. For Lothar, for the first time in his life, such things were of no concern. Today, he had not come to win. Not on the chessboard, at least.

Shortly after Lothar sat down, Bahl arrived. He was wearing his striped blazer with a new red shirt, a sign that he meant business. Lothar wondered if his compatriot would notice the attaché case that he had placed at the side of his table. If Bahl did spot anything unusual, he said nothing. Lothar suspected he was more focused on his own game.

After the customary last-round speeches and photographs, play commenced at two o'clock sharp. No matter how hard he tried to compose himself, he was unable to keep calm. Looking down to the VIP row below the stage, his heart racing, his breath short, he saw that Neuer had not yet taken his seat. That was good news. Their team leader was in the habit of taking his lunch late, and on most days he didn't arrive in the playing hall until three. Hopefully he would follow that habit again today. He checked to see if any of the other Stasi men were in the hall, but there was no sign of them yet. Good news again.

At precisely twenty minutes past two, he made his seventh move, leaned across to Jensen and whispered the words, 'Thomas, I offer a draw.'

Jensen peered up at him through his glasses with a bemused expression. Then he glanced at the case by Lothar's side. He looked back at him with recognition in his eyes and slowly stretched out a hand to shake his. 'Good luck, Lothar. I hope you know what you're doing.'

Signing his score sheet, Lothar stood up, picked up his jacket and case, and walked down the steps off the stage. His legs were shaking and it was all he could do not to fall over. Bahl glanced at him, puzzled, and shook his head before turning back to his own board. By agreeing a draw, Lothar had gifted him the opportunity to win the tournament.

As he walked down the corridor towards the exit, Lothar bumped into Neuer and Stein. They had arrived at the hall earlier than normal today.

'What's happening, Lothar?' asked Neuer. 'Where are you going?'

'I've got a splitting headache, Wolfgang,' he said, his voice shaking. 'I'm going out to get some fresh air.'

'Are you still playing?'

'Yes I am. Thomas agreed to let me leave the board. I'll be back in a moment.'

'I see,' said Neuer. 'Don't be long.'

'I won't be,' he said, carrying on towards the exit, his legs feeling like lead. Behind him, he heard Stein ask, 'Why does he have his attaché case with him?'

There was a pause, and then Neuer let out a shriek. The game was up.

'Get him!' shouted Neuer, as Lothar pushed open the swing door. Behind him, Stein lunged forward, in a desperate bid to grab him before he left Westminster Central Hall.

Stein was too late. Lothar was already through the door, and with Hans' written instructions imprinted on his brain, had broken into a sprint as he took a left turn out of Central Hall. Suddenly, the panic and fear which had been coursing through his veins had turned into adrenaline, giving a shot to his arms, to his legs, extra speed to his every movement. Thirty metres ahead, at the crossroads, he turned left again. He could hear Stein's footsteps behind. Twenty metres behind him were the heavy boots of Neuer.

Stein was closing in. For all his head start, Lothar was no longer sure that he would make it. He needed to take action. Seeing a market stall to his left, he turned and ran through the crowds, with no time to apologise for the unceremonious way in which he was shoving people aside. Stein did his best to follow him, but in the melee the Stasi man lost ground. At the end of the market, Lothar turned right and resumed his original path. Neuer was now some considerable way behind, and the bodyguard was the only man who could stop him. He had narrowed the gap, however, and Lothar didn't fancy his chances if Stein caught him.

At the top of the street he came to a main road, where he saw a crossing with traffic lights, just as per Hans' instructions. A group of Japanese tourists stood on the pavement, waiting to cross. To the right, a bus was approaching. Lothar looked at the lights. Green. Stein was nearly upon him. He did the calculations in his head, as if he were playing a game of chess. It was a tight decision, but if he ran at full speed, he figured he could run across the road and safely reach the other side, avoiding the bus by about half a second.

To the gasps of passers-by, he carried on running, over the pavement and into the middle of the road. A woman carrying three bags of shopping screamed and the driver slammed on his brakes. The bus came to a shuddering halt, millimetres away from him. He saw the bus driver wave his fist. Behind him, Stein had come to a stop, bemused.

Lothar turned back round and carried on running. It had been a close-run thing, but his judgement hadn't let him down. Straight ahead was the prize. Stein had resumed the chase, but he was too far behind now. Running up the steps, three at a time, with one final glance to make sure he was clear of Stein, he pushed through the heavy front door. Ahead was an oak desk behind which sat a police officer.

'Can I help you, sir?'

Lothar collapsed in a heap on the desk. He could see Stein outside the front door, scowling, bent double, out of breath, not sure whether to follow him in. In his left hand he still held the attaché case, containing *The Manifesto for a Free Society*. Hidden inside the back cover of one of his chess books, the little red pamphlet had made its way over one thousand kilometres, from Berlin to London, through perhaps the tightest security known to man at East Berlin airport, to find its rightful place in the free world.

'I'm Lothar Hartmann, Grandmaster,' he gasped, 'and I wish to claim political asylum.'

Chapter Twenty-Three

A New Life

Lothar settled quickly into life in London. It rained constantly and the sun never seemed to come out. The people were reserved and kept themselves to themselves. Strangers rarely approached him, but when they did they were invariably polite. Coming from East Berlin, this felt like home from home. The only thing he missed was German efficiency. It took a while to get used to the fact that trains did not run on time, buses turned up in groups of three, and if a state official said they would contact you in four days, you should expect an answer in four weeks.

The biggest change he noticed was the absence of the surveillance that had been such a constant in Berlin. He began to realise that he could make a phone call, and no third party would be listening on the other end of the line. He could give an opinion freely, and nobody would be ready to report him to the secret police. Best of all, he could buy luxuries unimaginable in East Germany – whisky, silk ties, blue jeans – without a sense of guilt or a fear that he would be arrested and interrogated afterwards for his crimes against the state.

Of course, one other big difference from being in the East was that he had no state income to rely on. Hans found him some work as a coach and, for the first time, the pay cheque he brought home each week was dependent upon the hours he worked, not the patronage of the government. He also focused seriously on his own game, training with Hans and with Tony Marlowe, who was now a London neighbour.

His defection had brought considerable publicity. Outwardly, the entire Eastern bloc regarded him as a pariah, an enemy of the state. The East German press denounced him as a traitor, and in an open letter to *Your Move* magazine, twenty Grandmasters from the Eastern bloc suggested that he be banned from international chess for 'a crime against humanity.' Several of his former teammates were supposed to have signed this, but he found out afterwards from Thomas Jensen that most of them knew nothing about the letter until it was published.

For all the outward fury, his former paymasters had at least done one decent thing. Realising that they could no longer stop the publication of *The Manifesto for a Free Society*, they had allowed Monika Kohler and Gregor Kramer to move to West Germany. This was something which would never have happened in the past. He reflected that even if *The Manifesto* itself had only made a small wave, Honecker and his regime were finally losing their grip.

Freed of his responsibilities to the East German state, Lothar regained the vigour in his play. Defeating in turn his old rivals Vasily Smirov and Lev Ivanov, he qualified for the finals of the World Chess Championships. Finally, his lifetime goal was in reach. Only one thing tempered his joy. To everybody's surprise but his own, his old enemy Sebastian Bahl had defeated both Tony Marlowe and Boris Korneev. Lothar and Bahl would now face each other for the title of World Champion. It would be a fight of East against West. Bahl, the East German hero, against Hartmann the hated defector.

The match was scheduled for April. David Laws, the President of the British Chess Federation, the man he had met back in Madrid, led the negotiations on his behalf, the British having adopted him as one of their own. Bahl insisted that he would not play in London, and Lothar refused to return to the

Eastern bloc, worried about his safety as much as anything, and so they settled on Switzerland as a neutral venue.

Before the match began, there was one other thing that he needed to do. Until now, they had not spoken about it. He saw Hans three or even four times a week, sometimes more. They talked almost exclusively about chess, and nothing else. But he had not broached the question. As they sat in Hans' study, analysing the games of Mikhail Voronin, Freya bringing them in periodic cups of coffee, it reminded him of those first days, when Hans had helped ignite his passion for the game.

'So will you do it?' he asked.

Hans looked at him blankly. 'Do what?'

'Help me take on Bahl. Become my coach again. I can't succeed without you.'

Hans smiled, and Lothar thought he saw a tear form in his eye. 'I thought you'd never ask. Of course I will. Now when do we start?'

As he took his seat for the first game of the 1987 World Championship, waiting for his opponent to arrive, Lothar wondered if Sebastian Bahl would try to put their old differences aside. Any hopes of this were dashed the moment Bahl strode onto the stage and took the chair opposite him. Not only did Bahl refuse to shake his hand, his former compatriot could not even bring himself to write his name on his score sheet, recording him simply as 'Enemy'. It was a petty gesture, and one that said much about Bahl's state of mind. The press in East Germany, he was told, did the same thing, referring to him only as 'the opponent', and refusing to name him in any match reports.

Lothar suspected that Neuer was behind much of this. He had spent enough time with the Stasi man to know that once play was underway he would try any trick he could to make him feel uncomfortable. The first sign of this was in the opening game, when Neuer and an army of Bahl's supporters sat in the front row, arms crossed, glaring at him. To his surprise, seated at the end of the row was a figure he had not seen in a long time. Frail now, with a walking stick and little hair, he had lost weight too. But it was still difficult to miss Udo Grosz, the old intriguer-in-chief, apparently now rehabilitated into East German chess after having served his time on the sidelines. Catching his eye, Grosz nodded and gave a small hand signal, the only one of the East German party to acknowledge him in any way. Lothar recognised the man sitting two seats along from Grosz, a small studious-looking individual with dark glasses, as Zhakov, a psychologist and allegedly also a trained hypnotist. Whether or not Zhakov really was able to influence him, he didn't know, but he finished each day feeling tired and with a blinding headache. On the eve of the fourth game, David Laws asked for Zhakov to be removed from the front row. Neuer refused, and when Laws lodged a formal appeal, a huge argument ensued, with the East German party threatening to withdraw from the match if Zhakov was forced to move.

When Laws' request was turned down, Lothar's team brought in their own fan club, two monks from Tibet, shaven-headed and clad in orange robes, who were on a trip across Europe. The monks knew nothing about chess, but as they sat directly behind Zhakov meditating, they helped bring Lothar a sense of calm. More significantly, they disturbed Bahl sufficiently that Laws and Neuer reached a deal, agreeing to leave the entire front four rows of the auditorium empty from then on.

As for the match itself, the games were as hard fought as any Lothar had ever played, with no quarter asked or given on either side. Bahl had adopted a more solid, careful style than usual, and his striped blazer, so often an indication of exuberance, was nowhere to be seen. Sensing his opponent's determination, Lothar fought equally hard, playing each move as if it were a fight to the death. In this hostile and unpleasant atmosphere, they broke all sorts of records: the most moves, the most checks, the most pieces captured, and the most draws. At the end of twelve games, there had not been a single decisive result. Some joked that neither of them wanted to win the World Championship and face the inevitable media pressures that came with being champion. Others accused them of playing fearfully, of being scared of losing. The truth was that they were so familiar with each other's games by now that they both knew how to blunt the other to a stalemate.

At the end of the twelfth round, the organisers announced a tiebreak. The two players would meet each other in a further four games, each lasting half an hour. In chess terms, a half-hour game qualifies as 'quick play' and it increases the chances of a decisive result. To the disappointment of the organisers and spectators alike, these further four games still could not separate them. There was only one solution left: a sudden-death playoff. For the first time in the history of the World Championship, a match would be decided on a so-called *lightning* game. Lothar and Bahl would have five minutes each to complete all their moves. Bahl had the advantage of the white pieces, and the first move, but he had to win. If Lothar managed to avoid defeat, he would become World Champion.

The game started at six o'clock in the evening, prime time for television. This single ten-minute affair attracted record viewing figures for a chess event, greater even than the Fischer–Spassky match of 1972. Reuters estimated that nine million people, or over half the population, were watching in Lothar's old country alone.

Perhaps, Lothar thought, given the magnitude of the game, and the huge television coverage, Bahl would break his habit and offer to shake his hand. Once again, his opponent dashed such hopes. Arriving at the board shortly after him, Bahl glared, crossed his arms firmly and then swivelled his head to look at the spectators, five hundred odd in total, sitting below them in the auditorium. Taking a deep breath, Lothar steeled himself and turned to look at the audience, trying to spot some familiar faces. There was Hans, seated alongside David Laws and Ernst Reisen. Hans smiled and gave a thumbs-up sign. In the row behind them, there were the two Tibetan monks, who had become firm friends with Lothar and his group, as well as chess aficionados. They seemed as serene as ever. Two rows behind the monks... he gave a start, rubbed his eyes and looked again. Could it really be? Spiky purple hair, two studs in her nose, a Boomtown Rats T-shirt. Yes, it was her. Catching his eye, Monika Kohler jumped up gleefully, waved at Lothar and mouthed the words 'good luck'. Next to her, Gregor Kramer smiled and clenched his fist encouragingly.

Almost overpowered with the positive energy from his friends, for the first time in the match Lothar felt a surge of optimism. Until now, the two players had been jostling with each other. Now it was time to fight. When the arbiter announced the start of play, he felt ready and alert. Bahl pushed forward his King's pawn firmly, before bashing down his hand on the clock with his fist. Game on.

With the eyes of the world now upon him, Lothar paused for a second before bringing out his own King's pawn. Bahl quickly developed his King's Knight, and Lothar defended his pawn with his Queen's Knight. When Bahl brought out his Bishop, they were in the famous Ruy Lopez opening, invented by a Spanish priest in the sixteenth century.

The usual move now would be to push forward his Queen's Rook pawn one square. Pausing for effect, Lothar looked up at Bahl, and then delicately, with two fingers, brought out his King's Knight. There was a commotion from the audience, and Bahl fell back in his chair like he had been shot. Lothar had just played the Berlin Defence. He knew exactly how Bahl would perceive this: a calculated insult from the man who had defected from East Germany to his former compatriot who still lived in Berlin.

Bahl paused, shook his head and looked over at Neuer, before gathering himself and castling on the Kingside. They both played their next few moves quickly, trading pawns in the centre before exchanging the two Queens. Lothar had now obtained exactly the type of position he was aiming for. Bahl had extra space for his pieces, but Lothar's position was solid and difficult to break down, just like the Berlin Wall.

On the twenty-fifth move, Bahl gave a check with his Bishop and Lothar quickly took the piece back with his Knight. Bahl now had a choice of three captures. With three minutes left on his clock for the rest of the game, Bahl still had ample time. Perhaps it was this that lulled him into a sense of security. Hovering his hand over first his Rook, and then a Knight, Bahl began shaking his head. A capture, but which way? It is often said that the choice between two good moves is one of the hardest decisions a chess player has to make. In this instance, there were three decent alternatives, and an increasingly bemused Bahl appeared to have no way of choosing between them.

As Bahl continued to stare at the board, Lothar caught a sideways glimpse of the clock to his right-hand side. What had started as a healthy three minutes had run down to two minutes, then sixty seconds. As his clock continued to tick, Bahl suddenly noticed his elapsed time. Thirty seconds left. Hardly time to complete all his moves, let alone administer checkmate. Still no move. Eventually, as Lothar's heart began to beat so hard he was sure the spectators in the back row must have heard it racing, louder than the ticking of the chess clock itself, with just fifteen seconds left, Bahl grabbed Lothar's Knight with his Rook, slamming down his hand on the clock as he made the capture.

Making the most of his extra time, Lothar allowed himself a few seconds before his next turn. Picking up his Bishop, he swept it along the long diagonal until it landed opposite the White King, giving check. The move itself may not have been the strongest, but it contained a cunning trap. Take the Bishop, and Bahl would allow Lothar's Rook to enter the game, threatening devastation on his back rank. As Bahl sat transfixed, staring at his Bishop, his clock ticked down three, two, one, time out. At zero, his flag fell, and the arbiter rushed across to the table, microphone in hand.

'Lothar Hartmann wins on time and is the new World Champion!'

He had done it. He had beaten his enemy with the Berlin Defence. Beneath him, the crowd broke into wild applause and started shouting 'Bravo!' Hans, Ernst and David Laws were jumping for joy. Behind them the two monks had produced a couple of tambourines, which they were shaking excitedly. Monika and Gregor were hugging each other and Monika was in tears. Only Neuer and the East German delegation sat in stony silence. Udo Grosz sat impassively, but when Lothar caught his eye, he nodded in recognition and gave a small smile. Opposite him, Bahl had his head in his hands, unable to believe what he had just done to himself. Perhaps he was regretting that fateful day, twenty years ago, when his parents had showed him an intriguing board game with sixty-four squares and thirty-two pieces.

After all their epic encounters, this was to be the last time that he would ever come face to face with Sebastian Bahl. Shortly afterwards, Bahl announced his withdrawal from the international chess scene. In his retirement speech, he blamed his defeat on a previously undiagnosed heart condition. He also said that he was no longer prepared to compete in a game populated by *enemies* such as Lothar and Viktor Gavrilov. Lothar replied that he was proud to be mentioned in the same breath as the great Gavrilov.

In the autumn of 1989 Lothar defended his title against the former champion and Soviet golden boy Vasily Smirov. On 9 November, as they sat down to play, he noticed that the crowd seemed particularly boisterous. During the game, he heard whispers breaking out in the auditorium, but the arbiter had shushed the spectators, and the noise had quickly subsided. Now, as he walked off the back of the stage to the rest area behind him, Hans was the first to grab him. His eyes were red-ringed and he pulled Lothar towards him and hugged him.

'You will not believe what's happened.'

'What is it, Hans?'

'They've opened the Wall! After all these years, freedom at last.'

EPILOGUE

ICH BIN EIN BERLINER

November 1994

Taking the tram two stops past Alexanderplatz, Lothar walked through the crowded marketplace, where red-faced men in aprons tried to sell him fish and women with their hair tied in buns beckoned him to their flower stalls. In his coat pocket was a battered copy of Brecht's Collected Works, which he was reading for the third time.

Five years since they had pulled down the Wall. Eight long years since he had set foot in East Berlin. It may as well have been a lifetime. Of course he could have returned sooner, should have done so, but the memories had been so deep, the betrayals so painful, he had put the moment off all these years.

Now that he was back, he marvelled at how things had changed. Goods that one could never have purchased in the old East Germany, not even on the black market, not even in the special shops that were open to senior Stasi officials, were now readily on sale to anybody who had the cash. French cheeses, exotic sauces, fine wines and spirits. Not simply vodka, but brandy, whisky, even liqueurs. As for the clothes: fine, tailored suits, in multiple colours, with silk linings. Fur coats, elegant dresses, expensive jewellery. He wondered what his mother would have made of it. Such delicacies would have been unimaginable before the Wall came down.

As he walked through the market, he spotted the poster. The Thin White Duke himself, David Bowie. A local museum was arranging a retrospective of Bowie's time in Berlin. He would book himself a ticket, for nostalgia's sake. He smiled as he thought of the evening with Bernd and Christiane, when Bernd had played him David Bowie for the first time. He wondered what had happened to Bernd? He had seen little of him, after the night they had gone to see the anarchist singer Karl Rauser, until they had gradually lost touch altogether. That's what the Stasi did to you. Used fear to destroy relationships, until you had nothing left except the state. He should seek his old friend out, find out what he was doing now. He hoped that life had worked out well for him, even if the odds were against that.

Fighting through the crowds, the noise and the odour of stale fish, he reached the end of the marketplace. To the left was a row of old-fashioned shops. Past the barbershop, the bank and the sausage shop, he found what he was looking for. Blumen: the finest florist in Berlin.

Lothar asked the young girl behind the counter to wrap his gift. Then he took the fifteen-minute walk down the hill out of town. He didn't know what to expect. Something grand perhaps. A detached little palace, with turrets, its own nameplate, space for two cars on the drive. The two-bedroom terrace, with peeling yellow paint on the front and a tiny unkempt patch of grass separating the house from a busy main road, was strangely comforting. Holding the present behind his back, he knocked softly on the front door. The wooden frame looked like it was rotting and he worried that if he exerted too much pressure his hand might go right through.

He heard footsteps and after a minute the door opened. She had aged since he had last seen her, but then so had he. They were both in their mid-thirties now, after all. Her hair was longer, and it had the merest wisp of grey. She looked comfortable in her blue jeans and a beige cardigan.

Lothar held out his gift. 'I'm afraid I couldn't find any roses. Had to make do with this old thing.'

Smiling, Anna took the yucca plant, clasping his hand as she did so. 'Lothar, is it really you? Come in, please, follow me.'

Anna led him through to the living room and motioned for him to take a seat on a sofa by the window. The wallpaper and the sofa were beige, matching her cardigan. Cards and flowers stood on the mantelpiece.

'Five years married this month,' said Anna, finding a spot for the yucca in the middle of the mantelpiece, and straightening the cards at the same time. 'Who would have thought that? Most people didn't think Dominik and I would last five months.'

'I always thought you'd stay together,' he said, 'as long as the state didn't get you.'

'Well that was certainly a possibility,' she said, 'at least in those early days.'

'Children?' he asked.

'A boy. He's at nursery school now. How time flies.' Anna paused. 'Are you married, Lothar?'

He shook his head. 'Still looking for the right girl, I guess.'

Anna smiled. 'Married to the chessboard. To be fair, you did become World Champion. Who would have thought it?' Anna walked across to the bookcase and pulled out a copy of *Your Move* magazine.

'Who would have thought you'd buy a chess magazine, Anna?'

'Well, you were on the front cover.'

'I used to think the only way I'd ever make the front cover of any magazine was if I was on a wanted list.'

Anna reached across and passed him her copy of the magazine. 'Coffee?'

He nodded. While Anna busied herself in the kitchen, he opened the magazine. On page two was a picture of Viktor Gavrilov. The old renegade. He seemed so harmless now. Back in the day, they had thought he might bring down the whole Eastern bloc.

Returning, Anna placed a tray with two coffees on the table next to him and sat down on the armchair opposite. 'I should have asked if you wanted anything stronger. I know you chess players.'

He smiled. 'That's OK, thanks, Anna. I've given up drinking.'

Anna sipped at her coffee. 'What brought on that decision?'

'I realised I was just trying to escape my demons. It's time to face the truth. I spent so many years treating life like a game of chess, seeing everything I did as if it were a strategy on the chessboard. In reality, the world isn't black and white. Sometimes you have to play with your heart and not your head.'

'Lothar, it was a brutal system. You survived. Give yourself credit for that.'

'Like the yucca plant,' he said.

'Like the yucca,' said Anna, 'although stronger at chess.'

New Year's Eve 1994. He thought of David Bowie and his song 'Five Years'. There were five years left in the millennium. How much had man accomplished in the last thousand years, how much had he achieved, in science, technology, engineering, the arts, culture? It was a time to celebrate and reflect on the genius of Da Vinci, Shakespeare, Edison, Einstein and Alexander Fleming. Yet that same world had also brought Hitler, Mao and Stalin. In East Germany, Simon Wiesenthal estimated that the Stasi employed a hundred thousand people to control a population of only seventeen million. Up to another two hundred thousand were used as informants, a degree of oppression, espionage and subversion unprecedented in modern times. Would mankind survive another thousand years? On his worst days, he doubted it.

Life, though, was for living. Time to return to action in the city, and the country, which he loved. *Ich bin ein Berliner*, after all. Taking his seat that evening on the first board for Germany, next to his friend Ernst Reisen, Lothar Hartmann nervously adjusted his tie, shook his French opponent's hand, and pushing forward his pawn to King's fourth, pressed the clock. After playing his move, he clasped his hands together. He thought about his parents, and his uncle, those he had lost. He remembered those who had disappeared from his life: Rolf Lehmann, Bernd and Joker. Above all else, he thought of Anna, his one true love. He knew that he had made mistakes. Finally, he was willing to acknowledge that, and to learn. Let a new game begin.

Printed in Great Britain
by Amazon

71231678R00092